T0303982

ROUTLEDGE LIBRARY EDITIONS:
THE ECONOMICS AND BUSINESS OF
TECHNOLOGY

Volume 45

TECHNOLOGY TRANSFER AND EAST-WEST RELATIONS

TECHNOLOGY TRANSFER AND EAST-WEST RELATIONS

Edited by
MARK E. SCHAFFER

Routledge
Taylor & Francis Group

LONDON AND NEW YORK

First published in 1985 by Croom Helm

This edition first published in 2018
by Routledge
2 Park Square, Milton Park, Abingdon, Oxon OX14 4RN

and by Routledge
711 Third Avenue, New York, NY 10017

Routledge is an imprint of the Taylor & Francis Group, an informa business

British Library Cataloguing in Publication Data
A catalogue record for this book is available from the British Library

ISBN: 978-1-138-50336-6 (Set)
ISBN: 978-1-351-06690-7 (Set) (ebk)
ISBN: 978-0-8153-6027-8 (Volume 45) (hbk)
ISBN: 978-1-351-11810-1 (Volume 45) (ebk)

Publisher's Note
The publisher has gone to great lengths to ensure the quality of this reprint but
points out that some imperfections in the original copies may be apparent.

Disclaimer
The publisher has made every effort to trace copyright holders and would welcome
correspondence from those they have been unable to trace.

Technology Transfer and East-West Relations

EDITED BY MARK E. SCHAFFER

CROOM HELM
London & Sydney

© 1985 Millennium Publishing Group
Croom Helm Ltd, Provident House, Burrell Row,
Beckenham, Kent BR3 1AT
Croom Helm Australia Pty Ltd, First Floor,
139 King Street, Sydney, NSW 2001, Australia

British Library Cataloguing in Publication Data

Technology transfer and East-West relations.
 1. Technology transfer   2. Technology transfer —
Communist countries
 I. Schaffer, Mark E.
 338.91'09171'7   T174.3

ISBN 0-7099-3325-8

Printed and bound in Great Britain by
Biddles Ltd, Guildford and King's Lynn

CONTENTS

FIGURES AND TABLES

ACKNOWLEDGEMENTS

This volume originates in the 1983 Millennium Conference on 'Technology Transfer and East-West Relations in the 80s', sponsored by *Millennium: Journal of International Studies* and held at the London School of Economics and Political Science. The Journal would like to thank the United States Embassy in London, the Department of International Relations at the LSE, and the School itself for their support of the conference. Some of the editing, and the writing of the Introduction, took place while the Editor was a US National Science Foundation Graduate Fellow. Any opinions, findings or recommendations expressed in this volume are those of the Editor and authors and do not necessarily reflect the views of Millennium: Journal of International Studies, the London School of Economics, the United States Embassy in London, or the US National Science Foundation.

For their participation in the conference, their efforts and advice in its organisation, their suggestions for this volume, and/or their helpful comments on the material presented in the Editor's Introduction, I would like to thank in particular Julian Cooper, Paul David, Matthew Evangelista, Carla Garapedian, Stanislaw Gomulka, Agota Gueullette, Malcolm Hill, Mark J. Hoffman, David Holloway, Hugh Macdonald, James Mayall, Lois Winner Mervyn, Robert Nurick, Hilary Parker, Iris Portny, Edward Rhodes, Susan Strange, Gautam Sen, Alexander Vershbow, Peter Wiles, Stephen Woolcock, Michael Yaffe, the participants in the strategic studies seminar of the LSE International Relations Department, the Management and Editorial Boards of *Millennium: Journal of International Relations*, and the speakers and panelists at the 1983 Millennium Conference.

MES
London

1 TECHNOLOGY TRANSFER AND EAST-WEST RELATIONS: EDITOR'S INTRODUCTION

Mark E. Schaffer

This volume is a comprehensive survey of technology transfer from West to East and its place within East-West relations. The subject cuts across the traditional boundaries of a number of academic disciplines, and this survey therefore examines the economic, political, strategic and legal aspects of West-East technology transfer.

The starting point of the book is the causes and implications of the 'technological gap' between East and West, and the nature of innovation in the Eastern economies. Among the major questions addressed are whether the deficiencies of the innovation process in the East are inherent in the system of central planning, and what kind of economic reform, if any, could remedy these problems. A related set of questions discussed below concerns the role of Western technology in Eastern economic growth. The size and structure of West-East technology transfer, and the relative economic importance to the Eastern economies of the various forms of this transfer, are both examined. The economic importance of trade in technology to the Western economies, and the experience of Western firms in this trade, are also analysed in detail.

One consequence of the adversarial relationship between East and West is that the West has sought to control the West-East transfer of technology which is believed could effect the military balance. But Western governments have also sought to influence West-East technology transfer for other reasons, such as influencing the behaviour of the Soviet Union or achieving economic gains through increased exports to the East. The attempted influence and control of West-East technology transfer by Western governments raises a host of interrelated questions addressed by the contributors to this volume. Clearly the structure of this transfer and its economic and military importance to the East have powerful implications for its direction by Western governments towards political or economic ends. On the other hand, the political environment has had a considerable influence on the course of West-East technology transfer, which in turn has caused economic and political repercussions felt by both West and East. Western policies on West-East technology transfer have also been the source of major disagreements within the Atlantic alliance. Both these policies and the disagreements have important legal aspects which are also discussed below. Finally, the contributions to this survey discuss important problems which go beyond the subject of West-East technology transfer: in particular, the conduct of economic relations between military adversaries, and the conflict between the control of information by the State and the maintenance of an open society.

The multidisciplinary nature of technology transfer and East-West relations means that a strict division of topics among authors was neither possible nor desirable. After an initial editorial division of the subject matter, each author proceeded more or less independently to examine a particular aspect of West-East technology transfer. The reader will note differences of opinion among the authors; but in general the authors share a 'European' perspective on the subject.

The purpose of this Introduction is threefold: first, to introduce and discuss the terminology and issues most frequently encountered in this volume; second, to give a short historical outline of West-East technology transfer; and third, to explain briefly the organisation of this volume and the place of the various chapters within it. The views expressed here are those of the Editor, and do not necessarily represent those of the contributors.

Definitions and Issues

The task of setting out a core of definitions is a difficult one, for the different specialists who study the subject at hand bring with them their own terminology and distinctions. What I shall try to do here is discuss the most common terms and concepts used in this volume, and in so doing offer a guide to the issues under debate. The definitions I suggest are by no means 'definitive'; rather, they are an attempt to delineate a common ground among the disciplines which are concerned with West-East technology transfer.

First of all, this book is concerned with the transfer of technology from the 'West' to 'East'. The term 'West' is usually used in two different senses. First, it can refer to the 'Western alliance', or, more specifically, to the members of the informal Co-ordinating Committee, CoCom, which co-ordinates the policies of its member states on West-East technology transfer. The membership of CoCom is the same as that of NATO, less Iceland and Spain, and plus Japan. Second, the term 'West' can refer to the 'developed West', the industrialised nations of Western Europe, North America, and Japan; or to the members of the Organisation for Economic Co-operation and Development (OECD).

The term 'East' generally refers to the European 'Soviet bloc', the seven active European members of the Council for Mutual Economic Co-operation (CMEA, or Comecon) which also make up the Warsaw Treaty Organisation (WTO): Bulgaria, Czechoslovakia, the German Democratic Republic, Hungary, Poland, Romania, and the Soviet Union.[1] The term 'Eastern Europe' usually denotes this group minus the Soviet Union. (The subject of technology transfer to the People's Republic of China is thus not discussed in the volume.) Because technology flows predominantly from 'West' to 'East', it is 'West-East' — rather than 'East-West' — technology transfer that is the main focus of the authors.

'Technology' itself requires a definition. Most simply, it can be thought of as 'useful knowledge'. Strictly speaking, therefore, a product is not technology, but 'embodies' technology. The term 'know-how' is sometimes used as a synonym for 'technology' in its 'disembodied' form. A narrower meaning for 'know-how' is, roughly speaking, 'practical knowledge'; for example, the knowledge necessary to run (rather than build) a factory.

'Invention' in our context is the creation of new technology. An 'innovation' is the first practical application of an invention in a firm or enterprise, industry, or country. 'Research and development' (R&D) describes the organised process of innovation. 'Imitation' occurs when innovation is based directly on another's previous innovation. The spread of an innovation through an industry, country, or the world, is termed 'diffusion'.

The concept of 'technological level' is usually used in two different ways. For example, a particular industry in two different countries may have access to the same 'useful knowledge', and in this sense are of the same 'technological level'. However, the two industries may have different 'technological levels' in the sense that their efficiency of production and their quality of product may differ because, say, different economic systems prevail in the two countries, or different resource constraints lead to the use of different techniques of production. A difference in technological level (however defined) is sometimes called a 'technological gap'. 'Lead-time' is one way of estimating a technological gap; others are economic efficiency and international trade performance.

The term 'rate of technological change', or 'rate of innovation', is used in two different contexts. First, it can refer either to the rate of appearance of inventions or innovations, or to the rate of diffusion of a particular innovation. The second context for the term 'rate of technological change' is the rate of economic growth attributable to innovations and their diffusion; the innovation/ diffusion process involves economic costs and benefits, and it is these economic consequences which are the focus of this context for 'technological change'.

To define 'technology' as 'useful knowledge' raises the question, 'Useful for what?' There are two possible answers — useful for 'economic' purposes and useful for 'military' purposes — but the overlap between these two categories is very complex, because economic resources are a prerequisite for military power. A very useful distinction here is that between the military *application*, or 'end-use', of a good or technology, and its 'military *significance*'.

The 'end-use' of a technology refers to its actual application. End-uses are usually said to be either 'civilian' or 'military'. For example, some hypothetical military end-uses for an imported computer are: to direct a missile guidance system; to direct automated production of military transport vehicles; or, through copying the computer's design ('reverse engineering'), to enable the production of identical computers to be used in military applications. The distinction between civilian and military end-uses may not in practice be clear cut. In the above examples, the same computer may direct production of both civilian and military vehicles; or the domestically-produced copies of the imported computer may find both civilian and military end-uses.

A term often employed in discussions of this problem is 'dual-use' technology: technology which can potentially be employed in either civilian or military end-uses. The term 'dual-use' can itself be used in two different contexts. First, there is the nature of the actual application of a technology, i.e. its eventual end-use. 'Dual-use' technology which is sold by the owner on the understanding that it be used only in 'civilian' applications, but which is in fact then used for 'military' purposes, is said to have been 'diverted'. The second context for the term 'dual-use' relates to the uses which a technology may find in its country of origin or in the international market, rather than the use it finds in its country of destination. The main point here is that, *ceteris paribus*, it is more difficult for a 'free market' society to control the export of a dual-use technology which has important military uses but which faces a large and predominantly civilian market, than it is to control a technology which has only military uses.

The term 'military significance', unlike the term 'military end-use', refers to the effect of a good or technology on the military balance. The question of what constitutes a 'militarily significant' good or technology — or, alternatively, what defines a 'strategic' good or technology — is a major issue in today's technology transfer debate. For example, a transfer of oil drilling technology may enable a country to increase its energy production. It can be argued that the country's military power has increased as a result of the technology transfer because the production and use of arms requires energy. Indeed, in the widest definition of 'militarily significant trade', the export of *all* technologies and goods is militarily significant regardless of their end-use, because the economic gains from such trade can be used to build military power. Thus in the example above, should increased oil production lead to increased oil exports, the resulting hard currency earnings could be used to purchase, say, machinery for the production of military goods. It is this broad definition of 'military significance' which underlies the strategy of 'economic warfare'.

On the other hand, a number of arguments can be made in favour of a narrower application of the concept of 'military significance': one which focuses only on goods and technologies with 'significant' military end-uses and which permits (or even encourages) other kinds of sales to a military adversary. Obviously, the seller as well as the buyer gains economically from trade. The buyer may possess a similar good or technology which has already been developed domestically or imported from abroad. The buyer may also be able to obtain the good or technology from another source ('foreign availability'). The seller may obtain political or strategic benefits which offset the 'military significance' (if any) of the sale.[2] Finally, although a sale of items with purely civilian end-uses may yield economic gains to the purchaser, these gains might not be used for military ends — because the recipient chooses to direct these gains toward, say, consumer goods, or because the economic gains are of limited fungibility.

Moving on to the forms of the *transfer* of technology, a useful distinction is that between the transfer of knowledge *per se*, or 'disembodied' technology transfer, and the transfer of technology as embodied in goods or machinery ('hardware'), or 'embodied' technology transfer. Some examples of disembodied technology transfer are sales of licences, subscriptions to technical periodicals, intergovernmental technical co-operation agreements, word of mouth, and industrial espionage. 'Reverse engineering' — the practice of copying a product design and deducing the method of manufacture using as a guide an example of the actual product itself — is another form of disembodied technology transfer: in this case the product itself is used essentially as a blueprint.

On the other hand, imports of actual products, and in particular capital goods, are generally labelled embodied technology transfer; and are the main focus of most economic and econometric investigations of West-East technology transfer, mostly because they are easier to quantify than disembodied transfer. In practice it may be difficult or impossible to distinguish between sales of capital goods which actually 'transfer' technology — that is, goods which the importing country lacks the technical expertise to produce on its own — and capital goods which the importing nation may be technologically capable of producing but buys to eliminate shortages, to take advantages of favourable terms of trade, etc. This is particularly problematic when analysing the economic impact of embodied technology transfer on the centrally planned economies of the East, as shortages are endemic in these economic systems.

The distinction between embodied and disembodied technology transfer may also in practice be difficult to make. For example, purchases of 'turn-key' plants — factories which are complete and need only have 'a key turned' to start production — typically include purchases of licences and know-how. An imported plant may also serve as a model for later, domestically built plants.

Another useful distinction between forms of technology transfer is that between 'active' and 'passive' channels of technology. Active channels involve direct interaction between the seller and the buyer of technology, such as the training of personnel or active guidance in the running of a turn-key plant. Passive channels are basically 'one-way' channels, involving the simple transfer of technology with no active assistance from the owner in how to use it properly. Know-how (in the narrower sense of 'practical knowledge') is thus not readily transferred via passive channels. More generally, active channels are usually conceded to be more effective in transferring technology than are passive channels.

Finally, it is useful to distinguish between 'legal' and 'illegal' technology transfer. This distinction is particularly relevant when analysing government attempts to control the export of technology. Legal technology transfer is decreased by expanding export controls to make more transfers illegal; whereas illegal technology transfer is decreased through greater efforts at enforcement of existing controls.

History

I now want to provide a brief historical sketch of post-war West-East technology transfer. In particular, I will address the following question: Why has an increasing amount of public, political and academic attention been devoted to this subject over the past 15 years or so?

Perhaps the most fundamental factor behind the rise of today's debate on West-East technology transfer lies in the post-war evolution of the CoCom embargo. In the cold war years following the Second World War, the Western allies, led by the United States, tried to engage in 'economic warfare' against the Soviet bloc — in other words, to deny to the East as much as possible the benefits of trade in general. To this end, CoCom was set up by the Western allies in 1949 to co-ordinate their individual national export controls. The CoCom embargo lists were and are classified; but it is clear that the current CoCom embargo is narrower than the original post-war embargo. The initial CoCom embargo, being part of a strategy of economic warfare, included, along with military goods, items with 'civilian' end-uses; these goods were regarded as 'strategic' or 'militarily significant' because they contributed to Eastern economic power and thus to Eastern military potential. Today's CoCom embargo, on the other hand, apparently focuses on goods which embody a high level of technology and on goods with military end-uses.

There are two main reasons for this shift in the focus of the strategic embargo: the course of the post-war East-West military competition; and the changing structure of East-West trade. With regard to the first point, a major feature of the post-war era has been the development of an East-West technological arms race. Indeed, one strategy of the West in the East-West arms race has been to offset the quantitative superiority of the East with technologically superior weapons. One reason, therefore, why many analysts and the CoCom embargo itself focus on *technology* is that over the past 40 years military technology has grown in strategic importance, and in abundance.

The second reason for the narrowed focus of the current CoCom embargo lies in the history of East-West trade relations. In the wake of the failure in the 1950s of the Western attempt at economic warfare against the East there began a trend of improving East-West political relations and increasing East-West trade. This growth in trade required a narrower definition of 'military significance' and thus a narrower CoCom embargo. It appears that as the embargo narrowed the least 'militarily significant' goods were removed from the embargo lists. At the same time, as noted above, the 'military significance' of technology was increasing. In short, CoCom came to focus on technology because technology became increasingly important militarily while open East-West trade became increasingly important politically and economically.

I would also like to suggest three other factors behind the increasing attention devoted to West-East technology transfer: the evolution of Eastern trading strategy; the course of East-West detente; and the increased difficulties faced by the West in controlling technology transfer.

In the 1960s Eastern trading strategy started to emphasise imports of capital goods from the West. A number of Eastern countries began to engage in a strategy of 'import-led growth' — large amounts of Western capital goods were imported, often using Western credit, the plan being to use these imports to increase export capacity and economic growth. Embodied technology imports increased steadily until their peak in the mid-1970s, and with this increase came increased attention in the West to the significance of this channel of West-East technology transfer.

After roughly the mid-1970s the level of embodied technology transfer began to decline. The major factor behind this was probably the failure of the Eastern strategy of import-led growth. Imports of Western capital goods achieved some notable successes, but in general Eastern exports and economic growth rates did not increase as much as planned, and embodied technology imports were cut back as this failure became evident and the pressures of servicing debt increased. But an additional factor in the decline in embodied technology transfer was the worsening of US-Soviet relations. For example, sanctions imposed by the US on the USSR in response to the Soviet invasion of Afghanistan and the declaration of martial law in Poland included embargoes on embodied technology exports. These actions reflected a continued willingness of the US — generally not shared by other CoCom members — to actively use East-West trade for foreign policy purposes.

With the fall of US-Soviet detente, US policy-makers also widened their definition of 'military significance' and in general began to disapprove of allowing the Soviet bloc the economic benefits of trade with the West. Some voices suggested in effect a move back towards the original economic warfare principles of CoCom — a suggestion particularly strongly resisted by the West Europeans, who have kept a narrower definition of 'militarily significant' trade. The recent negative approach of the US to East-West trade, coupled with the continued desire of the West Europeans for detente and East-West trade, led to major disagreements within the Western alliance, notably those arising out of the pipeline embargo attempted by the US following the Polish crisis. This last episode also raised legal questions concerning the issue of 'extra-territoriality', in this case US efforts to enforce its export controls on Western companies based outside the US.

The third factor behind the attention today towards West-East technology transfer is the increasing military importance of dual-use technologies such as microelectronics. These technologies face very large civilian markets; and because of the incentives provided by the market and because of the length of Western arms procurement cycles, the technological level of civilian goods which embody these technologies can today rival the technological level of Western (and Eastern) weapons systems. These trends have induced mounting concern and difficulties among Western nations over the control of the West-East flow of such dual-use technology. Efforts by CoCom members to slow the transfer of dual-use technologies to the East potentially interferes with their diffusion throughout the West, non-CoCom countries included. Furthermore, maintaining the open nature of Western Society while simultaneously allowing the State to control civilian trade is very problematic. The US response to the problems posed by the flow of dual-use technology has been to push strongly for revision of the CoCom embargo lists, for increased governmental supervision of the trading activities of Western firms, and for greater efforts toward preventing illegal technology exports. These measures have received at best only partial support from other

Western CoCom and non-CoCom countries.

In sum, major differences of policy on West-East technology transfer exist within the West. These differences include debates over the actual economic and military significance of the transfer of Western technology to the East, what Western policy on West-East technology transfer should be, and what legal and administrative methods should be used to control this transfer. The contributions to this volume are directed at these debates.

Organisation of this Volume

Generally speaking, this book first covers economic issues, and then moves towards political/strategic questions. The starting point of the volume is the nature of innovation in centrally planned economies and the 'gap' in technological level between East and West. *Stanislaw Gomulka* takes a very broad approach to the subject, examining the major features of innovation under both central planning and market socialism, the role of technology transfer in economic growth, and the relationships between capitalism, socialism and technological change. *Alastair McAuley* addresses his chapter to a more specific issue, namely the impediments to innovation under central planning and the prospects for an economic reform which could speed the innovation process.

The next three chapters look specifically at the economic side of West-East technology transfer. *John A. Slater* makes use of the newly developed OECD East-West technology transfer database to examine in close detail the structure and composition of Eastern embodied technology imports from the OECD area during the period 1970-80. *Julian Cooper* looks at the role of Western technology in the Soviet economy, arguing that the importance of West-East technology transfer is often overstated and the ability of the Soviet economy to sustain innovation is similarly frequently underrated. The role of Western firms is examined by *Malcolm R. Hill* who discusses the nature and importance of West-East technology trade to Western firms, the experiences of these firms in trading with the East, and the impact of the political climate on their East-West trade activities.

Dr Hill's chapter thus serves as a bridge to the second, political/strategic portion of the book. *Neville March Hunnings* begins by examining the legal aspects of East-West trade and in particular the legal nature of CoCom and other Western attempts to control exports of technology to the East. In the next chapter *David*

Holloway examines the very controversial question of the role of Western technology in Soviet military power, looking at the relationship of technological change to security, the relative levels of Soviet and Western military technology, and the historical evidence on the use of Western technology by the Soviet Union for military purposes. Western policies on East-West trade and technology are discussed by *Stephen Woolcock*, who first takes an historical look at the European and US approaches and the differences between them, and then examines the current situation and the prospects for the future. *Hugh Macdonald* looks critically at the nature of the strategic embargo pursued by the West and the rationales advanced for it, arguing that a coherent and practical embargo policy must be based on a sound approach toward East-West relations in general. In the last chapter, *Péter Margittai*, a Senior Economist at the Institute for Economic and Market Research in Budapest, discusses the general subject of West-East technology transfer from an Eastern perspective.

Notes

1. The CoCom embargo applies to the seven Eastern countries listed above, plus Albania, the PRC and other Asian communist countries. The controls thus do not apply to, for example, Yugoslavia and Cuba. Albania is still formally a member of the CMEA but ceased active participation in the 1960s. Cuba, Vietnam and Mongolia are full members of the CMEA, while Yugoslavia has an 'associate member' status.

2. These three reasons for trade with an adversary — economic gain, political/strategic gain, and availability of substitute goods — may also apply even if the items sold find military end-uses. In other words, the sale to a military adversary of goods or technologies which are actually directed to military end-uses may not in some circumstances be 'militarily significant', in the sense that the security interests of the seller may not be harmed and may even be advanced. As a possible example, Romania (admittedly the least integrated and most independent of the East European WTO nations) is currently producing helicopters for its air force under French licences. (See *SIPRI Yearbook 1984* (Taylor and Francis, London and New York, 1984), p. 271, and *The Military Balance 1983-1984* (International Institute for Strategic Studies, London, 1983), p. 24.) Another possible example is the suggestion that the two superpowers should share technology involved in the detection of surprise ICBM attacks; the idea is that such technology transfer would decrease the likelihood of a nuclear attack launched in response to a false alarm and would thus enhance the security of both sides (I am grateful to Maureen Zilliox Normann for suggesting this example to me).

2 THE INCOMPATIBILITY OF SOCIALISM AND RAPID INNOVATION

Stanislaw Gomulka

Introduction

One important aspect of the Marxian theory of economic development and social change is the strong emphasis given to economic efficiency and productivity levels as key factors that decide, in the course of history, the outcome of the competition between different forms of organisation of economic activity.[1] This idea rests on seeing societies as constantly searching for ways of achieving the highest standard of living. Systemic changes, whether evolutionary or revolutionary, are an outcome of that search. False or true, the idea has been and, despite present economic difficulties, probably continues to be, highly influential in shaping the ideological make-up of the political leaders and professional economists in the Soviet Union, China, and other centrally planned economies (CPEs).

Economic efficiency is measured in terms of the actual output taken as a proportion of the maximum (potential) output, given the quantities and qualities of the resources. The starting point for the USSR in 1917 was one of technological inferiority and, therefore, the productivity levels were initially low. Thus, to prove the superiority of the Soviet economic system, it has been and is essential for the USSR to achieve an internationally superior rate of innovation[2] for some time, at least until the gap in output per man-hour could be closed.

To this end, the USSR has given an extraordinary emphasis to technical education, research and development, and industrial technological innovation. The Soviet R&D sector has been expanding since 1928 at so high a rate that, according to a study by Nolting and Feshbach, the number of Soviet R&D scientists and engineers in 1978 was 'nearly 60 per cent greater than the US'.[3] The non-personnel expenditure on R&D is now probably of comparable size in both countries. The remarkable (quantitative if not yet qualitative) progress has been accomplished despite the

12

unusually high human and material losses that the Soviet economy had sustained in the war years 1914-23 and 1941-5, as well as those from the massive government terror, especially in the 1930s. The USSR was also successful in building up, in a short period of time, a vast educational sector which now supplies about twice as many technicians, engineers and scientists as the US sector.

The pace of industrialisation has been slower than in Japan, but of comparable speed or faster than that experienced in Western Europe. The result is that, in 1976, 'in ruble prices, Soviet GNP was 50 per cent of US GNP; in dollar prices, the USSR produced final goods and services equal to 74 per cent of the US national product'.[4] The geometric mean of the two size comparisons increased from 40 per cent in 1955 to 60 per cent in 1976;[5] it was probably not more than 25 per cent in 1928. The outputs of the two key industrial sectors, one producing machinery and equipment for investment purposes and the other defence goods, are also thought to have outpaced the corresponding outputs of the US industries.[6] Productivity performance has not been poor either. In Soviet industry, the trend rate of growth of output per man-hour, in the years 1928-75, was about 5.5 per cent according to Soviet data[7] and some 4 per cent according to Western estimates.[8] This is lower than the equivalent growth rate for Japan, but comparable to that for Western Europe and markedly higher than the rates in the United States and Great Britain in the same period.

On the other hand, a large body of microeconomic evidence has been accumulated in Eastern Europe and the USSR which indicates a high degree of resource misallocation both in conventional production and R&D, a large but rather slow and often wasteful amount of investment activity, and a generally high resistance to innovation, especially in existing enterprises. Despite its large size, equal to at least one-quarter of the size of world R&D, the contribution of Soviet and East European R&D activity to the world flow of new inventions is negligible. In the 1970s, member countries of the CMEA were importing about ten times more licences in terms of dollars paid than they exported, the exports representing merely 1 per cent of the estimated total of world exports.[9] The analogous ratio for Western Europe in recent years has been approximately 2, and for the US about 0.2.[10] Similarly insignificant is the Soviet and East European share of the Western world market for manufactured products, the countries continuing to exchange mainly raw materials and standard intermediate goods for Western imports.[11] Another indicator of poor efficiency is the apparently high use of primary and intermediate inputs per unit of final demand outputs. An aggregate indicator of this phenomenon is that the consumption of energy per unit of GNP in the CMEA is about twice what it is in the West. Moreover, following the 1973 price rise, this unit consumption has been falling in the West, but rising still further in the CMEA as a region.

Somewhat paradoxically, in the past this high micro-inefficiency has not prevented the USSR and other CPEs from achieving a respectable growth performance. However, since about 1975 the rates of output and productivity growth have fallen markedly in the USSR and most other CPEs. The fall which occurred in the small European CPEs can be attributed largely to the forced reduction of Western imports, following the failure of the import-led growth strategy of the 1970s to sufficiently stimulate exports to the West. The reasons underlying the Soviet growth slowdown are less self-evident. Are they similar to those which have caused the productivity slowdown in the developed capitalist economies? Or has the traditional method of running the Soviet economy exhausted its growth potential? If so, is there a feasible economic reform that can be effective in improving the Soviet and East European economic positions *vis-à-vis* the West?

These are some of the questions which I shall address in this chapter. I shall first discuss the innovation characteristics that appear distinctive for CPEs. I then take up the same topic in relation to Hungary under the New Economic Mechanism. This is followed by a discussion of the influence of West-East technology transfer on the East's economic growth. In the next section, broad relationships between innovation, competition and socialism, are suggested. The chapter ends with a section on the Soviet growth strategy, the present slowdown and the prospects for economic reform.

R&D and Innovative Activity in Centrally Planned Economies: Five Major Characteristics

The subject of R&D and innovative activity in the USSR and Eastern Europe — its organisation, size, and performance — has been studied particularly intensively since the late 1960s. Among the most systematic and substantial Western writings in this field are those by Zaleski *et al.*[12] and Cooper[13] on the organisation of R&D and science policy, and Berliner[14] on innovative activity itself. A concise and incisive survey of this by now extensive literature, Western and Soviet, has been made recently by Philip Hanson.[15] In what follows I shall, therefore, be very selective in the choice of institutional and policy detail, emphasising instead what appear to be the major organising principles, or distinctive characteristics, of innovative activity under central planning. At the same time, a number of empirical findings will be called upon to provide grounds for the interpretative analysis and theoretical generalisations in this and the following section.

Two Polish Empirical Studies: The First Three Characteristics

The two separate Polish studies differ considerably in method and scope, yet their empirical findings share a number of important characteristics that are likely to be common to all CPEs. One is the work by Poznanski, which represents an in-depth investigative study of 86 innovations in seven industries in the 1970s.[16] The other study, by Kubielas, reports the results of an extensive inquiry of some 7,600 innovations that were implemented by 55 large industrial firms in four manufacturing industries in the years 1973-8.[17]

Both samples exhibit a number of features that would also be familiar to investigators of Western innovation processes. For example, about 20 per cent of the innovations turned out to be technical failures; about 80 to 90 per cent of the total were small innovations, of which about half were really minor in-house improvements; only 2 per cent are classified as 'major structural innovations'. In Poznanski's sample, as many as 80 per cent of the innovations were of domestic origin. However, about three-quarters of these represented direct adaptation of, or were said to have been directly inspired by, foreign technology. Similarly, as in market-based economies, most of the innovations were initiated locally by the innovating firms or by the R&D staff. Only in about 5 per cent of the cases was the role of the decision-makers from above the firm decisive; but these were the really important innovations.

The two studies also provide evidence on the basis of which I shall suggest three characteristics of innovation which appear to be specific only to centrally planned, Soviet-type economies. One such characteristic is that *innovating firms are motivated primarily by the need to overcome supply difficulties.* The need to adapt to new demand conditions, especially in export markets, has also been found to be important, but enterprises are resource- rather than demand-constrained and, as a rule, take little initiative in exploiting new technological opportunities for the purpose of creating new demands, at home or abroad, something that happens often in market-oriented economies. The enterprise's innovation strategy would thus appear to be primarily defensive rather than offensive, with the resource-constrained rather than demand-oriented nature of the economy emerging as a key underlying factor.

The second characteristic is that *not product but process innovations appear to dominate* (about 60 per cent in both samples). When faced with supply difficulties, firms would use the same tools and equipment, but investigate the use of somewhat different intermediate inputs (ingredients) to produce essentially the same product. Consequently, many of the new process innovations reflect the widespread phenomenon of forced substitution, and as such represent technological necessity rather than actual improvement. This interpretation would appear to be consistent with the finding that, in the judgement of firms themselves, 30 per cent of the innovations in Kubielas's large sample were known to represent technological regress and that, in most cases, no serious cost-benefit analysis was undertaken.

The third systematic characteristic is that *financial incentive for undertaking an innovation is weak, and although industrial R&D personnel have considerable freedom in their work, the decision-making freedom and the resources available to enterprises for implementing inventions are severely limited.*

The average bonus for an invention is small, amounting to the average monthly salary, and is related to the expected, not actual, cost savings by the producer; it would be given even if the invention is not implemented at all. Inventors are expected to be motivated primarily by professional ambition rather than financial benefit or promotion prospects. In large enterprises the management and workforce would have a great number of different 'bonus titles', but few or no separate titles for implementing the innovative part of the directive plan. The enterprises in the sample were aware that some of the innovations they implemented had a positive influence on value-added and profits, but these categories were much less important than gross output in determining the sum of wages and bonuses per employee.

Other Empirical Studies: Two Further Characteristics

The fourth characteristic is that *enterprises in CPEs tend to be large in scale and to trade off choice and quality for quantity.*

Market-oriented economies are characterised by the presence of large risk capital, the purpose of which is to sustain a high rate of birth of enterprises set up to exploit promising domestic or foreign inventions. The innovation/investment decision is thus diffused and decentralised, and these numerous small-scale enterprises are often used as a testing ground for new inventions. The market is thus used as a screening device for the purpose of channelling resources from old to new industries in a rational way.

In centrally planned economies, the original stimulus to innovate comes from the (domestic or foreign) inventor. This is inevitable in any economy. However, screening of almost all innovation possibilities which involve significant investment expenditures is centralised, and risk-taking is almost fully nationalised. The limited screening capacity of the centre would call for the construction of new firms that are limited in number and large in scale. Such a bias for large size has indeed been confirmed by studies of size distributions of firms in the two types of economies. If scale economies are present, as they often are in the manufacturing sector, then suppressing choice and emphasising scale is also an effective method of raising output levels. It appears that Soviet decision-makers have used this method extensively, and not only in consumer goods industries. For example, summarising his survey of a major industry, James Grant notes:

> The Soviet machine tool industry, developing independently of Western assistance, has become the world's largest producer of machine tools. However, emphasis has been on large-scale production of relatively simple-to-produce, general-purpose machine tools at the expense of special-purpose and complex types.[18]

But the preference for vertically-linked large organisations and the inevitable presence of many organisational barriers (plans, directives, committees) leads to certain costs. These arise because of high economic inertia in the form of limited output and innovative flexibility of individual firms, something which Balcerowicz

The Hungarian New Economic Mechanism and the Five Innovation Characteristics

The small East European countries appear to share with the USSR the main weakness of its innovative activity, without enjoying some of its strengths, such as a large R&D sector, the possibility of exploiting economies of scale, and presumably considerable competitive pressures in military-related research and innovation. These small countries are not without advantages of their own, however, the main being that they trade relatively more with the developed West. In particular, the share of machinery imports in total machinery investment in Eastern Europe, at about 10 to 30 per cent, is roughly five times greater than the share of imports in Soviet investment.[22] The presumably much larger technological transfer from the West compensates to some extent for their much smaller (original and imitative) R&D activity. The greater exposure to Western markets for manufactured goods has also produced some competitive pressures of its own. In order to withstand these pressures, the East European governments have been forced to think seriously about introducing systemic changes that would give greater managerial and financial autonomy to the exporting firms. In the case of two countries, Hungary and Poland, major changes of this kind have actually been undertaken. The Polish reform of 1981-2, while still fluid, is unlikely to be more radical than the Hungarian New Economic Mechanism (NEM), introduced in January 1968.

Under this system, prices are much more flexible and rational, enterprises nominally have no centrally-imposed output targets and input quotas, and the role of the profitability principle in the firms' own choices is significantly larger. Since plan fulfilment is no longer the main criterion of management evaluation, the negative economic consequences of the practice of bargaining for low output targets and high input quotas are almost absent. Yet most of the major investment and price decisions and key managerial appointments continue to be made centrally, and they are used, apparently to great effect, for the purpose of influencing the production, market and innovation decisions of enterprises, especially large enterprises. As the Hungarian forint is not freely exchangeable into foreign currencies, domestic markets remain well sheltered from foreign competition. Since the economy is small, these markets tend to be dominated by one or a few firms. The

absence of bankruptcies is a further indication that financial constraints continue to remain rather soft and market competition
low, although in both these areas there has probably been a
marked improvement compared to the pre-reform years. The
national plans continue to be ambitious, producing a high degree of
tautness in the economy. Consequently, resource constraints are
often binding more than is socially desirable, micro-imbalances are
present, and forced substitution is widespread.

The reformed Hungarian economy also retains some of the
essential innovation characteristics of the other centrally planned
economies. From among the five characteristics I have discussed
above, the first (supply difficulties a primary stimulus of innovation), the third (limited resource capability of enterprises in
implementing inventions), and the fifth (high time-lag between
innovating and inventing, and slow diffusion) appear to be valid
for Hungary too. They place the Hungarian economy closer to the
other CPEs than to market-based Western Europe. Yet a somewhat greater degree of decision-making flexibility and much
greater exports of manufactured goods to competitive Western
markets do induce firms to put greater stress on quality and product innovation. Consequently, the second and fourth characteristics
are less in evidence. The case study of the Hungarian motor
industry by Bauer and Soós[23] provides a good deal of evidence in
support of the points made above. In particular, it brings into sharp
focus the relation between innovation and foreign trade. The firms
of the CMEA countries which provide components for the
Hungarian motor industry are found to largely ignore innovative
requests from their Hungarian customer, because, it is suggested,
the Hungarians have practically no choice of suppliers within the
CMEA. On the other hand, the local R&D input is insignificant
compared with that of the West European motor industry, and
hence little attempt is made to enter the dollar market. The import
of suitable licences is a possibility, but, it is suggested, this would
bring in large imports of components from the West without
necessarily resulting in high dollar exports.

The Influence of West-East Technology Transfer

Over the last two decades or so a significant number of studies
have attempted to estimate net gains to a recipient — whether firm,

industry or country — that come from the international transfer of technology. The literature pertaining to the USSR and Eastern Europe has been recently surveyed in OECD-initiated studies by George Holliday,[24] and Alec Nove and myself.[25] It is transparent that the subject of technology transfer is a very complex one, and our knowledge of it not yet satisfactory. The description of the various channels of technology transfer and the evaluation of their relative significance and total net effect shows remarkable variation among different case studies. Despite this variety, resisting generalisation, the literature does offer a few helpful facts, estimates and interpretations. They may be summarised as follows.

The well-known S-shaped diffusion curves for the cumulative spread of individual innovations within industries or among households — curves indicating that the diffusion process is slowest at the start and towards the end — have their aggregate equivalent in the world economy in the form of a hat-shaped growth path of the type indicated in Figure 2.1. For any particular country, the innovation rate tends to be highest at medium levels of development, when the country in question still has much to learn from the outside world and, at the same time, has already developed the means — a high level of education, an R&D sector, an investment goods sector, an export capability — of transferring directly or being

Figure 2.1: The Growth Path of a Latecomer in the Course of Technological Catching-up, in Terms of the Innovation Rate and the Relative Technological Gap

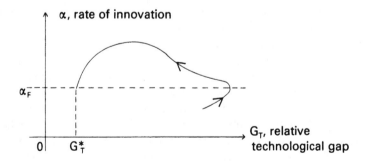

Note: α_F denotes the rate of innovation, assumed constant over time, in the technologically most advanced area, such as the US for most of the twentieth century. The relative technological gap increases whenever $\alpha < \alpha_F$ and declines otherwise.

otherwise capable of absorbing outside knowledge. The magnitude by which the actual rate of innovation may exceed the equilibrium rate (the distance between α and α_F in Figure 2.1) is country-specific, depending critically on the volume of resources being allocated to capital accumulation and technological change and on the efficiency with which these resources are utilised. A country which has a highly inefficient economic system may still enjoy a high innovation rate provided that G_T is greater than G_T^* and that the country is prepared to compensate for that inefficiency with larger quantities of labour and investment resources. In particular, although the rate of diffusion of a given new product or process may be low, a high growth rate of investment effort would ensure that the volume of all newly-introduced products and processes increases rapidly, with the consequence that the resulting overall innovation rate may also be high. This is the reason why in an economy such as that of the Soviet Union, low static efficiency need not be inconsistent with high dynamic efficiency, the paradox to which I alluded in the Introduction.

Eventually, a state of international growth equilibrium is reached in which the innovation rate is the same in all countries, but the aggregate relative technological (and labour productivity) gaps are also country-specific, probably depending above all on countries' systemic and cultural characteristics, things which usually change slowly. In Figure 2.1, G_T^* denotes such an equilibrium relative technological gap. When the actual relative gap is near the equilibrium one, a continuing large transfer of technology would usually be indispensable to keep it there, and yet the innovation rate would be, by past standards, low and, given systemic and cultural factors, not very responsive to any further increase in the flow of technology. In other words, the average return on accumulated investments in technology transfer capability is high, but, in the neighbourhood of G_T^*, the marginal return is low.

An aspect of the Soviet strategy of growth has been a limited use of foreign trade as an instrument of transferring Western technology. With the notable exception of the years 1928-32, when trade was used on a large scale across industries, and the years 1945-51, when forced acquisition of German technology was significant, it was largely the Soviet R&D sector that had been given the task of imitating or adopting Western technology or, based on world-shared science, of inventing independent technology. (There are, to be sure, a few sectoral exceptions where capital imports

have been crucial, such as chemicals and the motor car industry.[26])
The purpose of the extraordinary emphasis on technical education,
R&D and industrial innovation to which I referred in the Introduction, has been in part to serve this end. The strategy has so far
been largely successful despite a high degree of allocative
inefficiency and resistance to innovation in existing enterprises, as
the innovation rate has benefited from the Soviet economy starting
out, in 1928, on the high segment of the hat-shaped curve.

However, the Soviet method of compensating for allocative
inefficiency and innovation resistance with larger conventional and
innovation inputs would cease to be feasible as a way of sustaining
a high innovation rate once the initial reserves of these inputs have
been exhausted and, consequently, when the output and investment
growth rates have declined substantially. Especially important is
the growth rate of industrial output. In the years 1928-55, war
years excepting, that rate was unusually high due to an extraordinary investment effort in industry at the expense of other
sectors, and to a rapid absorption by that sector of a large fraction
of the underemployed labour reserve. In the years 1955-75 the
growth rate of industrial capital stock continued to be high. It is
only since the 1970s that the growing investment claims of the
non-industrial sectors, the growth-limiting influence of the underdeveloped productive and social infrastructure, and the exhaustion
of the labour reserve, have forced a substantial fall in industrial
employment and capital stock. The expansion of Soviet R&D has
also slowed down substantially. A slowdown in the growth rate of
labour productivity has followed, and this indicates that the USSR
may have entered the phase when the Soviet economy is near the
international growth equilibrium, characterised by both the technological gap G_T^* and the innovation rate α_F in Figure 2.1. If so, in
the absence of substantial efficiency-enhancing institutional
changes, the Soviet Union's relative (technological, productivity,
and standard of living) position *vis-à-vis* the developed West
would in the future continue to remain approximately the same as
it is at present.

As a proportion of total machinery investments, imports of
Western machinery are known to amount to, depending on year
and exchange rate assumed, some 3 to 8 per cent in the USSR and
some 10 to 30 per cent for the East European countries.[27] The latter
countries have developed considerable R&D capability, but there
seems to be little international co-operation and much duplication

of effort and, in any case, their total inventive and imitative capability is much weaker than that of the Soviet Union.[28]

Relationships Between Innovation, Competition and Socialism

After reviewing the reality of innovation under Soviet-type socialism, with some occasional comparisons with market capitalism, I now turn to considering a number of generalisations that are in part implied by that reality and in part are intended to interpret it. Three propositions are suggested, each followed by a brief comment.

First Proposition
Rapid innovation is incompatible with idealised (Marxian) socialism; such innovation not only sustains high inequality and competition by constantly supplying many new products for few, but it also requires high inequality and competition as incentives.

That rapid innovation produces inequality is obvious, but that it requires competition is much less so. It was Schumpeter who warned us that in a highly competitive economy, where firms are many and therefore small, there may be too much R&D effort, but too little innovation.[29] The point is that in such an economy duplication of R&D effort would be very extensive, and hence total R&D effort large. But the small size of operations of each firm would prevent taking advantage of economies of scale, and since as a consequence both the incentive to innovate and the inventive effort by each firm would be small, so too would the economy-wide innovation rate. Moreover, the presence of risk would hinder the assimilation of potentially useful inventions which require large capital expenditure. Thus, Schumpeter suggested, there operates a trade-off between static efficiency (meaning the best use of existing technology) and dynamic efficiency. A recent theoretical model of innovation and market structure by Dasgupta and Stiglitz[30] does exhibit this Schumpeterian property.

The interesting implication of this argument, also confirmed by the Dasgupta-Stiglitz model, is that the innovation rate would be highest in a socially-managed, competition-free economy. This implication was often used by socialist writers to argue that the planned socialist economy provides basic preconditions much more favourable to innovation than those afforded by the capitalist economy. However, this argument appears to be contradicted by the evidence we have about the innovation rates under different economic systems, and, in Eastern Europe, is now rarely used and even openly questioned.

It is certainly true that industrial inventive and innovative activity often requires substantial set-up costs. Consequently, rapid innovation does appear incompatible with perfect competition. But the Schumpeterian theory must not be stretched so far as to miss the vital point that in a competitive economy the incentive for a firm to innovate is, above all, *survival,* rather than the gain of windfall profits. Such opportunity costs — the costs which would arise if the firm did not innovate — are the driving force behind the innovation effort that originates from within the firm, the point which Schumpeter himself stressed. However, that force would be declining as competition declines; it would be small under monopoly and virtually absent under socialism. It follows that to secure a maximum rate of innovation, the degree of competition must be intermediate, neither high nor low.[31]

Second Proposition

As long as the scope for innovation (in an economy, in the world as a whole) remains high and, at the same time, the satisfaction of material needs is perceived by most to be (strongly) inadequate, the innovation-conducive forms of organisation of economic activity will continue to be in demand, despite the (income and status) inequalities and competitive pressures such forms may entail.

This conjecture is an empirical generalisation of how today's societies, both in the East and in the West, appear to respond to the choice of an economic system, when they have any say in that choice.[32]

Third Proposition

Since material needs are likely to remain virtually unlimited forever, it follows from propositions one and two that for idealised socialism to come about at all, it is necessary, though it may not be sufficient, that the innovation and growth explosion of the past two centuries run its course.

Substantial innovation slowdown may or may not occur in the future, but if it does, for instance for reasons which I spell out elsewhere,[33] then the rate of improvement in *per capita* consumption would also drop substantially. In such circumstances, there would clearly be less incentive for the bulk of the population to accept arrangements which imply a privileged position for the inventive and innovative social groups. The inherent inequality among people in terms of wealth-creating abilities may then be of lesser or even little consequence, as even the most able would not be particularly more productive. Moreover, when innovation is slow, the pace of allocative adjustments needed to conduct business efficiently could also be slow and, therefore, the inflexibility of non-competitive or mildly competitive economic systems would be less costly than it is at present.

As is well known, both Marx and Schumpeter argued that capitalism would give way to socialism, and it is interesting that their different arguments also rest on particular assumptions concerning the characteristics of innovations. These assumptions have so far proved to be wrong (Marx) or doubtful (Schumpeter). Innovations have indeed been largely labour-saving, but, contrary to Marx's expectations, have not caused the increasing and eventually massive unemployment which was supposed to lead to the overthrow of the capitalist system. For Schumpeter, the capitalist economic system was one in which the individual initiative of the entrepreneur, rather than the collective efforts of organisations, was central. However, the innovation economies-of-scale argument apparently led Schumpeter to believe that small firms would be at a disadvantage compared with large firms, and so the latter would eventually dominate. Firms would be increasingly so large and complex that they would have to be run by hierarchical organisations. A bureaucratised economic system would emerge, 'an order of things which it will be merely matter of taste and terminology to call Socialism or not'.[34] Such a system would be less competitive and could in due course become less innovative than the initial capitalist system. Thus for Schumpeter the direction of causality runs from entrepreneurial capitalism to increasing concentration of production and bureaucratisation of management (which at some stage he would be prepared to call socialism), and only then to possible innovation slowdown. So far the nature of the innovation process would appear to have been different, however, since the innovation activity and economic significance of small-scale firms continue to be large. Moreover, both advances in information technology (making market information more readily available) and the opening of national borders for trade have tended to sustain a high degree of competition, especially for internationally traded goods, despite the emergence of super-large firms. Our argument, on the other hand, is that the major causality runs from slowdown in R&D growth to innovation slowdown and to systemic changes in the direction of idealised socialism. Furthermore, such a development would be largely a matter of social or political choice made possible in part by the satisfaction of economic preconditions (of high output and slow change).

The Soviet Growth Strategy and the Recent Slowdown

The present Soviet economic system shares some of the features of what Marx called crude or primitive communism.[35] The emphasis in such a system is on rapid economic growth rather than the strict application of socialist ideas. The growth strategy of the Soviet planners has been to activate quickly two major growth reserves: underemployed domestic labour and underemployed world-best technology. The strategy is not particularly Soviet — it is in fact common to all developing, industrialising countries — but its implementation does bear the imprint of the peculiar Soviet system. In particular the system has been instrumental in the past in rapidly raising not only the rate of capital accumulation and the rate of labour participation, but also the expansion rate of the educational and R&D sectors. The strategy has been largely successful until recently, despite the systemic characteristics that make the Soviet economy rather inefficient and resistant to innovation.

However, as noted earlier in this chapter, the state of the Soviet economy may now be one of international growth equilibrium, in the sense that in the absence of substantial efficiency-enhancing institutional changes, its position relative to the developed West would continue to remain approximately the same. Such an equilibrium state would thus imply freezing the present Soviet inferiority in technology and consumption per head indefinitely. The suggestion that this is an inevitable consequence of the present economic system would probably be challenged by the Soviet leadership. But should the evidence in its support continue to accumulate, the pressure to initiate a substantial economic reform would probably continue to build up as well. In any case, such a reform in the USSR is unlikely to be adopted in the near future.

The experience of the Soviet and East European countries in the 1970s has exposed vividly the weaknesses and limits of the strategy of import-led growth. The prevailing Western view — that at this quite advanced stage of Soviet and East European development, such a strategy cannot be effective in further closing the technological gap between the East and the West without substantial exposure of the Eastern economies to market competition and financial discipline — has apparently been vindicated by this experience. It is interesting that after what happened in the 1970s, many East European economists, especially Polish and Hungarian ones, would now probably agree with this Western view. It may be noted that the imports of machinery and expertise from the West have fallen substantially in the 1980s, in order to arrest the rise in a sizeable dollar debt. It seems that disillusionment — a feeling that increased Western technology imports alone cannot pull their economies up — might also have been a contributing factor.[36]

The responses of the communist elites, in terms of economic reforms and foreign trade policy, may differ significantly between those of the USSR and those of the East European countries. The USSR does not need to import Western machinery on a large scale to take good advantage, although admittedly with some delay, of Western innovative activity. The pressure there to decentralise is therefore weaker than, say, in Poland or Hungary, where domestic R&D activity is too insignificant to be an effective instrument of international technology transfer and where, consequently, larger export capability must instead be developed in order to sustain larger imports of technology embodied in machinery. By the same argument, reform designed to enhance economic efficiency and trade competitiveness would become less pressing for Eastern Europe if an embargo on technology exports to this region is imposed. Should such an embargo hold successfully, Eastern Europe might consider moving towards still closer technological integration with the USSR, even though any attempt of this kind may be unpopular in Eastern Europe — and perhaps not very attractive for the USSR either. In any case, Eastern Europe is probably the weak spot of the Soviet bloc and is likely to suffer more than the USSR from any determined policy of the West to reduce substantially the West-East technology flow.

Summary

The propositions and the arguments of this chapter fall into two categories. One concerns the grand relationships which are suggested to operate worldwide between innovation dynamics and the type of economic system. At that high level of abstraction the primary aim was to provide an interpretation of the paradox of increasing interest in CPEs in returning to market-based systems, even though these systems are known to entail strong material rather than moral incentives, competition rather than co-operation, and high income, wealth and status inequalities. The other category deals with the CPEs of the present day. At that lower level of abstraction the main purpose was to interpret another paradox, namely that there is a high resistance to innovation in those economies and yet high innovation rates have been achieved until recently. The hat-shape relationship explains at once this paradox and the recent innovation slowdown. By linking the type of economic system with the size of equilibrium technological gap, it also helps to interpret the first paradox.

Notes

*An earlier version of this chapter appeared under the same title in *Millennium: Journal of International Studies*, vol. 13, no. 1 (1984); and, in French translation, in *Revue d'Etudes Comparative Est-Ouest*, vol. 15, no. 3 (September 1984). I wish to thank Mark Schaffer, the Editor of the first journal, for many useful discussions and comments, as well as for the invitation to write this paper in the first place. I am also grateful to Philip Hanson and Alan Smith for their helpful criticisms.
   1. John E. Elliot, 'Marx and Contemporary Models of Socialist Economy', *History of Political Economy*, vol. 8, no. 2 (1976), pp. 151-84.
   2. For the purposes of this chapter, 'invention' and 'innovation' usually have their standard economic meanings — an 'innovation' is the first application by a firm or enterprise of an 'invention'. However, the 'rate of innovation', or the 'rate of technological change', is also meant to include the effects of the spread of innovation, or diffusion.
   3. Louvan E. Nolting and Murray Feshbach, 'R&D Employment in the USSR — Definitions, Statistics, and Comparisons' in United States Congress, Joint Economic Committee, *Soviet Economy in a Time of Change* (US Government Printing Office, Washington, DC, 1979), p. 747.
   4. Imogene Edwards, Margaret Hughes, and James Noren, 'US and USSR: Comparisons of GNP' in United States Conrgess, *Soviet Economy*, p. 377.
   5. Ibid., p. 370. These percentages should be reduced by a fifth for *per capita* comparisons.
   6. Ibid., p. 378, Table 1.
   7. Stanislaw Gomulka, 'Slowdown in Soviet Industrial Growth 1947-1975 Reconsidered', *European Economic Review*, vol. 10, no. 1 (1977), pp. 37-50.
   8. Abram Bergson, *Productivity and the Social System: The USSR and the West* (Harvard University Press, Cambridge, MA, 1978).
   9. Eugene Zaleski and Helgard Wienert, *Technology Transfer Between East and West* (OECD, Paris, 1980), p. 116, Table 29, n. 8.

10. Christopher Freeman and Andrew J. Young, *The Research and Development Effort in Western Europe, North America and the Soviet Union* (OECD, Paris, 1965), p. 74, Table 6.

11. Eugene Zaleski and Helgard Wienert, *Technology Transfer*, p. 75, Table 7.

12. Eugene Zaleski, J.P. Kozlowski, H. Wienert, R.W. Davies, M.J. Berry and R. Amann, *Science Policy in the USSR* (OECD, Paris, 1969).

13. Julian Cooper, 'Research, Development and Innovation in the Soviet Union' in Z.M. Fallenbuchl (ed.), *Economic Development in the Soviet Union and Eastern Europe*, vol. 1 (Praeger, New York, 1975), pp. 139-96; Julian Cooper, 'Innovation for Innovation in Soviet Industry' in Ronald Amann and Julian Cooper (eds), *Industrial Innovation in the Soviet Union* (Yale University Press, London and New Haven, 1982), pp. 453-513.

14. Joseph Berliner, *The Innovation Decision in Soviet Industry* (MIT Press, Cambridge, MA, 1976). See also Herbert S. Levine, 'On the Nature and Location of Entrepreneurial Activity in Centrally Planned Economies: The Soviet Case' in Joshua Ronen (ed.), *Entrepreneurship* (Lexington Books, Lexington, MA, 1983), pp. 235-67; and Alastair McAuley's chapter in the present volume. The latter paper is in part a response to the present essay, but one which significantly develops and strengthens this author's case.

15. Philip Hanson, *Trade and Technology in Soviet-Western Relations* (Macmillan, London, 1981).

16. Kazimierz Poznanski, 'A Study of Technical Innovation in Polish Industry', *Research Policy*, vol. 9, no. 3 (1980).

17. Stanislaw Kubielas, 'Mechanism of Technological Progress Under the Economic/Financial System in Polish Industry', unpublished manuscript in Polish (1980).

18. James Grant, 'Soviet Machine Tools: Lagging Technology and Rising Imports' in United States Congress, *Soviet Economy*, p. 555.

19. Leszek Balcerowicz, 'Organizational Structure of the National Economy and Technological Innovations', *Acta Oeconomica*, vol. 24, nos. 1-2 (1980), pp. 151-67.

20. John A. Martens and John P. Young, 'Soviet Implementation of Domestic Inventions: First Results' in United States Congress, *Soviet Economy*, pp. 505-6.

21. Julian Cooper, 'Iron and Steel' in Ronald Amann, Julian Cooper, and R.W. Davies (eds), *The Technological Level of Soviet Industry* (Yale University Press, London and New Haven, 1977), p. 96, Table 3.11; p. 98, Table 3.12.

22. Philip Hanson, 'The End of Import-Led Growth? Some Observations on Soviet, Polish and Hungarian Experience in the 1970s', *Journal of Comparative Economics*, vol. 6, no. 2 (1982), p. 136, Table 3.

23. Tamas Bauer and K.A. Soós, 'Inter-Firm Relations and Technological Change in Eastern Europe: The Case of the Hungarian Motor Industry', *Acta Oeconomica*, vol. 23, nos. 3-4 (1979), pp. 285-303.

24. George D. Holliday, 'Transfer of Technology from West to East: A Survey of Sectoral Case Studies' in *East-West Technology Transfer* (OECD, Paris, 1984).

25. Stanislaw Gomulka and Alec Nove, 'Econometric Evaluation of the Contribution of West-East Technology Transfer to the East's Economic Growth', in OECD, *East-West Technology Transfer*.

26. Hanson, *Trade and Technology*, pp. 154-5.

27. Stanislaw Gomulka and Jerzy D. Sylwestrowicz, 'Import-led Growth: Theory and Estimation' in Franz-Lothar Altman, Oldrych Kyn, and Hans-Jurgen Wagener (eds), *On the Measurement of Factor Productivities* (Vandenhoeck and Ruprecht, Gottingen, 1976); Stanislaw Gomulka, 'Growth and the Import of Technology: Poland 1971-1980', *Cambridge Journal of Economics*, vol. 2, no. 1 (1978).

28. Gomulka, 'Growth and the Import of Technology: Poland 1971-1980'.

29. Joseph A. Schumpeter, *Capitalism, Socialism and Democracy* (George Allen & Unwin, London, 1976).

30. Partha Dasgupta and Joseph Stiglitz, 'Industrial Structure and the Nature of Inventive Activity', *Economic Journal*, vol. 90, no. 358 (1980), pp. 266-90.

31. For a recent survey of the empirical literature on this point, see Morton I. Kamien and Nancy L. Schwartz, *Market Structure and Innovation* (Cambridge University Press, Cambridge, 1982), Chapter 3.

32. This is discussed further in Stanislaw Gomulka, 'Economic Factors in the Democratization of Socialism and the Socialization of Capitalism', *Journal of Comparative Economics*, vol. 1, no. 4 (1977), pp. 389-406.

33. Stanislaw Gomulka, *Inventive Activity, Diffusion, and the Stages of Economic Growth* (Aarhus University, Aarhus, Denmark, 1971); Gomulka, 'Economic Factors in the Democratization of Socialism and the Socialization of Capitalism'.

34. Joseph A. Schumpeter, 'The Instability of Capitalism', *Economic Journal*, vol. 38, no. 151 (1928), p. 386.

35. According to Elliot's interpretation of Marx, 'Crude or primitive communism is the form which communism takes when it emerges in a preindustrialized, underdeveloped economy ... The institutions of crude communism are merely primitive versions of capitalism. Ownership of capital is vested in the community as a "universal capitalist" instead of a private-property-owning capitalist class ... Lacking control over production and investment, workers are both alienated — from their output, the work process, their own human nature to control and direct the forces of nature, and from other men — and exploited, and focus upon satisfactions from consumption rather than creative work.' Elliot, 'Marx and Contemporary Models of Socialist Economy', p. 156.

36. This observation is due to Peter Wiles of the London School of Economics.

3 CENTRAL PLANNING, MARKET SOCIALISM AND RAPID INNOVATION

Alastair McAuley

Introduction

Technological and organisational innovation leading to increases in productivity play a determining role in the Marxist theory of social change. And, because Marx himself was a product of nineteenth-century European culture, this technical change is seen as a progressive force: it embodies the potential for improving the conditions under which mankind lives and works. This conception of technological change is echoed in Soviet thinking. Soviet ideology also contains the claim that Soviet-style socialism is more effective at achieving rapid technical progress than is advanced capitalism. (Indeed, this assertion of greater effectiveness forms part of the Soviet claim that socialism is more progressive than capitalism.)

Innovation, as the word is used in this chapter, consists of three related processes: invention, development and diffusion. *Invention* refers to the moment of illumination: the occurrence of a bright idea for a new product or a new way to produce an existing one. *Development* describes the realisation of inventions: this consists of finding solutions to the engineering problems involved in production on a commercial scale and assessing the economic viability of product or process. Development often results in further improvements. *Diffusion* relates to the introduction of a new product or process into successive plants, its spread throughout the industry. Diffusion can spill over into a further process of *dissemination*: the devising of new uses for products in other industries — or the adaptation of processes to other materials.

The distinctions between development, diffusion and dissemination are made for analytical convenience. They can be difficult to identify in practice. And, in any case, development continues after a product's first commercial manufacture; indeed, it is frequently the case that the improvements adopted during the diffusion process are more significant than those generated during the pre-launch development phase.

The Soviet claim to superiority in innovation is based on three presumed advantages that central planning and state ownership enjoy over the market and the private entrepreneur. Central planning, it is claimed, allows the USSR to eliminate the wasteful duplication of effort in research while at the same time ensuring that sufficient resources are available for the exploration of all likely avenues of advance. Second, since all enterprises are state-owned, the dissemination of relevant information about technological matters is not obstructed by commercial secrecy or considerations of private advantage. This means that new products or processes can be adopted more simply (and hence more quickly) in a socialist economy than in a market environment. Finally, it is easier to make rational decisions about new technology in a socialist society; since production is for social need rather than for private gain, choices of technique will not be distorted by the chase after profits.

Whether these claims are valid and whether they constitute a sufficient basis for asserting the superiority of socialism in generating innovation is the theme of this chapter. The argument proceeds in three stages. First, Soviet performance in the area of innovation is reviewed — or rather, a brief assessment of other Western studies of this topic is given. This suggests that there are grounds for doubting the Soviet claim. But it also seems to me that Western analyses of this topic too often identify the wrong features of the Soviet (or socialist) environment as responsible for the relatively poor performance in this field. The second part of the argument is a discussion of those systemic factors that I believe do most to inhibit the diffusion of new technology in a centrally planned economy. But the weaknesses of socialism as an environment conducive to technical change do not depend solely on Soviet-style central planning. The third stage of the argument is that market socialism, at least in its Hungarian variant, may be conducive to rapid innovation only under certain conditions, and meeting these conditions involves overcoming political as well as economic obstacles. The chapter concludes with a reassessment of the validity of Soviet claims to superiority.

Technological Innovation: Soviet Performance

Soviet research and development — the ability of the socialist economy to stimulate and direct innovation and technological achievement in the USSR — has attracted considerable interest among Western scholars and policy-makers. There now exists an extensive literature on these subjects which I will not attempt to survey or criticise in detail.[1]

The findings of these and other studies can be summarised in the following stylised facts. All agree that there has been significant technical change in the USSR since 1917 — or, more particularly, since 1928. But, it is usually accepted that the technological level of most Soviet industries remains below that of their counterparts in Western Europe and North America.

Much of the advanced technology that has been incorporated into Soviet industrial practice since the beginning of central planning has been imported from the West. Indeed, some observers have argued that Western technology has formed the basis of Soviet productivity growth; indigenous innovation and development have been of secondary importance. Few Soviet industries have yet attained a level of sophistication that would permit them to export machinery or industrial processes to the developed West, and there is little to suggest that key sectors will be in a position to do so in the foreseeable future.

The Soviet system has shown that in particular areas it is capable of concentrating resources and generating a level of technology that is equal to Western achievement. By all accounts, Soviet military hardware is comparable to that of other major arms producers. And this has been attained with only modest help from abroad.

These 'facts' are widely accepted, but there are differing interpretations of their significance. It has been argued, for instance, that the way in which Soviet planners have combined advanced (capital-intensive) technology for key production processes in particular industries with more primitive (labour-intensive) techniques for auxiliary phases constitutes a rational response to the relative scarcities of capital and labour in the USSR. More generally, it has been claimed that the selection of techniques in different industries has been appropriate to the level of development of the Soviet economy — and that as this has changed so has the emphasis of technological policy. The general rationality of Soviet tech-

nological choices, runs this argument, is demonstrated by the fact
that the USSR has enjoyed rapid economic growth for upwards of
half a century and that this has succeeded in narrowing the difference in development level between itself and the industrial economies of the West. But the general rationality of choices of
technique — even if a characteristic of Soviet technological policy,
and I argue below that there is reason to doubt this — is not the
same as the encouragement of rapid innovation, that is, the
encouragement of frequent invention and rapid development and
diffusion of new technological choices. This argument is thus mis-
placed.

Alternatively, some Western economists have argued that the
evidence shows that the USSR is incapable of developing and producing advanced technology — and that this inability stems directly
from shortcomings in the planned economy. Among those who
argue in this way, there is a further difference of opinion. Some
suggest that Soviet failure is a consequence of inappropriate
policies; they imply that changes in policy would result in a much
improved performance. Most Soviet economists who have
expressed concern at faltering growth rates in the USSR appear to
share this opinion. It has also been claimed, however, that the poor
record of innovation should be attributed to systemic factors. This
means that nothing short of the abandonment of socialism, at least
in its Soviet form, will lead to a significant improvement. This case
has too often been argued in ideologically loaded terms; but it can
also be made on more neutral economic grounds, which is what I
shall try to do.

All three phases of the innovation process defined at the start of
this essay are important but specialists have tended to concentrate
on the first two and to neglect the third. This is probably because
they have been concerned to analyse the impact of science policy
and the organisation of research and development on technical
change. Clearly, the assignment of more or fewer resources to particular projects at the development stage can make a difference to
the final outcome. But, arguably, it is the third, diffusion, phase of
innovation that has the greatest economic impact. The slow diffusion of cost-reducing innovations may lead to slow growth of
productivity and output and will certainly ensure that the overall
technological gap will never be closed. In many cases, even
efficient development will have a limited impact on overall economic performance so long as the new product or process is con-

fined to only a few plants. Consequently, it is on the question of whether there exist systemic impediments to the diffusion of new products or processes in the USSR that I shall concentrate in the rest of this essay.

Diffusion involves decisions to produce new products or to adopt new processes. In a Soviet-type economy, this will be a question of whether or not such products and processes have been written into enterprise plans. It might be thought that that is all there is to it: if planners schedule the widespread adoption of new products or processes, diffusion will be rapid; if diffusion is sluggish, the fault must lie with planners' failure to include more novelties in their plans. But the issue is not so simple. If enterprise managers possess any discretion over what is produced or how to produce it, the rate of diffusion will also depend upon the nature of the incentives that the system provides for compliance with such plans. And a common explanation of the slowness of the diffusion process in the USSR (at least among Western economists) is that the Soviet system does not provide managers with adequate incentives for the adoption of new products. According to Joseph Berliner,

> Our guess is that the differential reward for innovation relative to the reward for competent but non-innovative management is too small to induce a high rate of innovation [i.e. diffusion] and that the small differential is a major obstacle to innovation.[2]

Berliner also points out that managers may be deterred from innovating because, if the new process or product does not work out, plan targets may not be met and bonuses will be lost. The implication of this analysis is, of course, that if the Soviet authorities were prepared to reward the innovating manager adequately, they could achieve a much more satisfactory rate of diffusion of new technology. It is socialist egalitarianism that must bear much of the blame for poor performance in this area.

But such an explanation misses the point. It does not focus on the systemic impediments to a change in managerial incentive structures. These systemic features were also missed by the 'perceptive' manager whom Berliner asked whether the chance of becoming a millionaire from the profits of innovation would lead him to become more active in introducing technical change. He replied,

What would anyone do with so much money in our country? One can't invest in the ownership of productive property, as in yours. And one would soon run out of consumer goods to buy. Large incomes would do no good at all.[3]

Berliner alludes to the *difference in reward* between the innovating and the non-innovating but competent manager. But in his subsequent discussion he only asks whether the rewards for innovation might not be raised within the socialist context. He does not ask whether a reduction in rewards (or an increase in the penalties) for non-innovation is consistent with socialism. These alternatives are not equivalent: managerial responses are not symmetric with respect to reward and penalty. Indeed, this lack of symmetry is a crucial element in the argument of this chapter.

Abram Bergson is aware that non-innovation may incur penalties in a market economy:

In the west, an enterprise is penalized when an innovation turns out awry, but it may also be penalized for not innovating, for a more venturesome competitor may encroach on the market of a less venturesome one. The competitive threat that is thus posed must be a major spur to innovation generally.[4]

But Bergson too fails to go on to ask whether socialist economic organisation makes it impossible to introduce a similar structure of penalties in the USSR.

Such is my contention. First, I would argue that it is not the absence of the promise of substantial financial rewards that discourages rapid innovation. After all, the successful manager may expect promotion, political power and privilege; these will confer many of the benefits that are bought with money in a market economy. But, so long as his enterprise fulfils its output plan, the non-innovating manager has little to worry about. In effect, the central planners undertake to dispose of anything that is produced. The manager does not have to concern himself with loss of custom or falling market share. And, while plans are fulfilled, he will continue to receive salary and bonuses. His status is secure; he may even be promoted! In short, sluggishness in the diffusion of new products and processes is to be attributed to the absence of substantial penalties for laggards.

But I would wish to go further. I intend to argue that this failure to penalise the laggard is a consequence of the character of central planning as a system rather than the result of a specific policy or set of policies. Thus, it is difficult to see how the structure of incentives for innovation could be changed without a radical reform of the system of economic administration. Indeed, one can argue that even a move from central planning towards market socialism would not provide a solution to this problem: there exists a fundamental incompatibility between socialism and rapid, autonomous innovation. These topics are explored in the next two sections.

Systemic Obstacles to Diffusion

In this section I argue that the system of central planning introduced by Stalin in the 1930s and developed in a number of ways since his death operates in such a way as to prevent the authorities in Moscow from introducing insecurity into the enterprise manager's environment in a form that would act as a spur to technological dynamism. I do this by first providing a summary characterisation of Soviet-style economic administration, and then by discussing the constraints that the logic of this system imposes upon planners' freedom of action.

Bornstein has suggested that the traditional Soviet economic system possesses the following nine interrelated characteristics:[5]

(1) All significant means of production outside agriculture are nationalised.
(2) In agriculture, the dominant pattern is collectivisation, with nominal co-operative ownership.
(3) Economic organisation is hierarchical and decision-making is concentrated near the top.
(4) Output and its distribution are planned in detail in physical units.
(5) Means of production are rationed by administrative orders: labour is controlled through controls on wage funds; investment is controlled through the central distribution of investment funds, and through controls on construction materials and the distribution of machinery and equipment.
(6) Prices are set centrally and are changed infrequently. These are cost-plus prices which generally allow the various branches to cover current costs and earn a small profit.

(7) Money is passive; planners adjust financial flows to planned physical flows through taxes, subsidies and credits.
(8) Incentives to managers and workers emphasise the fulfilment of quantitative targets.
(9) Multiple exchange rates (effected through the tax and subsidy system) separate domestic and foreign trade prices.

Although this characterisation of the Soviet system contains nine separate points, it is important to recognise that they are in fact interdependent. They reinforce each other. Change to any one feature thus necessitates appropriate adjustments elsewhere if it is to result in significant and permanent modification to the way in which the system as a whole works. Absence of appropriate changes will result in pressures for a return to the *status quo ante* — or for more radical reform.

For the purposes of this chapter, interest focuses on the way in which this system impinges upon the structure of incentives that face the enterprise manager. This is alluded to in points (3), (4), (5) and (8). The Soviet system of central planning was developed to permit the central political authorities to impose their own priorities upon the allocation of resources. This degree of centralisation was a feature of Stalin's view of socialism and it remains characteristic of Soviet thinking to the present time. Central control was (and is) maintained in the short run through the system of indents and allocation certificates (*zayavki* and *naryady*) through which intermediate inputs are distributed. In the longer term it is effected through control over access to capital equipment — as described in points (4) and (5).

The hierarchical organisation of the Soviet economy allows central planners to exercise significant control over what should be produced in the USSR. They can 'instruct' subordinate enterprises to produce particular goods or services; through their power to issue or withold *naryady*, and through the requirement that only enterprises with a valid allocation certificate as well as money are entitled to obtain supplies of key resources, they can influence how different goods are produced. But, at the same time, hierarchy imposes obligations on the planners. The planning of output involves acceptance of responsibility for the disposal of what is produced. However obsolete, however poor the quality of an enterprise's output, the planners are obliged to find a customer for it. To do otherwise would 'unbalance' the plan.

This 'logic of balance' is reinforced by one of the distinguishing political characteristics of socialism: its commitment to full employment. The state's guarantee of a job of some kind for *every* citizen who wishes to work would be threatened by any widespread preparedness on the part of planners to abandon responsibility for the disposal of output. If planners were to reject obsolete and poor quality products, enterprises might be rendered incapable of 'paying' their suppliers; they might have to lay off workers; they might be forced into liquidation. This would (or at least might) result in unemployment.

The 'logic of balance' and of the full employment policy mean that planners in a Soviet-type economy cannot allow inefficient or laggard enterprises to go to the wall. At most, planners can have recourse to administrative solutions. Enterprises which make persistent losses may be re-organised; incompetent or negligent managers may be transferred or demoted. Under Stalin some were even brought before the criminal courts. But even such draconian measures do not achieve their end: the insecure manager seeks to propitiate his superiors and to produce alibis for failure. He does not seek ways of attracting new custom or cutting costs.[6] In fact, it appears that since Stalin's death, the authorities in Moscow have come to accept that little purpose was served by the extreme personal insecurity of managers in the 1930s.

> ... Soviet [managerial] careers in the middle 1930s were highly mobile and apparently included a good deal of movement in both directions between enterprises and higher organisations. By the 1960s, to the contrary, tenure in post throughout industry had become extremely lengthy ... The position of factory director was normally a terminal one.[7]

Also, those who penetrate the magic circle of the *nomenklatura* are seldom deprived of that status. Rather, if they fail in one position, they are transferred to another managerial or administrative post, where, as often as not, they continue the same bad habits.

Thus, it is the logic of central planning, the requirements of the indent-allocation permit system, that make it impossible to create the sort of managerial uncertainty that acts as a stimulus to diffusion. But the influence of *zayavka* and *naryad* is more pervasive — and more pernicious — than this. Balance, the ability to supply all the products that appear in the *naryady* that the planners have distributed, depends upon plan fulfilment. It is this, *inter alia*, that results in the importance attached to gross output as a success indicator described in point (8) above. But the fact that managerial reputation depends more on an ability to meet targets than to attract custom means that the risks attached to innovation will more often seem greater than those of doing nothing. Managers will tend to display greater technological conservatism and firms will be slower to introduce new products than in a more demand-oriented environment. Also, since plan fulfilment is the goal and since plans are more likely to specify output targets than techniques of production, such innovation as does occur is more likely to involve the adoption of new processes than the introduction of new products. In the absence of appropriate marketing facilities, new processes are likely to be diffused more slowly than new products.

The classical Soviet system involves central control over the allocation of capital equipment. This is described in point (5) above. Only the planners can authorise the production and distribution of new machines. And it is alleged that planners tend to take these decisions bureaucratically, without paying sufficient attention to economic factors. Such was the message, at least, in that popular post-war Soviet novel *Not by Bread Alone.* The so-called Kosygin reform of 1967 attempted to introduce a measure of flexibility into the traditional system. Enterprises were given the right to retain a certain proportion of their accumulated profits and were authorised to spend it on the acquisition of new capital equipment. This whole experiment failed, as logically it had to. And it failed because it conflicted with the imperatives of the indent-permit system.

First, as pointed out above, the Soviet system is characterised by stable average-cost prices. Such prices provide managers with little guidance in their search for economically advantageous investments. Just because a particular machine promises to reduce costs, to increase enterprise profits, at ruling Soviet prices, does not allow one to infer that it will entail a saving of resources for the economy as a whole. It is the economic meaninglessness of prices that, too often, forces planners to choose between alternative technologies in a bureaucratic way. All the same, it must be admitted that central planners, by their position within the system, do have some inchoate appreciation of economy-wide scarcities. They are more likely to make sensible decisions than are individual managers. And their greater knowledge is likely to make them critical of enterprises which seek to use their new-found freedom.

Even if managers had been aware of the right set of scarcity prices, of course, there is no reason to assume that allowing them to accumulate investible funds would have resulted in a more efficient allocation of resources. There is no reason to assume that the pattern of investment opportunities in an economy should correspond to the structure of profits or profit-rates. The Kosygin scheme did not go so far as to allow enterprises to borrow from each other — nor did it commit the authorities to allocate the funds at their disposal according to any microeconomic performance criteria.

Although the technological choices made by Soviet managers under the Kosygin decentralised investment scheme were essentially arbitrary, this was not the main reason why the 'experiment' failed; it only made it easier for the authorities to encroach upon enterprise autonomy. More fundamental was the logical incompatibility of decentralised investment decisions and the *zayavka-naryad* system. Suppose, for the sake of argument, that planners decide to allow enterprises to undertake 10 per cent of investment in a decentralised manner. This implies that the *central* plan should contain targets which equal 90 per cent of the capacity of the capital goods sector. But how can planners know which 10 per cent to leave idle? Should they create special firms which have no output targets? Should they allow 10 per cent excess capacity in each firm? Also, how does one incorporate this 'slack' in the distribution of current inputs? And what if they get it wrong? What if some of their specially created firms are unable to secure enough orders? Or what if some capital goods firms cannot make up through private orders for the excess capacity left by the planners? Either the full-employment commitment will be breached or the planners themselves must step in and make up for the shortfall in demand. But, the knowledge that the planners are always there — as customer of last resort, as it were — will change enterprise behaviour. Also, the additional cost of the last-minute need to dispose of unsold output will encourage planners to encroach upon enterprise prerogatives — to crowd out 'private' demand.

Thus Soviet-style central planning involves the authorities (at the ministerial level or in Gosplan) in deciding what should be produced. This in turn involves a commitment to dispose of what is produced. (It is this, as much as the soft budget constraint, by the way, that makes sellers' markets so prevalent in Eastern Europe.) This commitment is built into the system, as it were, and could only be eliminated by radical reform. It has a number of consequences. First, it means that the non-innovating manager enjoys much more security than his equivalent in a market economy. It is difficult to see how the structure of incentives that face him can be modified to introduce a sufficient degree of productive insecurity.

Second, the system does not generate and disseminate the information necessary to allow individual managers to make sensible decisions about technological alternatives. Decentralised investment decisions, where they are permitted, are arbitrary.

Third, since managers cannot be encouraged and guided to make informed decisions, autonomous innovation is unlikely — and probably undesirable. But planners are ill-informed about consumer demand, and about the microeconomic consequences of using particular machines. Their technological choices are likely to be imperfect. There are significant systemic impediments to rapid autonomous innovation in a Soviet-type economy.

Market Socialism and Diffusion

Does the fact that there are systemic obstacles to the diffusion of new technology in a centrally planned economy constitute an argument in favour of market socialism? After all, the absence of indents and permits, the absence of a commitment to dispose of anything produced should make it possible to restructure managerial incentives and to introduce a degree of competition. This may be so, but the experience of Hungary and Yugoslavia, both of which have eliminated much of the paraphernalia of Soviet-style planning, suggests that it is not altogether straightforward. In this section I will argue that the adoption of a market-socialist system which could promote the rapid diffusion of new technology appears to imply among other things the abandonment of the full-employment policy associated with Soviet-style socialism, and that therefore a shift to market socialism would face obstacles which are political as much as administrative or economic.

A Western economist might argue that there are two types of inefficiency that economies can suffer from, two reasons why actual output might fall below the maximum potential output which can be produced from available resources. First, there is misallocation: the marginal rates of substitution between factors may differ in different sectors. If this occurs it will be possible to increase output of at least one product without reducing production anywhere else.[8]

The second reason why the level of economic output might fall below its potential maximum is if some of the available factors remain unused. It is this 'visible' waste of resources, together with the production of goods that cannot be sold, that constitutes the tangible evidence of economic inefficiency for Marx. And it is this conception of inefficiency that predominates in Soviet economic thinking. Economists and planners are much more concerned to ensure that available resources are fully utilised than they are to see that factors are efficiently allocated.

If there are two possible types of inefficiency, either of them (or both) may be responsible for losses in potential output. Which imposes the greater welfare cost is an empirical question — and may differ from case to case. But the answer is relevant to an understanding of the appeal of market socialism. It is usually argued that the switch from central planning to market socialism will make it more likely that marginal rates of substitution between factors in different sectors will be brought into equality. Thus, the welfare cost of the misallocation of resources is likely to be lower in an economy organised on market-socialist principles than under Soviet-style central planning. Indeed, advocates of market socialism believe that the welfare gains from a reduction in misallocation will outweigh any additional losses attributable to an increase in visible waste (for example, as a result of unemployment).

Even if the introduction of market socialism does result in a net increase in total output and hence a reduction in the global welfare-cost of inefficiency (and there have been few attempts to *calculate* the gains from such a change in Eastern Europe), this does not mean that such a policy should be adopted. Welfare judgements should also involve a consideration of the distributional impact of policy changes.

In a centrally planned economy with full employment and a substantial misallocation of resources, the loss of potential output will appear as relatively low factor productivity. If factor earnings — and, in particular, wages — are related to apparent productivity, they too will be low. (That is, earnings per man-hour will be lower than they would have been under an efficient allocation of resources.) Since it is to be assumed that this misallocation is general rather than being confined to a small number of sectors, the welfare cost of the inefficiency will be widely distributed.

Consider now what would occur if a market-socialist system were introduced. Let us accept the market-socialist hypothesis; let us assume that the misallocation of resources is eliminated — but that some proportion of available resources are unable to find employment. Since factor earnings are related to productivity, and since total output has increased, the incomes of those factors that are still in employment will have risen. But the earnings of those factors that are not being used will have fallen to zero. The full cost of the remaining inefficiency will be borne by a sub-group of factor-owners.

In *Kaldorian* terms, the switch of regime should be adopted if the gainers could compensate the victims. But things are not so simple in the real world. What is required for compensation to be viable is an administrative mechanism to make the transfer and an ideological legitimation to make it acceptable.

The relevance of all of this to the adoption of market socialist solutions in Eastern Europe may seem obscure but it is as follows. The introduction of dynamic insecurity into the incentive structures of managers requires the abandonment of central planning. But this in turn will threaten the unconditional commitment to full employment implicit in Soviet-style socialism. Unless the reformers introduce administrative procedures to compensate those who lose their jobs, and develop an ideological legitimation for unemployment compensation, it will be possible to construct a coalition of interests to oppose the change; and that coalition may well be decisive.[9]

There are other issues of an ideological nature that affect the acceptability of market-oriented systems under socialism that I will mention briefly. If the market socialist system is adopted, enterprises will enjoy considerable autonomy in decision-making. Those responsible for enterprise decisions will acquire effective control over substantial resources. They will hence enjoy considerable economic power. If this accession of power is to be acceptable, it needs to be legitimated through an appropriate social myth. In Yugoslavia, for instance, the device of workers' councils and the principle of workers' control has for many years permitted enterprise managers to exercise effective authority. The failure of the

Hungarian authorities to adopt similar principles — or to replace them by an appropriate alternative — also contributed to the partial failure of the NEM. There is no widely accepted principle of right that would legitimate the manager's opposition to ministerial tutelage, that would justify the manager making mistakes. In consequence, the pressure for a creeping return to the Soviet-style of economic administration has been very strong.

These intangible factors call into question the ability of an East European government to move sufficiently far in the direction of market solutions to be able to stimulate managers to innovate in their search for custom. They thus reinforce the doubt expressed in the previous section.

Conclusion

The evidence of the various Western studies cited above suggests that the technological level in much of Soviet industry is lower than in most Western industrial countries. Also, these scholars could find little reason to argue that the differences in levels, the so-called technological gap, had closed appreciably in the last 20 years or so. This calls into question the Soviet claim that socialist economic organisation is more suited to rapid innovation than is capitalism.

In particular, it suggests that the three presumed advantages of Soviet-type systems set out at the beginning of this chapter are not sufficient to guarantee the superiority of socialism. First, it may be the case that central planning eliminates wasteful duplication of effort in research and development (although even this might be questioned by Western observers) but, as has been argued at length here, central planning constitutes a significant impediment to the rapid diffusion of new products or processes.

Second, it may be true that socialism eliminates commercial secrecy, but the Soviet political and economic systems impose other significant barriers to the diffusion or dissemination of new ideas. For instance, the obsessive secrecy that surrounds all things military in the USSR must make it more difficult for the civilian economy to benefit from spillovers from military research and development programmes. Equally, ubiquitous censorship, limits on contacts with colleagues in other countries, and a refusal to allow research workers open access to such technological aids as xerox copiers (or typewriters) must restrict the speed with which ideas can circulate.

Third, it may be that the profit motive is absent in a centrally planned economy, but the absence of scarcity prices, which is a consequence of the elimination of markets, makes it difficult if not impossible for rational choices about techniques to be taken in a decentralised manner.

But the argument of this paper has been stronger. It is not only that the presumed advantages of socialism and central planning are not sufficient to ensure superiority in innovation for the USSR; it is that there are systemic impediments to the diffusion of new products and processes in Soviet-type economies. The fundamental reason for the inability of the Soviet system to stimulate a rapid flow of autonomous innovations is to be found in the inability of planners to provide an appropriate structure of incentives at the enterprise level. In particular, planners have been unable to introduce uncertainty over market shares in a form that would encourage managers to seek to woo customers with the rapid adoption of new products. Planners have been unable to generate this uncertainty because the insecurity it entails is inconsistent with the 'logic of balance', with the Soviet commitment to full utilisation of resources and with the *naryad* system that implements it. Since this inability is a result of the system of central planning itself, changes in policy would have only a limited impact on the rate of innovation.[10]

I have also argued that, in the absence of changes to East European socialist doctrine — and hence to ideas about the legitimacy of conferring control over resources on specific groups — attempts to stimulate innovation through the adoption of Hungarian-style systems of economic administration will evoke political opposition and may well fail. Here too, although in a somewhat different form, the argument is made that the authorities may be unable to introduce a sufficient degree of insecurity to make innovation attractive for managers — and employees.

If the argument of this paper is valid, it implies that the benefit to a Soviet-type economy from the impact of Western technology will be limited by its failure to provoke a creative response, although periodic injections of Western capital (and the new ideas and know-how that these embody) may play a vital role in the introduction of new products and processes.

At a deeper level, the paper's argument implies the existence of

48   *Central Planning, Market Socialism, Rapid Innovation*

a trade-off (or conflict) between social stability and the personal security of managers on the one hand and, on the other, a system's ability to engender innovation. It is often argued that Western industrial economies are more dynamic, more innovative, than socialist ones because capitalism offers greater opportunity, more scope for individual advancement. On the contrary, I suggest that the innovative capacity of industrial market economies is a reflection of the insecurity experienced by their entrepreneurs. Managers and workers in a Soviet-type economy enjoy a measure of job security, a greater measure than their Western counterparts, and *therefore* they have less need to innovate or to adopt the innovation of others.

Notes

1. See, for example, R. Amann, J. Cooper and R.W. Davies (eds), *The Technological Level of Soviet Industry* (Yale University Press, London and New Haven, 1977); R. Amann and J. Cooper (eds), *Industrial Innovation in the Soviet Union* (Yale University Press, London and New Haven, 1982); Joseph Berliner, *The Innovation Decision in Soviet Industry* (MIT Press, Cambridge, MA, 1976); Philip Hanson, *Trade and Technology in Soviet-Western Relations* (Macmillan, London, 1981); Anthony C. Sutton, *Western Technology and Soviet Economic Development, 1917 to 1965* (3 vols., Hoover Institution Press, Stanford, CA, 1968, 1971, 1973); Eugene Zaleski, J.P. Kozlowski, H. Wienert, R.W. Davies, M.J. Berry and R. Amann, *Science Policy in the USSR* (OECD, Paris, 1969).
2. Berliner, *Innovation Decision*, p. 490.
3. Ibid., p. 491.
4. Abram Bergson, 'Technological Progress' in Abram Bergson and Herbert S. Levine (eds), *The Soviet Economy: Toward the Year 2000* (George Allen and Unwin, London, 1983), p. 60.
5. M. Bornstein, 'Economic Reform in Eastern Europe' in United States Congress, Joint Economic Committee, *East European Economies Post-Helsinki* (US Government Printing Office, Washington, DC, 1977), pp. 103-4, as cited by E. Hewett, 'Soviet Economic Reform: Lessons from Eastern Europe', paper given at the 1984 BNASEES Conference, Cambridge.
6. The reasons for this are complex and cannot be fully discussed here. But, in addition to the economic aspects developed below I would suggest that there is a psychological difference between the way in which one responds to an identifiable and threatening person and impersonal forces beyond anyone's control.
7. D. Granick, *Managerial Comparisons of Four Developed Countries: France, Britain, United States and Russia* (MIT Press, Cambridge, MA, 1972), p. 245.
8. Stated as succinctly as this, the proposition may appear opaque; what is being asserted can perhaps be seen more clearly within the framework of a two-good two-input model. In an Edgeworth-box diagram, unless techniques chosen in each sector are such as to yield a point on the so-called contract curve (and thus to ensure equality in marginal rates of substitution) it is always possible to increase the output of at least one good.

9. This is not the place to develop the argument at length, but it is possible to suggest that the failure of the Hungarian reformers to attach sufficient importance to arguments of this type was responsible for the partial failure of the NEM in the early 1970s. See E. Hewett, 'The Hungarian Economy: Lessons of the 1970s and Prospects for the 1980s' in United States Congress, Joint Economic Committee, *East European Economic Assessment* (US Government Printing Office, Washington, DC, 1981), pp. 483-524, for a statement of this argument.

10. I have also suggested that the type of personal insecurity experienced by Soviet managers in Stalin's time is not a viable substitute for market uncertainty. although I have not developed the arguments in favour of this assertion in any detail.

4 WEST-EAST TECHNOLOGY TRANSFER: THE TRADE COMPONENT*

John A. Slater

Introduction

The object of this chapter is to introduce and describe the set of trade data developed at the OECD as an aid to quantify and assess the effects of Western technology exports to the six countries of Eastern Europe (Bulgaria, Czechoslovakia, the German Democratic Republic, Hungary, Poland and Romania) and the Soviet Union (henceforth referred to as the Eastern or CMEA countries). A survey of the criteria according to which data on West-East and intra-CMEA embodied technology trade (mainly capital goods) were selected, and the main difficulties encountered in doing so, is given in the first section. In the second section, comparisons between the data taken from OECD and Eastern sources are made, and some of the shortcomings thereby revealed are discussed. In the final section, the main indicators of the value of Eastern embodied technology imports, both from the West and also from other Eastern countries, are presented and compared, and the main conclusions set out.

It should be stressed that the data are described rather cursorily. The presentation of the data concentrates on total flows and their allocation by sectoral end-users, and within the industry sector by industrial branch end-users, without reference to flows by type of good, though these are also available in the databases used. Furthermore, the conclusions presented are general and preliminary. This is deliberate, since the chapter anticipates both a fuller description of the methodology, and more detailed findings concerning West-East technology transfers, by the OECD. This work will be made available in a more substantive and up-to-date form in 1985.[1]

The Databases

It is not intended in this presentation to belabour the concept of

50

'technology' — either by offering alternatives to definitions proposed by other authors in this field or by justifying those definitions which, implicitly or explicitly, were the starting point for the work described. Suffice it to say that we first distinguished between 'embodied' and 'disembodied' technology and in fact limit our comments to the former. While this could be interpreted as avoiding the issue, it is a fact that no definition of technology, even of embodied technology, can be reckoned suitable for all purposes: if the definition is broad, data constraints will inevitably limit full analysis, while the available data may also contain material irrelevant to the particular question under analysis. In this chapter, we have attempted to show the size and development of only a certain relatively simply definable component of technology, with a view to highlighting changes in its magnitude during the 1970s — a decade which witnessed a shift in attitudes to economic development in the Eastern countries as the previous easy availability of basic production factors (labour and capital) began to run out.

All we have done, therefore, is to use two classes of traded goods which seem relevant to the technology transfer issue on *a priori* grounds. The first type is capital goods (investment goods), chosen because they directly augment domestic production capacity. It should be noted that we do not distinguish between investment goods imported to remove more or less temporary capacity constraints, and those which fill gaps due to specific, long-term shortcomings in domestic technology. All investment goods are retained for our purpose, whether or not they can be considered as particularly technology-intensive or not. The second type of goods we examined are intermediate goods with a significant technological content. Here we have, in fact, tried to distinguish between different classes of intermediate goods by selecting imports, the domestic production of which might be expected to have a high opportunity cost; we have done so, however, simply on the implicit assumption that it is goods with a significant technology content which have the highest opportunity costs. Again, while part of these imports of intermediate goods fills gaps in (or helps to improve) domestic production *technology*, others simply supplement domestic output *capacity*. However, as in the case of investment goods, we make no systematic attempt to distinguish between the two.

The selection of capital goods has been made first on the basis of OECD statistics of East-West trade, and secondly on the basis of East European and Soviet *national* statistics. However, Eastern-reported data are insufficiently detailed to enable the selection of intermediate goods with a significant technology content, and so this part of the exercise was thus limited to West-East flows based on OECD trade statistics.

It may be asked why, apart from the general desirability of assembling as much data as possible on any phenomenon, a considerable effort has been made to gather together data on flows of Western capital goods flows to the Eastern countries from both OECD and CMEA country sources — why, that is, it is useful to look at essentially the same phenomenon using two different data sets. The reason is that, prior to the OECD project, little systematic information was available on the breakdown of technology flows of any kind by economic sectoral or industrial branch end-uses. The presentation of capital goods (but not intermediate goods flows) by end-uses is a unique future of the OECD exercise. To accomplish it, we first used total OECD trade flows with the seven Eastern countries individually, based on the UN Standard International Trade Classification (Revision I). The SITC is essentially a classification by *type* of good, which, as will be discussed later, leads to difficulties in allocating capital goods by end-uses. However, whatever its shortcomings in this respect, the OECD data are both more complete and more consistent over time than the trade statistics of the Eastern countries themselves.

To check on the breakdowns derived from the OECD data when disaggregated by end-uses, it was also considered desirable to perform as nearly as possible the same operation on the Eastern countries' own trade figures. Despite a number of omissions which will be discussed below, the Eastern countries' trade statistics do contain a large number of capital goods items already classified by end-use. It was in any case desired to exploit Eastern countries' own data to examine intra-CMEA trade in investment goods by end-use sector and branch: to examine its implications for West-East technology trade, to set the size of the latter in context and, where possible, to assess the complementarity or substitutability of supplies from the two sources. It was thus relatively simple to include data for total trade and hence, by subtraction, to obtain data on CMEA exports to and imports from the Rest of the World. In the case of Eastern imports, the Rest of the World means, effectively, the OECD countries (though other suppliers which are not included in the OECD aggregates — notably

Yugoslavia — are not altogether negligible). CMEA countries' own import data thus provide an independent check on the OECD data in aggregate as well as by end-uses.

The Western data cover exports by 24 OECD countries (excluding Yugoslavia and trade between the Federal Republic of Germany and the German Democratic Republic). As mentioned, they include both capital and intermediate technology-based goods. Capital goods are as specified in the United Nations Classification by Broad Economic Categories (BEC),[2] and correspond to category 41 (machinery, other capital equipment except transport, excluding parts and accessories) *plus* item 521 (industrial transport equipment). It should be noted that in both cases parts and accessories are excluded from capital goods. The BEC listing was slightly expanded to include pipeline, within which large diameter pipe for the transport of oil and gas is included; and also a few other items such as rails which are clearly also capital goods items.

Intermediate goods with a significant technology content are selected first from the BEC intermediate goods listing, and second according to a method of classifying output by industrial branches according to the R&D intensity of the producer branch.[3] The broad headings under which they were classified for this purpose are: parts and accessories of machinery and equipment; ditto of transport equipment; paper manufactures; textile manufactures; synthetic fibres; special manufactures of leather, wood, glass and minerals; miscellaneous mineral manufactures; iron and steel; non-ferrous metals; organic and inorganic chemical elements; final chemical manufactures; chemical and plastic materials; and a very small miscellaneous component.[4]

The selection of capital goods items made on the basis of the East European and Soviet country data is based upon a 'control group' — CMEA Standard Foreign Trade Classification[5] (SFTC) group 1 (machinery and equipment), for which a number of items have been added (pipes) and others subtracted (mainly a few intermediate goods such as ballbearings, cable and wire and metals, etc.). Investment goods imports from and exports to other CMEA countries and also to and from Rest of the World were both extracted. This gives not only the possibility of checking on OECD-reported exports to the East in total and by end-uses, but also enables intra-CMEA shipments by country to be completed; since the data cover both exports and imports, they enable 'mirror'

data to be used to supplement gaps in individual reporting countries' data on intra-CMEA trade.

End-use sectors and branches were specified according to the
more or less similar national accounting and industrial classifica-
tions used by the Eastern countries. First, the total economy was
divided between the 'material' and 'non-material' spheres — that is,
between activities resulting in material output and services such as
trade, transport and communications which contribute directly to
the production of goods; and consumer services, notably medical
and administrative services which are the main ones which involve
identifiable trade flows in capital goods. Within the material
sphere, four end-use sectors were identified: industry, construction,
agriculture and transport (including pipeline and ancillary equipment for the transport of oil and gas). Within industry, there is a
good deal of variation in branch classification between Eastern
countries, but nine branches (see the Notes to Tables 4.3 and 4.4)
were selected; differences in their coverage are summarised in the
Note to Table 4.3.

Both sets of statistics are presented in current US dollars.
OECD data are, of course, reported in this currency. CMEA
country flows are based on national currencies; intra-CMEA data
were first converted into transferable roubles at official rates, and
then into US dollars on the basis of official rouble/dollar rates. Data
on trade with the Rest of the World were derived from national currency at the official dollar rate. (The rouble/dollar cross-rates implied
diverge from the Soviet dollar/rouble rate.) National currencies
used (except for Hungary after 1976) are *valuta* ('foreign trade')
currencies. However, it needs to be borne in mind that the *valuta*
currencies are accounting units which bear no relation to domestic
price levels or inter-branch and sectoral relative prices. Moreover,
while the resulting dollar values for East-West transactions presumably reflect accurately the hard currency values in which they were,
in most cases, originally designated, the indicative value of the dollar
data for intra-CMEA trade is more limited. Even though intra-
CMEA trade prices are in theory fixed on the basis of world market
prices, a certain unquantifiable arbitrary element remains since it will
not always have been possible to find equivalent products traded on
world markets for the purpose of price setting, whilst it can be
expected that many transactions are designated in prices reflecting
the particular circumstances of a given bilateral flow at a particular
time.

This short résumé does not do justice to the problems involved. First, in the attribution of OECD (SITC) data to Eastern end-uses, there were inevitably many cases where instinct and experience rather than precise knowledge guided the attribution of a particular item to a particular end-use. This was unavoidable; as noted, the SITC is, essentially, a classification by type of good rather than by end-use. While some SITC end-uses are fairly obvious (the energy branch in the case of electricity generation equipment, the transport branch for railway engines or rolling stock and, within industry, textile machinery, etc.), other items may be destined for a range of different end-users (structural parts; electrical or non-electrical machinery in general). In these cases, the approach used was one of cautious common sense — which does not, however, exclude the possibility of error. In the event, it was found possible to attribute over 90 per cent of investment goods flows to one or other sector of the material sphere (industry, construction, agriculture, transport and communications) and of the non-material sphere (office machinery, medical items); within industry, branch attribution covered about 65 per cent of the total allocated to the industry sector. Of the industry residual, approaching half was accounted for by SITC item 719.8 (non-electrical machinery and equipment not elsewhere specified). Much of the 35 per cent not attributed is probably destined for the chemical and engineering branches, which are substantially understated in some years and in some countries by the OECD-reported figures when these are compared with the data reported by the East European countries and the Soviet Union.

Allocation problems were smaller in the case of East European and Soviet-reported figures, which contain many more categories relating trade directly to end-users than does the SITC. However, other problems arise as a result of the very poor detailed commodity coverage of a number of CMEA countries: Bulgaria, where many items are shown in physical units only; the German Democratic Republic and Romania, for which only data at relatively high levels of aggregation are published; and the practice of including certain items in some years but not in others, a feature of the Soviet statistics which are otherwise among the most complete. OECD-reported data were used to fill in some gaps in the coverage of trade with the Rest of the World. In general, the Czechoslovak, Hungarian, Polish and Soviet data give the most complete and consistent end-use breakdowns. But the figures reported by Eastern European countries as a whole (but not the Soviet Union) do reveal a considerable degree of understatement of aggregate flows in trade with the Rest of the World.

With regard to intra-CMEA flows, these difficulties can be resolved to some extent by filling obvious gaps in the end-use items in particular countries' reported figures by the use of 'mirror' statistics. A serious deficiency is the existence of a substantial unexplained residual between the sum of capital goods inputs identified by country of origin, and capital goods imports in total, which amounted in 1975 and 1980 to some $US 5 billion and 7.5 billion respectively — some 16 per cent of the total identified in both years for the seven countries taken together (Table 4.1).

This brief and oversimplified description of the sources and methods used to create the database already perhaps suffices to show that it can make no claim to completeness in measuring embodied technology flows (or even of capital goods flows); in addition, it omits disembodied technology of all kinds — patents, licences, other transfers of know-how via documentation or personnel training, etc.[6] In the East-West dimension, the OECD-reported figures do capture total Eastern investment goods purchases — as well as a selection of trade in intermediate goods as defined — though the data are incomplete given the ommission of trade between the German Democratic Republic and the Federal Republic of Germany. We also exploited all relevant Eastern statistics, but gaps remain. Finally, our retention of capital and some intermediate goods is somewhat undifferentiated in terms of the various definitions of embodied technology which have been offered by different scholars.

The Quality of the Data

Aggregate West-to-East Flows of Capital Goods

As a first step in assessing the quality of the data sets described above, the OECD and CMEA country reported data on West-to East flows are compared in Table 4.1. It can be seen that the ratio between the total of Eastern countries' acquisitions of capital goods from the OECD area (OECD-reported export data) and Eastern countries' reported imports of such goods from the Rest of the World (that is, from non-CMEA countries) falls from about 90 per cent in 1973, and 80 per cent in 1975 and 1978, to only 72 per cent in 1980. However, when the OECD data are adjusted to include spare parts and accessories (for all countries but Hungary and Czechoslovakia), and also exports of capital goods by Yugoslavia, the ratio improves considerably — and the adjusted OECD data give results which average plus or minus 5 per cent of the CMEA-reported totals in the years shown. In aggregate, therefore, CMEA-reported capital goods imports from the Rest of the World and corresponding OECD-reported exports can be reconciled rather closely.

However, this agreement is due in part to offsetting discrepancies. In the first place, the Eastern country import data should yield higher figures because of the inclusion of imports by the German Democratic Republic from the Federal Republic of Germany. Second, as noted by Paul Marer in his investigation of mirror-image statistics in East-West trade, Eastern-recorded imports — particularly of machinery and equipment items — may be bigger than OECD-recorded exports because 'Soviet statistics include in imports the cost of technology and know-how associated with machinery purchases, which Western countries report as invisible exports'[7] and the same is presumably true of other countries using the SFTC or a similar system.

The close correspondence in the seven country aggregate conceals moreover some substantial differences between OECD- and Eastern country-reported data for the individual Eastern countries. In the first place, the adjusted OECD-reported data for the Soviet Union are, for years after 1970, duly smaller than the Soviet-reported figures (the former fell from 102 to 83 per cent of the latter between 1970 and 1980). But the converse is true for Eastern Europe as a whole and for all of the six countries individually. In part, this reflects the paucity of data identifiable by origin and type of good. Data not so identifiable (henceforth referred to simply as the 'unidentified' item) are sometimes large — notably in the German Democratic Republic, where OECD partner-country 'mirror' data accounted for roughly two-thirds of the sector and branch detail within the 'control group' of total imports of Western machinery and equipment; and in Romania, for which only OECD partner-country data are available. In Bulgaria, the contribution of partner-country data was also high (about half). For most countries, the total sector and branch totals reported by them (purchases identified by region), appear to underestimate the actual purchases from OECD countries even when supplemented by OECD data. However, for Hungary,

Table 4.1: Comparison of OECD Exports of Investment Goods to the Eastern Countries (A) and (B) with Eastern Countries' Imports from the Rest of the World (C) ($US Billion and Percentages)

	1970			1973			1975			1978			1980		
	A	B	C	A	B	C	A	B	C	A	B	C	A	B	C
Bulgaria	0.09	0.12	..	0.15	0.18	0.13	0.51	0.60	0.46	0.38	0.47	0.37	0.56	..	0.38
— per cent of C	..	..		115	138		111	130		103	127		147	..	
Czechoslovakia	0.26	0.28	..	0.39	0.40	0.40	0.64	0.67	0.68	0.85	0.89	0.98	0.92	..	1.48
— per cent of C	96	100		98	100		94	99		87	91		62	..	
German Dem. Rep.	0.16	0.19	0.16	0.17	0.23	0.18	0.33	0.42	0.41	0.33	0.43	0.41	0.52	0.68	0.59
— per cent of C	100	119		94	128		80	102		80	105		88	115	
Hungary	0.13	0.13	0.13	0.23	0.24	0.23	0.41	0.42	0.45	0.84	0.86	1.20	0.73	0.76	0.63
— per cent of C	100	100		100	104		91	93		70	72		116	121	
Poland	0.22	0.27	0.26	1.09	1.27	1.18	2.19	2.58	2.56	1.82	2.26	2.22	2.10	..	1.94
— per cent of C	85	104		92	108		86	101		82	102		108	..	
Romania	0.25	0.30	0.21	0.51	0.62	0.50	0.64	0.87	0.76	1.07	1.40	1.38	0.81	1.18	0.96
— per cent of C	119	143		102	124		84	114		78	101		84	123	
Total, Eastern Europe	1.12	1.29	(1.04)	2.54	2.94	2.65	4.72	5.56	5.32	5.29	6.31	6.05	6.20	..	5.98
— per cent of C	108	124		96	111		89	105		87	104		104	..	
Soviet Union	1.10	1.32	1.30	1.89	2.15	2.43	4.93	5.81	6.75	6.54	7.90	8.78	7.32	8.82	..
— per cent of C	85	102		78	88		73	86		74	90		70	83	
Total, Eastern Europe and Soviet Union	2.22	2.61	(2.34)	4.47	5.09	5.08	9.65	11.37	12.07	11.83	14.21	14.84	13.52	..	14.80
— per cent of C	95	112		88	100		80	94		80	96		91	..	

Notes: Column A (OECD data) *excludes* spare parts and accessories; column B (also OECD data) *includes* them (except for Hungary and Czechoslovakia), plus the value of Yugoslav capital goods exports to all countries concerned. Components may not sum due to rounding.
(. not available; .. not applicable; ( ) estimate.)
Source: OECD East-West Technology Transfer Database.

Poland, and for Czechoslavakia in the earlier years, national statistics do give a reasonable correspondence with the corresponding OECD-reported export flows.

These apparent discrepancies focus upon one of the principal shortcomings of the data set based on the Eastern countries' own trade returns. The relatively large size of the residual import of capital goods which cannot be identified by country of origin can be traced, in the first place, because of the method used to identify total capital goods imports. Since this starts from the extraction of the total imports of machinery and equipment 'control group' (adjusted, as noted earlier, to exclude non-capital goods items and to include pipeline),[8] it is the difference between this total and imports of capital goods identified by origin which gives the 'unidentified' item shown in Table 4.2.

This residual was large in all countries of Eastern Europe at the beginning of the 1970s — about 30 per cent of the total for all East European countries in 1973. But it was much higher in some countries (for example, Bulgaria, Czechoslovakia and the German Democratic Republic). It fell somewhat in most countries towards the middle of the decade (mainly because statistical reporting improved in some countries), especially in Hungary (19 per cent) and Poland (14 per cent) but remained high in the German Democratic Republic (40 per cent) and even rose in Bulgaria (to 32 per cent). The average in 1975 was 25 per cent for all six Eastern European countries combined. By 1980, it ranged between 18 per cent (Poland) and 32 per cent (Bulgaria). The lack of statistical information on the German Democratic Republic prevented calculation of its residual in that year; mainly for this reason, the residual averaged only 18 per cent for the six countries.

In the Soviet Union, the unidentified residual has been relatively small throughout most of the 1970s (5-7 per cent), but rose somewhat toward the end of the decade (to 18 per cent in 1978 and 13 per cent in 1980). Thus, in very summary terms, it can be seen that, excluding Poland, about one-third of East European imports of capital goods cannot be identified by country of origin, while in Poland and the Soviet Union the unidentified item amounted to between 5 and 20 per cent in the second half of the 1970s.

In sum, while it is thus not possible fully to reconcile the OECD- and Western-reported totals for capital goods imports of each Eastern country, the two sets of figures taken together pro-

Table 4.2: Eastern-reported Capital Goods Imports of Eastern Europe and the Soviet Union by Region or Origin ($US Million and Per Cent of Importing Country Totals)

	1970				1973				1975			
	From CMEA	From rest of world	Unidentified	Total	From CMEA	From rest of world	Unidentified	Total	From CMEA	From rest of world	Unidentified	Total
Bulgaria	.	.	.	.	932.4	133.2	472.4	1538.0	1141.4	456.5	752.4	2350.4
					60.6	8.7	30.7	100.0	48.6	19.4	32.0	100.0
Czechoslovakia	552.0	279.9	371.6	1203.5	1037.6	404.8	806.2	2248.6	1526.9	677.0	1106.5	3310.4
	45.8	23.3	30.9	100.0	46.1	18.0	35.9	100.0	46.1	20.5	33.4	100.0
German Democratic Republic	620.2	156.3	914.4	1690.8	1150.0	178.6	1318.7	2647.3	1751.0	406.7	1415.6	3573.4
	36.7	9.2	54.0	100.0	43.4	6.7	49.8	100.0	49.0	11.4	39.6	100.0
Hungary	288.1[a]	201.3[a]	297.3[a]	786.7[a]	389.9	233.2	174.9	798.0	754.4	446.2	281.4	1482.0
	36.6[a]	25.6[a]	37.8[a]	100.0[a]	48.9	29.2	21.9	100.0	50.9	30.1	19.0	100.0
Poland	648.6	257.1	489.2	1394.9	1436.7	1184.7	859.5	3480.9	1742.5	2558.7	711.2	5012.3
	46.5	18.5	35.1	100.0	41.3	34.0	24.7	100.0	34.8	51.0	14.2	100.0
Romania	281.1	211.4	.	492.5	518.3	503.4	.	1021.6	533.0	760.5	.	1293.4
	57.1	42.9		100.0	50.7	49.3		100.0	41.2	58.8		100.0
Total, Eastern Europe[b]	(2852.0)	(1038.0)	(2160.2)	(6050.2)	5464.9	2637.9	3631.7	11734.4	7449.2	5305.6	4267.1	17021.9
	(47.1)	(17.2)	(35.7)	100.0	46.6	22.5	30.9	100.0	43.8	31.2	25.1	100.0
Soviet Union	2750.4	1303.9	218.4	4272.7	4522.5	2433.9	514.8	7471.1	6514.3	6746.7	641.8	13902.8
	64.4	30.5	5.1	100.0	60.5	32.6	6.9	100.0	46.9	48.5	4.6	100.0
Total, Eastern Europe and Soviet Union[b]	(5602.4)	(2341.9)	(2374.6)	(10322.9)	9987.4	5071.8	4146.5	19205.5	13963.5	12052.3	4908.9	30924.7
	(54.3)	(22.7)	(23.0)	100.0	52.0	26.4	21.6	100.0	45.2	39.0	15.9	100.0

	1978				1980			
	From CMEA	From rest of world	Unidentified	Total	From CMEA	From rest of world	Unidentified	Total
Bulgaria	1680.1 / 53.1	372.6 / 11.8	1111.9 / 35.1	3164.6 / 100.0	1941.1 / 56.6	376.6 / 11.0	1110.1 / 32.4	3427.8 / 100.0
Czechoslovakia	2593.4 / 51.6	976.5 / 19.4	1458.2 / 29.0	5028.1 / 100.0	2552.3 / 46.8	1483.1 / 27.2	1420.5 / 26.0	5455.9 / 100.0
German Democratic Republic	2500.8 / 56.4	405.2 / 9.1	1531.3 / 34.5	4437.2 / 100.0	2416.0 / 80.3	592.3 / 19.7	.	3008.3 / 100.0
Hungary	1176.7 / 47.4	703.0 / 28.3	604.6 / 24.3	2484.3 / 100.0	1286.5 / 47.6	625.2 / 23.2	788.7 / 29.2	2700.3 / 100.0
Poland	2762.6 / 45.6	2218.5 / 36.6	1075.4 / 17.8	6056.6 / 100.0	3276.2 / 51.7	1942.9 / 30.7	1115.2 / 17.6	6334.3 / 100.0
Romania	1021.1 / 42.6	1377.6 / 57.4	.	2398.7 / 100.0	1086.0 / 53.0	962.9 / 47.0	.	2049.0 / 100.0
Total, Eastern Europe	11734.7 / 49.8	6053.4 / 25.7	5781.4 / 24.5	23569.5 / 100.0	12569.0 / 54.7	6291.0 / 27.4	4115.6 / 17.9	22975.6 / 100.0
Soviet Union	9630.2 / 43.1	8783.1 / 39.3	3924.9 / 17.6	22338.2 / 100.0	12430.0 / 51.0	8816.1 / 36.2	3138.3 / 12.9	24384.4 / 100.0
Total, Eastern Europe and Soviet Union	21364.9 / 46.5	14836.5 / 32.3	9706.3 / 21.1	45907.7 / 100.0	24999.0 / 52.8	15107.1 / 31.9	7253.9 / 15.3	47360.0 / 100.0

Notes: a. 1971. b. 'Eastern Europe' and 'Eastern Europe and Soviet Union' aggregates for 1970 incorporate rough estimates for Bulgaria and Hungary in that year. (. not availble; .. estimate.)
Source: OECD East-West Technology Transfer Database.

vide, first, a reliable aggregate time series for Western exports to
the East (the OECD data). Second, the Eastern-reported data
provide at least a minimum basis for assessing the size of imports
from the West relative to those from CMEA partner countries —
and, as will be investigated in the following sub-section, useful
information to supplement the OECD data broken down on a
sector/industrial branch end-use basis.

The Sectoral and Branch Allocation of Eastern Capital Goods Imports from the OECD Area

Given the discrepancies at country levels between aggregate
Eastern country- and OECD-reported data outlined in the previous subsection, it is not surprising that there are some differences
between the sectoral and industrial branch end-use allocations of
Eastern capital goods imports from the West as revealed by the
two data sets. The main source of discrepancies *within* the aggregates is that the OECD-reported data contain much bigger resi-
duals which cannot be satisfactorily allocated either to sectors of
the economy as a whole, or to branches within industry.

For reasons of space, comparisons of the two data sets are presented for only the two years 1975 and 1980; they are, however,
sufficient to illustrate the general pattern (Table 4.3). The table
shows that for most Eastern countries the OECD data set points to
a much smaller share of capital goods imports for the material
sphere than do the Eastern-reported data. The broad magnitude of
the sectoral end-user patterns revealed by the two data sets within
the material sphere are rather similar — though the CMEA figures
tend to understate the share of industry and overstate that of transport and communications. The OECD-reported data do not,
moreover, enable investment goods for the construction industry
to be shown separately (all tractors, for instance, have been allocated to agriculture) whereas Eastern country data show that this
sector took 2-6 per cent of imports destined for the material
sphere of the economy in most years. This, together with the
OECD's understatement of imports of agricultural equipment,
contributes to the residual unattributable by sector of about 10 per
cent of capital goods imports in the total for the material sphere in
the OECD data.

Within industry, the overall magnitudes of the share of imports
by branch end-users shown by the two data sets are again broadly
similar, but there are, none the less, some differences. This relates

first to the fact that the OECD data contain a non-attributable residual of considerable size — generally between 30-40 per cent of the total and even higher in Bulgaria.[9] It is thus not surprising that the share of most industrial end-users appears to be under-estimated by the OECD-reported data. Given the apparent under-statement of industry as a whole in the totals reported by CMEA countries, no detailed reconciliation by industrial end-users is possible. However, despite these demonstrable discrepancies, the *relative* orders of magnitude of the various industrial end-users are (fuels and chemicals excepted) not dissimilar.

Intra-CMEA Capital Goods Trade

The data on intra-CMEA exchanges of capital goods is fairly complete despite the failure of Romania — and subsequently the German Democratic Republic — to produce detailed commodity breakdowns of foreign trade since the early 1970s. Improved coverage was attained for these and other countries by the use of 'mirror' statistics for intra-CMEA exchanges; the general principle has been to retain an individual reporting country's own import or export data, except where discrepancies are particularly large, and to fill in gaps due to apparent substantial underestimates, or missing components, by inserting the sum of the other CMEA countries' exports to that country.

While it should be borne in mind that the end-use detail of exports excludes shipments from Romania to the German Democratic Republic and vice versa, the aggregate dimension of CMEA *imports* from other CMEA countries, as well as their composition by end-use, are surprisingly consistent with the corresponding CMEA *export* data (Table 4.4). Leaving aside Romania, whose import figures after 1972 are in fact wholly derived from partner-country export data, discrepancies for Bulgaria, the German Democratic Republic, Poland and the Soviet Union are in a range of 2-5 per cent. In Hungary, the much lower figure for recorded imports in both 1975 and 1980 compared with the sum of partners' exports may result in part from exchange rate inconsistencies, and in Czechoslovakia (years prior to 1980), the roughly 10 per cent excess of recorded imports over partners' exports may reflect some inflation in the totals due to the limited availability in earlier years of the commodity detail needed to adjust the 'machinery and equipment' item in order to separate out capital goods only.

Table 4.3: End-Use Sector and Industrial Branch Distribution of Eastern Countries' Capital Goods Imports from the West: OECD and CMEA Reporting Country Data Compared (Percentage Shares of Respective Totals and Sub-totals; Grand Total in $US Million)

End-Users	Bulgaria 1975 OECD	Bulgaria 1975 CMEA	Bulgaria 1980 OECD	Bulgaria 1980 CMEA	Czechoslovakia 1975 OECD	Czechoslovakia 1975 CMEA	Czechoslovakia 1980 OECD	Czechoslovakia 1980 CMEA	GDR 1975 OECD	GDR 1975 CMEA	GDR 1980 OECD	GDR 1980 CMEA	Hungary 1975 OECD	Hungary 1975 CMEA	Hungary 1980 OECD	Hungary 1980 CMEA
Material sphere																
Industry	60	58	62	51	75	72	78	78	50	70	70	64	65	49	68	50
Construction	–	2	–	6	–	5	–	4	–	2	–	6	–	–	–	3
Agriculture	2	3	3	4	3	4	1	–	2	2	2	2	9	6	6	10
Transport and communications (including gas and oil distribution)	26	38	23	39	13	20	9	9	42	39	20	28	19	45	15	37
Non-attributable	11	–	12	–	10	–	11	11	7	–	8	8	8	–	9	–
Total	100	100	100	100	100	100	100	100	100	100	100	100	100	100	100	100
– per cent of grand total	98	89	96	79	93	83	94	83	97	81	94	67	94	78	94	72
Industry (detailed)																
Energy	2	7	3	12	3	13	4	5	11	14	13	23	6	13	4	16
Fuel	5	–	5	10	6	7	7	5	8	9	17	5	8	16	10	9
Metallurgy	7	2	7	37	10	9	8	8	3	1	2	8	4	1	6	3
Engineering and metalworking	8	12	9	10	10	23	11	11	7	9	13	13	5	13	7	7
Chemicals	11	11	11	–	11	9	11	–	14	1	17	–	1	16	16	9
Construction materials	6	7	–	2	–	1	–	12	–	9	8	8	–	1	1	3
Wood and paper	21	20	2	11	8	11	17	7	29	7	40	8	19	15	–	5
Light industry	9	17	5	–	15	18	11	11	4	17	17	25	4	16	13	13
Food	30	–	46	–	6	8	5	5	23	2	2	3	35	–	5	18
Non-attributable	–	–	–	–	31	–	27	–	–	41	41	–	–	39	39	–
Total	100	100	100	100	100	100	100	100	100	100	100	100	100	100	100	100
Non-material sphere																
Administration and public health																
– per cent of grand total	2	11	4	21	7	17	6	17	3	19	6	33	6	22	6	28
Grand total	100	100	100	100	100	100	100	100	100	100	100	100	100	100	100	100
– in $ millions	515	457	404	377	639	677	848	1483	334	407	516	592	411	446	735	625

End-Users	Poland				Romania				Soviet Union			
	1975		1980		1975		1980		1975		1980	
	OECD data	CMEA data	OECD data	CMEA data	OECD data	CMEA data	OECD data	CMEA data	OECD data	CMEA data	OECD data	CMEA data
Material sphere												
Industry	59	59	59	59	64	63	68	67	57	50	57	50
Construction	3	3	3	3	.	3	.	4	.	5	.	3
Agriculture	2	3	1	2	.	4	.	5	3	1	2	1
Transport and communications (including gas and oil distribution)	31	35	32	36	29	29	23	24	34	44	34	39
Non-attributable	9	.	8	.	7	.	9	.	7	.	7	.
Total	100	100	100	100	100	100	100	100	100	100	100	100
— per cent of grand total	98	87	97	83	97	89	96	85	98	89	97	90
Industry (detailed)												
Energy	4	7	5	8	6	13	5	12	4	3	2	9
Fuel	6	6	9	22	7	8	7	7	5	12	5	13
Metallurgy	11	16	9	9	10	15	8	15	9	14	5	7
Engineering and metalworking	12	22	11	26	17	17	20	23	18	32	21	27
Chemicals	11	14	11	18	13	26	12	25	18	17	19	28
Construction materials	.	6	4	1	.	.	1	1	.	2	.	1
Wood and paper	4	5	8	5	4	9	.	7	3	6	2	6
Light industry	14	12	4	5	9	8	10	9	8	9	4	4
Food	5	12	4	5	3	3	1	2	3	4	4	6
Non-attributable	32	.	40	.	31	.	35	.	32	.	39	.
Total	100	100	100	100	100	100	100	100	100	100	100	100
Non-material sphere												
Administration and public health												
— per cent of grand total	2	13	3	17	3	11	4	15	2	11	3	10
Grand total	100	100	100	100	100	100	100	100	100	100	100	100
— in $ million	2,186	2,559	1,578	1,943	635	761	806	963	4,935	6,747	5,723	8,816

Note: OECD data exclude spare parts and accessories and all shipments by Yugoslavia, and trade between the Federal Republic of Germany and the German Democratic Republic. Chemical branch in Bulgaria, the German Democratic Republic and Hungary includes oil refining. Light industry includes textiles, clothing and footwear plus (except in the Soviet Union) glass, ceramics and printing. In the German Democratic Republic and Hungary it also includes wood and paper. Components may not sum to totals due to rounding. (. not available.)

Source: OECD East-West Technology Transfer Data Base.

Table 4.4: Comparison of Intra-CMEA Imports and Exports of Capital Goods (Percentage Shares of Respective Total and Sub-totals; Grand Total in $US Million)

	Bulgaria				Czechoslovakia				German Democratic Republic				Hungary			
	1975		1980		1975		1980		1975		1980		1975		1980	
	Imports from CMEA	CMEA exports to country	Imports from CMEA	CMEA exports to country	Imports from CMEA	CMEA exports to country	Imports from CMEA	CMEA exports to country	Imports from CMEA	CMEA exports to country	Imports from CMEA	CMEA exports to country	Imports from CMEA	CMEA exports to country	Imports from CMEA	CMEA exports to country
Material sphere																
Industry	44	47	47	48	27	29	37	43	42	41	37	38	27	26	33	35
Construction	6	4	6	6	4	5	6	6	5	4	5	4	5	5	3	3
Agriculture	14	13	12	11	23	26	14	14	9	9	15	12	23	20	13	13
Transport and communications (including gas and oil distribution)	37	36	35	34	46	40	43	36	44	46	44	45	45	50	52	49
Total	100	100	100	100	100	100	100	100	100	100	100	100	100	100	100	100
– per cent of grand total	88	89	91	90	75	66	72	71	77	78	82	81	77	80	79	83
Industry (detailed)																
Energy	33	30	33	31	27	19	24	34	32	32	39	39	28	29	48	51
Fuel	7	14	6	14	8	9	9	8	4	4	3	3	10	12	7	9
Metallurgy	9	7	14	12	5	6	10	9	11	11	10	10	4	3	2	6
Engineering and metalworking	13	11	17	15	33	35	27	22	22	22	22	22	20	19	22	15
Chemicals	11	13	8	7	2	3	6	5	9	10	5	5	8	7	2	3
Construction materials	8	7	8	6	·	1	1	4	3	3	1	1	3	2	2	5
Wood and paper	3	4	4	3	2	2	4		1	1	2	2	2	2	1	7
Light industry	11	9	6	6	15	17	14	12	13	12	12	12	19	18	9	7
Food	4	4	4	5	7	8	5	6	5	5	6	6	6	7	6	5
Total	100	100	100	100	100	100	100	100	100	100	100	100	100	100	100	100
Non-material sphere																
Administration and public health																
– per cent of grand total	12	11	9	10	25	34	28	29	23	22	18	19	23	20	21	17
Grand total	100	100	100	100	100	100	100	100	100	100	100	100	100	100	100	100
– in $ million	1,141	1,165	1,941	1,974	1,527	1,398	2,552	2,587	1,751	1,657	2,416	2,356	754	913	1,286	1,778

	Poland 1975		Poland 1980		Romania 1975		Romania 1980		Soviet Union 1975		Soviet Union 1980	
	Imports from CMEA	CMEA exports to country	Imports from CMEA	CMEA exports to country	Imports from CMEA	CMEA exports to country	Imports from CMEA	CMEA exports to country	Imports from CMEA	CMEA exports to country	Imports from CMEA	CMEA exports to country
Material sphere												
Industry	41	42	33	32	56	56	57	57	37	38	46	45
Construction	5	4	6	5	4	4	7	7	1	1	2	2
Agriculture	14	14	17	17	3	3	3	3	9	9	11	9
Transport and communications (including gas and oil distribution)	40	39	45	46	36	36	34	33	53	53	41	43
Total	100	100	100	100	100	100	100	100	100	100	100	100
– per cent of grand total	78	77	82	82	85	85	89	89	78	77	80	78
Industry (detailed)												
Energy	14	16	21	21	24	24	14	14	21	21	23	20
Fuel	13	13	11	14	6	6	10	10	6	6	10	10
Metallurgy	12	11	16	13	13	13	9	9	5	5	7	7
Engineering and metalworking	30	28	21	22	30	30	35	35	17	19	16	19
Chemicals	4	5	6	4	9	9	9	9	19	19	15	16
Construction materials	5	6	4	5	.	.	.	.	4	4	3	2
Wood and paper	.	1	.	.	2	2	3	3	2	1	2	1
Light industry	16	17	15	15	14	14	19	19	14	14	15	15
Food	6	6	5	6	2	2	1	1	11	11	10	9
Total	100	100	100	100	100	100	100	100	100	100	100	100
Non-material sphere												
Administration and public health												
– per cent of grand total	22	23	18	18	15	15	11	11	22	23	20	22
Grand total	100	100	100	100	100	100	100	100	100	100	100	100
– in $ million	1,742	1,717	3,276	3,356	533	533	1,086	1,086	6,514	6,310	12,430	12,333

Note: 'Imports from CMEA' are those reported by the importing country; 'CMEA exports to country' are the sum of the other six countries' exports to that country. For coverage of industrial branches, see Note to Table 3. Components may not sum to totals due to rounding. (. not available.)

Source: OECD East-West Technology Transfer Data Base.

It should of course be stressed that, since the data presented reflect the use of 'mirror' adjustments, a fair degree of consensus between the direct import and partner country export-derived data is to be expected. Nevertheless, coverage by the two sets of figures for most countries does seem to be relatively complete and consistent — not only in aggregate but also in terms of end-use sectors and industrial branches.

Eastern Countries' Capital Goods Imports, 1970-80

This concluding section provides a commentary on the data presented in Tables 4.2-4.4 above. It first details the size of global capital goods imports of the Eastern countries over the 1970s and their geographical origins, and also comments on the development of Eastern imports of intermediate goods with significant technological content relative to capital goods in East-West trade. The sectoral and branch distribution by Eastern end-users is then considered, and differences with regard to the end-use pattern of purchases from the West and from other CMEA countries are highlighted. Finally, some of the Eastern countries' policy orientations as suggested by the size, development and pattern of embodied technology imports as defined earlier are discussed in the light of the economic growth slowdown of the Eastern countries in the late 1970s.

The Magnitude of Eastern Capital Goods Imports

As shown in Table 4.2, total investment goods imports of the Eastern countries from all sources were around $US 50 billion in 1980, making allowance for the omission of the German Democratic Republic's imports from unidentified geographical areas in that year. This compares with about $US 31 billion in 1975, and an estimated $US 10 billion in 1970. Thus the very fast rates of growth of 1970-5 were not maintained after the latter year — and after 1978, an absolute decline in volume terms probably occurred. As noted earlier, the above aggregate data, taken from Eastern sources, probably understate the absolute levels, particularly in the early years of the decade, and hence the rates of increase over the periods.

Both at the beginning and the end of the decade, the CMEA countries themselves supplied at least half of their own imports of capital goods identified by region — though it fell to substantially less than one-half in the 1975-8 period. Imports identified from the Rest of the World (virtually all of which were from OECD countries and Yugoslavia) ranged between one-quarter of the total from all sources in 1973 to 40 per cent in 1975, and 32 per cent in 1978 and 1980. Imports unidentified by region of origin amounted to 16-23 per cent of the totals throughout the period.

This residual unidentified by area of origin amounted to $US 4-5 billion in 1973 and 1975, and around twice that in 1978 and 1980. At least part of it originated in non-CMEA countries. As noted earlier, after 1970 it was much bigger relative to the totals in Eastern Europe (20-30 per cent) than in the Soviet Union (5-18 per cent). There is thus an observed relationship between the apparent understatement of Eastern Europe's own reported imports of capital goods relative to OECD-reported data, discussed above, and the large size of the residual unidentified by geographical origin; by contrast, in the Soviet Union — and also in Poland in the later years — the residual is small.

In this regard, it should be borne in mind that the OECD-reported figures are bigger than the countries' own reported data. Thus, it seems likely that a relatively large share of the unidentified residual of Eastern Europe other than Poland originates in the Rest of the World, and a relatively smaller share in the cases of Poland and the Soviet Union. It should also be noted that a possibly large share of the residual may be accounted for by complete plant, since of the East European countries concerned, only Hungary (for imports from the Rest of the World only) and Poland now report this item as such.

As the changing percentage shares shown in Table 4.2 imply (it is recalled that Table 4.2 is based on Eastern-reported data), the share of supplies from the Rest of the World rose substantially in the totals between 1970 and 1975, but began to fall rather faster after 1975 and particularly after 1978. The share of the Rest of the World probably rose to more than half the total imports of capital goods in Poland, Romania and the Soviet Union in 1975. Making use of the more consistent OECD data set, OECD exports of capital goods to the seven countries rose by more than fourfold between 1970 and 1975 — from just over $US 2 billion to just under $US 10 billion in value terms. A further rise to nearly $US 12 billion in 1978 was followed by a fall to below $US 11 billion in 1980 as this class of imports was cut back in the wake of domestic and foreign debt adjustment policies throughout the area — including in the more favourably placed Soviet Union which, unlike Eastern Europe, had benefited from favourable terms of trade movements over virtually the whole period.

For the OECD-reported series, it has proved possible to make use of price data to approximate the rise in Eastern imports of capital goods in volume terms.[10] Because of the very high rates of price inflation over the 1970-5 period, and the more moderate but still fairly high rates which persisted between 1975 and the end of the decade, the rise in Eastern imports was of course much less spectacular than the value changes quoted above. Nevertheless, they were quite impressive — particularly in Poland — up to the final years of the decade. Between 1970 and 1975, Eastern imports of capital goods from the OECD countries more than doubled in volume and were maintained at roughly the same level until 1978. Thereafter, their volume declined quite sharply — by about 20 per cent between 1978 and 1980 for the seven countries taken together.

As a further step in setting the scale of capital goods imports from the West into perspective, the aggregate volume figures quoted above can also be evaluated in terms of changes in the volume of investment. First, however, it should be noted that it is not possible to calculate the share of capital goods imports in total capital expenditures by using the regularly offered series of investment statistics in volume terms published by the Eastern countries for 1970-80. As noted the internal pricing systems in the centrally planned economies do not necessarily bear any relationship to prices on world markets. However, a comparison of relevant trade and investment volume data can show *changes* in the relationship between capital goods imports and investment (Table 4.5). The data show that between 1970 and 1975, the original (unknown) share of capital goods imports from the West in investment in the total economy had risen considerably in four countries: in Bulgaria (by 71 per cent), in Hungary (by 20 per cent), in Poland (by 113 per cent) and in the Soviet Union (by 54 per cent). The share of Western capital goods imports in industry's investment generally increased in these countries by slightly more than their share in total investment except in Poland. In three countries the share of capital goods imports from the West apparently declined: this movement reflected very cautious policies towards foreign technology by Czechoslovakia, while the fall in the German Democratic Republic was due to the slow growth of imports from OECD countries other than the Federal Republic of Germany compared with imports from the latter (which, as noted earlier, are not included in total data). In Romania, capital goods imports from the OECD countries were already high at the beginning of the decade; that they did not, in fact, increase their share in investment reflects largely the very rapid rate of growth investment expenditures over the period. By 1980, the share of imports in investment was very much lower than in 1975 in all countries but Hungary, and substantially less than in 1970 in four countries (Bulgaria, Czechoslovakia, the German Democratic Republic and Romania). It reverted to 1970 levels in the Soviet Union, but was still 10-20 per cent higher than in 1970 in Poland and Hungary.

It is of considerable interest to contrast the size of capital goods imports from the West with those of intermediate goods with a significant technology content over the 1970s. Such imports for the region as a whole were slightly smaller than capital goods during 1970-8, but by 1980 were 50 per cent higher, having closely followed, and in Eastern Europe substantially exceeded, the rise in capital goods imports throughout the 1970s. This reflects, first, large rises in imports of parts and accessories of machinery and equipment; these accounted for about 20 per cent of the total increase. It is also tempting to see in this one consequence of the

Table 4.5: Relationship Between OECD Investment Goods Exports to the Eastern Countries and Gross Fixed Investment in 1970, 1975 and 1980[a] (Indices, 1970 = 100)

	Industry		Material sphere		Total economy	
	1975	1980	1975	1980	1975	1980
Bulgaria	172.8	64.2	173.9	71.6	170.5	69.7
Czechoslovakia	78.7	49.3	81.8	52.9	81.5	55.4
German Dem. Rep.[b]	60.6	61.4	87.1	70.9	81.9	65.8
Hungary	122.5	120.0	130.0	131.6	119.6	120.9
Poland	152.7	90.1	203.2	112.4	213.3	109.1
Romania	63.2	32.2	73.5	37.8	74.6	39.9
Soviet Union	159.3	92.3	146.5	93.6	154.0	100.5

Notes: a. Volume index of growth of OECD investment goods exports to each country shown divided by the volume index of each country's total gross fixed capital formation. b. Excluding exports by the Federal Republic of Germany to the German Democratic Republic.
Source: OECD East-West Technology Transfer Data Base.

expansion of capital goods imports; given shortfalls in the quality of output of some domestic products, recourse may have been made on a substantial scale to imports of intermediate goods from the West which are more suitable than the domestic product for use with imported plan: — or which could supplement domestic shortfalls. In fact, intermediate chemicals account for some 40 per cent of the increase, and metals for a further one-quarter.

We might conclude from the development of capital goods imports from the West in 1970-5 by the seven countries taken together that while the movement was not particularly large relative to investment in some countries of Eastern Europe, it was considerably more significant for Bulgaria, Poland and also for the Soviet Union. The growth of capital goods imports from the OECD countries was moreover the biggest single contributor to the deteriorating balance of trade of the seven countries with the OECD, both in Eastern Europe as a whole and in the Soviet Union. Secondly, and for this reason the phenomenon was rather short-lived and was quickly reversed in most countries, capital goods imports in value and volume terms bore the brunt of the readjustment process which took place after the middle of the decade. Finally, while the increase in capital goods imports in most countries during 1970-5 was greater than the generally rapid rates of growth of investment, the slowdown in the growth of investment expenditure in most countries in 1975-80 was much smaller — except in Hungary — than the cutbacks of investment goods imports. This contrasts sharply with the maintenance of high levels of imports from OECD of intermediate goods with a significant technology content. Some of the implications of these findings will be discussed in the concluding section of this chapter.

Sectoral and Branch Distribution of Capital Goods Imports

Within the total economy, imports of capital goods from the OECD countries for material sphere activities clearly predominate and by a large margin, with identified imports to the non-material sphere (mainly medical equipment and office machinery including computers) taking between 5-10 per cent only of identified totals in most cases (Table 4.3). This compares with the 20-30 per cent share of the non-material sphere in total investment. Within the material sphere, capital goods imports for the industrial sector have usually taken the biggest share, though this is closely followed — and in a few cases exceeded — by transport and communications equipment. Within the latter is included pipeline and other equipment for oil and gas transportation, which is a large item accounting for some 20-25 per cent, depending on year, of the material sphere subtotal derived from OECD data on capital goods exports to the seven countries. With very few exceptions, both agricultural and construction equipment are minor items in the totals, although the Eastern-reported data suggest that these items were of some importance in Hungary (6-10 per cent and 7-9 per cent respectively). Within industry, the main end-use branches were the heavy industrial branches — notably engineering, chemicals and to a lesser extent, and declining over time, metallurgy — though in some countries of Eastern Europe, but not in the Soviet Union, the wood and paper, light industry and food branches were also smaller but still significant importers.

Taking account of the rough correspondence between the two data sets, but also of the fact that the specification of industrial end-users in the Eastern-reported statistics is more complete than in the OECD series, the data set based on CMEA sources is used in the rest of the present subsection to compare the end-use pattern of Eastern capital goods imports from the Rest of the World and from CMEA suppliers.

Differences in the sector and industrial branch end-use destinations from the Rest of the World and from CMEA suppliers in 1975 and 1980 can be seen by comparing data in the respective first columns for each year of Tables 4.3 and 4.4. At the level of the total economy, the Eastern countries appear to have allocated a bigger share of hard currency resources to imports from the OECD area for the industry sector, compared with this sector's share in imports from the CMEA (in the Soviet Union over half compared with just under half, and in Eastern Europe 60-70 per cent in the former case compared with 30-45 per cent in the latter). In contrast, and despite the generally large share of imports of Western capital goods for the transport and communications sector in all imports destined for the material sphere (30-40 per cent except in Czechoslovakia where the share was much lower), the share of these two sectors in Eastern countries' intra-trade flows have typically ranged between 40-50 per cent. This reflects, in particular, mutual CMEA deliveries of rail and road transport equipment (and also ships and aeroplanes), whereas purchases from the West consist more than half of gas and oil pipeline and ancillary equipment. And whereas imports of Western capital goods for the agricultural and construction sectors have been generally rather small (except for Hungary in the case of agriculture), the share of both these sectors combined in imports from CMEA partners amounted to a 10-20 per cent in all countries but Romania. This pattern of imports already suggests that the West enjoys a comparative advantage with regard to the supply of industrial and oil and gas transportation capital goods, both sectors in which technology levels are relatively high.

This pattern is to a large extent repeated within the industry sector itself. Taking as the high technology branches fuel extraction, chemicals and metallurgy, engineering and energy, the former three branches alone accounted for 20-70 per cent of all capital goods imported for industry from Western sources; the corresponding figures for their share in imports from Eastern partners is 15-30 per cent in 1975 and 1980. Reliance on Western chemical plant is particularly high. In contrast, the share of capital goods for engineering in East European imports from the West was substantially lower than in imports from other CMEA countries — but not in the case of the Soviet Union.

With regard to energy capital goods, the data confirm the relatively high degree of self-sufficiency of the CMEA area. Though the share of energy capital goods in imports from the West of capital goods designated for industry rose substantially in Eastern Europe over the decade — to 8-16 per cent in 1980 — this is still low compared with the 15-50 per cent share of energy capital goods in industrial capital goods imported from CMEA partners.[11] Soviet imports of this item from the West were small. With regard to fuel extraction, there is no general pattern. In both Poland and the Soviet Union, such imports accounted for substantial shares in industrial capital goods imported from the West in 1980 (22 and 13 per cent) — in the Polish case a substantial rise relative to 1975. In both countries these shares exceeded the branch's share in capital goods imports from Eastern countries. In the other countries, the latter share tended to be somewhat higher.

A final feature of relative branch share has been the average 10-20 per cent share of light industry in industrial capital goods imports from the East. However, this share was also high in some countries' industrial capital goods imported from OECD — notably Bulgaria and the German Democratic Republic. In general, this branch has lost priority over the 1975-80 period in imports from both East and West.

*Preliminary Conclusions Concerning Eastern Countries' Capital
Goods Imports in the 1970s*

It is not intended in this subsection to offer more than preliminary
comments on the strategies and impact of Eastern countries'
embodied technology imports in the 1970s. In the first place the
subject is complex and cannot be satisfactorily treated in a short
survey. Secondly, a fuller evaluation, based on the statistical
information presented in the preceding sections is, as noted earlier,
being published by the OECD.

An examination of the shares of capital goods in total imports
of the Eastern European countries from the West suggests that
given the priorities currently accorded to other categories of goods,
it did not prove possible on a sustained basis to increase capital
goods purchases at rates much different to other categories of
imports, without increases in indebtedness. In the Soviet Union,
interpretation is more complex because of the particularly large
rise in imports of Western food items — not only grain but also
meat and processed foods. This resulted in a sharp drop in the
share of capital goods within generally fast rising imports throughout the early 1970s; the share exceeded 1970 levels only in the
1976-8 period, which was made possible by higher earnings from
rises in the price and volume of fuel exports, but it fell very sharply
subsequently. In contrast, in both the Soviet Union and Eastern
Europe, the share of intermediate goods with a significant technology content was the same or higher at the end of the decade as
at the beginning.

It should also be recalled that the big rise in capital goods
imports initiated in the early 1970s was not general. Neither
Czechoslovakia nor the German Democratic Republic registered
the large rise in the volume of capital goods imports from the
OECD countries relative to investments up to 1975 which was
registered in Bulgaria, Poland and the Soviet Union and, though to
a much smaller extent, in Hungary and Romania. (In Hungary, the
relative rise was smaller but persisted until the end of the decade.)
But as noted earlier, the phenomenon was short-lived. This is consistent with the interpretation that a decisive factor in the strategies
of the Eastern countries concerned was to increase export
potential. When export prospects declined as a result of the
Western recession, rising debt and debt servicing costs made
redressment policies essential. The sector of imports most affected
was capital goods, with continued import priority being accorded

to imports of food and intermediate goods. The fact that, among the latter, technology-based intermediate goods for which imports of Eastern capital goods may have generated an increased demand, remained particularly buoyant was perhaps an outcome that may not have been entirely expected by Eastern policy-makers.

In the readjustment which took place after 1975, and at an increasing tempo as the consequences of the rising debt burden became apparent, it can be hypothesised — though not proved from the data presented — that export expansion as such lost priority and that greater emphasis was placed on importing capital goods to increase output for domestic use.[12] While the need to repay debt did not obviate the need for export expansion, most of the Eastern countries' balance of trade adjustments in the 1980-3 period have in fact — *faute de mieux* perhaps — been achieved by an overall import reduction. The changing end-use patterns of identified capital goods imports from the Rest of the World, which fell from 23 to 16 per cent of all East European imports from non-CMEA countries and from 30 to 18 per cent in the Soviet Union between 1975 and 1980 (CMEA-reported data), suggest that such imports have been directed to an increasing extent to the satisfaction mainly of priority domestic needs — notably that of the fuel branches of industry; oil and gas transportation in the Soviet Union; chemicals; and also, though to a lesser extent, energy and the engineering industry. The latter branch will play the basic and indispensable role in the improvements in output efficiency and product quality called for under the 'intensification' programme.

In assessing the role of capital goods imports from the West between 1970 and the mid-1970s, it should not be forgotten that intra-CMEA imports also rose very rapidly during the same period — by nearly threefold using Eastern country data — though less fast than imports from OECD, which grew over fourfold using OECD data on West-East flows. The 1971-5 period was one of rapid investment expansion. However, the corresponding data for 1976-80, when a slowdown in investment growth took place, still show a near doubling for intra-CMEA flows but only a rise of just over 10 per cent for those from OECD. All these rates are based on current prices. Thus, in the first period (taking into account the fact the intra-CMEA transaction prices appear to have risen con-siderably more slowly than world market prices), capital goods imports from both CMEA and Western sources may have grown, in volume terms, at not dissimilar rates. In the later period, intra-CMEA trade prices probably also grew less than those on the world market, but the difference in the growth in value terms indicates that imports from CMEA sources continued to rise — albeit at lower rates — whereas purchases from the OECD in value and volume terms declined very substantially.

Given these different directions of change, it can be asked to what extent the cutback in Western capital goods supplies up to 1980 led to the substitution of Western goods by CMEA supplies. The reduction in imports of Western goods obviously resulted in a considerable shortfall in what, up to 1975 at least, had been considered the desirable, and increasing, proportion of Western investment goods in total investment. In contrast, and given the slower growth rates of investment as a whole, the share of investment goods from other CMEA countries in the total certainly increased. There has clearly been a tendency to import from the Western countries a larger share of capital goods for the high technology sectors industry as a whole, as noted in the previous subsection, at the expense mainly of the consumer-oriented branches. But imports for industry, a high technology sector, have also increased their share in the total imported from CMEA countries in the later years of the decade, though within industry no decisive change in branch distribution towards or away from particular branches emerges. Thus, while some substitution may have taken place, the cutback in the growth of investment must have been accomplished largely by the reduction or abandonment of projects particularly dependent on a Western capital goods component.

Though the magnitude of the readjustment with regard to capital goods imports from the OECD was to some extent a case of *force majeure*, dictated by balance of payments constraints, it should also be recalled that it began very soon after 1975 in most countries — before the debt crisis became acute. This, and the sheer magnitude of the adjustment, suggest a substantial and fairly early reappraisal of policies towards Western technology imports. The reasons for this are far from clear, but a number of theories can be suggested. First, the Eastern countries themselves may have begun to doubt the efficiency of such imports in generating the gains in productive and export potential required to liquidate the debts incurred for their purchase — at least as far as imports of capital goods for the manufacturing sectors are concerned. This argument is reinforced by recent work showing the poor competitive performance of Eastern exports on OECD markets — the notable exceptions being the Soviet fuel industry, which benefited from the large scale import of Western pipeline, and the chemical branch in the Soviet Union and some other countries.[13] Second, it may suggest a certain dissatisfaction with the performance of imported capital goods in an Eastern context — either because expectations about their efficiency had been too high, or because absorption problems muted their enhancement of production or quality. Perhaps the maintenance of technology-intensive intermediate goods imports from the OECD countries is one reflection of this; it is noteworthy that it was not paralleled by a similar movement in the case of intermediate goods categories in intra-CMEA trade.[14]

Whatever the reasons, a much more critical view seems to have been taken in making import decisions from a relatively early date. At the same time, it is clear that such imports are still considered to be an important element of Eastern investment strategies. CMEA industrial co-ordination at all levels continues to be directed toward improvements in economic efficiency, including technical co-operation, which are designed to improve technology levels on a broad front. The role of Western technology is likely to continue to be an important complementary ingredient in this and in the intensification programme in general. Balance of payments constraints may well continue to ease, leaving more room for an expansion of Western capital goods purchases in the future. But the experience of the 1970s is likely to dictate a much more cautious attitude — in particular to the question of the degree to which future exports earnings, which as in the 1970s may not materialise, can be mortgaged to pay for current investment needs.

Notes

*The author is a member of the United Nations Secretariat. This paper is contributed in a personal capacity, and does not necessarily reflect the views of the UN Secretariat.

1. The author would like to thank Mrs Helgard Wienert-Çakim, and also previous consultants who have contributed to this work — notably Mr Zdènek Drábek (extraction and classification of OECD trade statistics) and Mr Israel Borenstein (who performed a similar operation on the Eastern countries' trade statistics).
2. *Statistical Papers*, Series M, no. 53 (United Nations, NY, 1971).
3. Regina Kelly, *Alternative Measurements of Technology-Intensive Trade,*

United States Department of Commerce, Office of Economic Research, Paper
OER/ER-17, Washington, DC, September 1976. The listings therein were slightly
expanded — notably to cover all metals.

4. The BEC intermediate goods categories from which this selection was
made are 111: primary food and beverages mainly from industry; 121: processed
food and beverages mainly for industry; 2: industrial supplies not elsewhere
specified; 31: primary fuels ard lubricants; 322: other fuels and lubricants; 42:
parts and accessories of machinery and other capital equipment (except transport);
and 53: parts and accessories of transport equipment.

5. The Standard Foreign Trade Classification (SFTC) of the Council for
Mutual Economic Assistance was supposed to be introduced in all CMEA member
countries from January 1971. In fact only three countries (Bulgaria, Romania and
the Soviet Union) did so. Hungary, Poland and the German Democratic Republic
follow their own classification systems — which have, however, many points in
common with SFTC — while Czechoslovakia publishes trade data according to
SITC.

6. However, Eastern-reported data do include some purchases of know-how
and licensing fees in cases where such costs are included in the price of plant
bought on a package deal basis. This cannot be quantified (see following section).

7. Paul Marer, 'Towards a Solution of the Mirror Statistics Puzzle in
East-West Commerce' in Friedrich Levcik (ed.), *Sfûdien über Wirtschaftsvergleiche*
(Springer Verlag, Vienna and New York, 1978).

8. Except for Romania, where insufficient geographical or commodity detail is
available.

9. For the seven countries taken together, SITC item 719.8 alone
(miscellaneous non-electrical machinery and equipment) accounted for 52 per cent
of the total of SITC items not allocated by branch in 1970, falling to 46 per cent in
1975 and 38 per cent in 1980.

10. The price data used are based on United Nations trade unit values where
possible and on the price indices of the Federal Republic of Germany for particular
types of machinery and equipment exported to the Eastern countries. This method
is described in the *Economic Bulletin for Europe*, vol. 31, no. 1 (1979), pp. 54-183.
It should be noted here that the same prices have been used for individual
commodities whatever the Eastern country destination. Inter-Eastern country
differences therefore arise exclusively from differences in the commodity
composition of OECD exports to these countries.

11. The 55 per cent share of this category of industrial capital goods imports
from the Rest of the World reported by Czechoslovakia in 1980 results from a
steady rise over the 1975 figure and a big jump in 1980; however, this is not borne
out by the OECD-reported data and awaits a satisfactory explanation.

12. Export industries, however, coincide with the branches given priority for
development in the 1981-5 Five Year Plans.

13. *Economic Bulletin for Europe*, vol. 35, no. 4 (December 1983), pp.
441-500.

14. *Economic Survey of Europe in 1981* (United Nations, NY, 1982) p. 288,
Table 3.6.4.

5   WESTERN TECHNOLOGY AND SOVIET ECONOMIC POWER

Julian Cooper

Introduction

In public discussion of the Soviet economy in recent years a number of propositions relating to Western technology have figured prominently. They can be summarised as follows:

(1) The Soviet Union imports, or otherwise acquires, a substantial volume of advanced Western technology, and such technology is predominant in Western exports to the USSR.

(2) The Soviet Union is incapable of developing and producing its own advanced technology, except for weapons, and this failure stems from the inherent shortcomings of the socialist planned economy.

(3) Almost all Soviet technical achievements, with the possible exception of some weapons systems and space technology, owe their origin to Western technology, either through direct acquisition or imitation.

(4) Western technology has been crucial to the development of the Soviet economy since 1917.

(5) The state of the Soviet economy is now such that the acquisition of Western technology is a decisive factor alleviating (or averting) a real (or incipient) economic crisis, or even complete economic collapse.

(6) The dependence of the Soviet Union on Western technology offers the possibility, through its denial, of exerting influence on Soviet policy or of exacerbating the difficulties of the economy.

These propositions, frequently met in the press and in the statements of politicians and other public figures, have proved remarkably impervious to criticism. Yet there has been no lack of dissent. With a few exceptions, more frequently encountered in the United States than in Western Europe, the propositions as stated

80

find little support within the community of academic Soviet studies specialists, although dilute variants do have some currency. In this chapter an attempt is made to explain this phenomenon, and to examine some issues pertaining to the contribution of the technology of industrially developed capitalist countries to the development of the Soviet economy.

There can be little doubt that the apparent rapid expansion of Soviet imports of technology from the West during the 1970s and the visibility of some of the large-scale contracts have been extremely important in shaping public and official perceptions. In the United States the impact was greater because the transition from modest to large-scale involvement in the Soviet market was more abrupt and dramatic. It was also more politically charged, inextricably linked with the broader issue of detente. Awareness of the findings of research into the comparative technological level of Soviet industry may also have exerted an influence, strengthening the conviction that the Soviet economy is inherently non-innovative and vitally dependent on external injections of technology.[1] More recently, the well-publicised cases of the interception of computers and other electronic equipment allegedly destined to the USSR in contravention of United States and CoCom export regulations has served to reinforce these attitudes. At a time when the major capitalist countries have been experiencing economic problems unprecedented in the post-war era, with persistent high levels of unemployment and inflation, some reassurance has been found in the belief that capitalism can still manifest greater technological dynamism than the socialist alternative.

But it can also be argued that the wide currency of strong propositions relating to the incapacity of the Soviet Union to generate advanced technology and to its dependence on the West owes much to perceptions of technology itself. Technology has been fetishised, being widely seen as almost the sole source of economic growth, in abstraction from the essential economic and social conditions for its effective use. In particular, Western technology has acquired an almost mystical significance. Not only is it Technology in its fetishised sense, but it is Western, and, as such, inherently superior to Soviet technology. It appears to be widely believed that this Western Technology, born of the inherently dynamic and innovative capitalist market economy, offers the only possible means of solving a wide range of technical and economic problems. It is regarded as non-substitutable. In the face of 'capital' in its brute technological form, even economists nurtured in the marginalist tradition are not immune from this misconception. Soviet writers may be correct in detecting signs of 'technological chauvinism' in recent discussion in the West.[2] This phenomenon is not without historical irony. At the outset of the Cold War in the late 1940s, many Soviet writers proclaimed the superiority of Soviet (or, frequently, Russian) natural science and technology and referred dismissively to their alien bourgeois equivalents. This crude, oversimplified class or 'systemic' approach to science and technology was soon rejected, although its faint echoes were heard occasionally in later years. Thirty years later, with the breakdown of detente and the slide into a new cold war, it is the West that is afflicted with the mirror-image of this ideological aberration.[3]

It must be acknowledged, finally, that it is not easy to assemble the evidence required to demonstrate conclusively the untenability of all the six propositions. (*Per contra*, it is even more difficult, in the author's opinion, to demonstrate their validity!) While it is possible to provide some relevant data illuminating quantitative dimensions of the problem, there are important issues requiring qualitative judgement for which adequate evidence is lacking. By its very nature, the available evidence is skewed. Despite commercial secrecy, it is possible to assemble a considerable amount of information from Western sources on outflows of technology to the Soviet Union, but it is much more difficult to gather evidence on the subsequent fate of the technology and on the real technological levels and capabilities of the recipient industries and sectors of the Soviet economy. Since the early 1930s, Soviet writers have been reticent in acknowledging the Western origin of technology in use in the economy and it is rare that detailed statistical data on its scale and contribution are published. As often happens with Soviet secretiveness, whether from considerations of security or national pride, in the face of an absence of hard information Western observers are free to draw the most unfavourable conclusions. In these circumstances, it should be incumbent on analysts and publicists alike to explicitly concede the limits of our knowledge and the inherent biases of the sources available.

Technology

In discussing the role of Western technology in the Soviet economy, it is usual to adopt a broad definition of technology that embraces both hardware (machinery, equipment, instruments, etc.) and knowledge and practices associated with the creation and use of this hardware, including organisational forms and methods of management. In general this approach is unobjectionable and, indeed, often useful, so long as it is understood that the different elements have their own specific features and conditions of production, transfer and application. The distinctions are especially important if one is attempting to analyse the impact of different social and economic systems on the processes of technology acquisition and assimilation. While most individual items of hardware are, in principle, equally applicable in both capitalist and socialist economies, this may not be true of systems of hardware, and even less so for knowledge, organisational forms and managerial practices in so far as they possess intrinsic social and economic attributes. Some Western technology may be considered completely inappropriate for use in the socialist economy; other technology may require adaptation and modification. Organisational and managerial forms and techniques, for example, may have to be changed to conform to the conditions of a non-market economy and purged of unacceptable, specifically capitalist features, and production systems may require alteration to secure satisfactory conditions of work.[4] To the extent that it is considered necessary to introduce such changes, the process of assimilating Western technology will be more protracted and costly. The end result may not be the simple transfer of Western technology, but the adoption of 'Sovietised' variants. This aspect of the problem has received little attention in the literature of recent years.

Channels of Acquisition of Technology

The principal channel of acquisition of Western technology is through the normal commercial processes of foreign trade, as imports of hardware, or knowledge in the form of licences and know-how. This is also the most visible, easily quantified form and, from the point of view of its contribution to the Soviet economy, the most significant. It therefore forms the main focus of the present chapter. However, Western technology is also acquired through other channels, including the collection and dissemination of freely available scientific and technical information, trade fairs and exhibitions, study visits abroad by Soviet scientists and engineers, the copying and 'reverse engineering' of products and processes, the illegal or regulation-bending acquisition of items of advanced technology (e.g. CoCom-proscribed goods obtained via non-member countries), and the use of intelligence agencies. It should be noted that some mechanisms of technology transfer usual between capitalist countries are not available to the Soviet Union, in particular the transfers which occur within multinational companies between wholly-owned affiliates. Furthermore, transfers through the movement of personnel play a much more restricted role, and normal commercial access to a wide range of advanced technologies is denied or obstructed by CoCom and national export control regulations and periodic politically-motivated embargoes. In general, it is precisely the most effective, 'active' forms of transfer that are the least available to the Soviet Union, enforcing dependence on the less effective 'passive' acquisition mechanisms.[5] Before turning to normal imports of technology, a few observations on other forms of acquisitions are called for.

The Soviet Union has created a substantial and elaborate national scientific and technical information system for servicing the needs of the economy. The effort devoted to this information system could be interpreted as an attempt to compensate for the weakness of more active transfer mechanisms. Employing some 190,000 people, this network of informational agencies is much concerned with the gathering, processing and dissemination of information on foreign technology. Major institutions include the All-Union Institute of Scientific and Technical Information (VINITI), jointly administered by the USSR Academy of Sciences and the State Committee for Science and Technology, which processes a wide range of domestic and foreign periodicals and other publications; the All-Union Research Institute for Patent Information (VNIIPI); a service for the collection and dissemination of foreign industrial catalogues and trade information; and the All-Union Institute for Inter-branch Information (VIMI), which services the needs of the defence industry and also channels information from the defence sector to the civilian economy. There is also a national translation agency, the All-Union Centre for

Translations (VTsP), which services clients throughout the economy. Each industrial ministry has its own central information service and a network of information departments and offices attached to R&D organisations and enterprises. This system is being gradually computerised to form an integrated, automated, national information service. It is impossible to measure the contribution of this form of Western technology transfer to the Soviet economy, but from Soviet accounts it is apparent that it provides a systematic monitoring of foreign developments as an aid to Soviet project planning, and provides standards of comparison against which domestic technical achievements can be assessed. However, it is also apparent that the system is not without problems which reduce its practical effectiveness as a transfer mechanism.[6]

It has often been claimed that the Soviet Union copies Western technology on a substantial scale, and there is no doubt that the practice was widespread during the pre-war years. But the reproduction of modern, advanced technology from the hardware alone, without the associated technical documentation, is itself an extremely complex process requiring technological knowledge and skills of a high order. While there may be benefits in terms of cost and time during the early learning stages of a new technology, copying cannot be considered a viable strategy for technology acquisition in modern conditions. Furthermore, as was already apparent before the war, to systematically copy is to permanently lag behind. Nevertheless, Soviet industry does base some of its new products on proven Western designs. The first Soviet large-scale integrated circuits and microprocessors, for example, were based on successful US products, although not precise reproductions in all respects.[7] In the case of microprocessors, the adoption of a strategy of first copying the best foreign models and then developing original designs has been explicitly acknowledged by Soviet electronics specialists.[8]

Probably more important than the detailed reproduction of specific items of hardware is the use of information on the general design configuration of technical systems; but once new systems have appeared, or have been publicised prior to marketing, such information becomes part of the international stock of technical knowledge open to all. The fact that the Soviet Union makes use of this form of information is hardly remarkable. Thus, it has been claimed that the Il-86 wide-bodied transport aircraft 'looks much like' the Boeing 747, while the Il-76 'resembles' the C-141; however, 'neither system is an identical copy'.[9]

Although impossible to confirm on the basis of the available evidence, it would seem likely that the direct pirating of foreign designs without payment of royalties has diminished since 1965 when the USSR joined the Paris Convention on the protection of industrial property. Soviet involvement in international patenting and licensing has greatly expanded in recent years and to this extent the necessity and wisdom of unauthorised copying have both declined. There is a parallel with the use of foreign technical literature. Prior to 1973 foreign journals were reproduced and distributed within the Soviet Union without payment and acknowledgement, but in 1973 the USSR adhered to the Universal Copyright Convention; 'since signing the Convention the Soviets have agreed to pay royalties for copyrighted materials. Negotiations with foreign publishers have been initiated and have led to a considerable number of information-exchange agreements, including royalty payments.'[10]

Another channel of acquisition which has received considerable publicity in recent times is resort to covert and illegal transfers of advanced technology, ranging, it has been alleged, from electronic components, computer and manufacturing equipment to a high-bypass turbofan engine with potential cruise missile application. This issue is discussed in greater detail in other chapters. Such transfers may indeed provide valuable information on certain critical technologies and cannot be entirely discounted, although in the author's opinion the whole question has been overdramatised and granted quite excessive attention. While it may be known, or suspected, that certain technologies have been transferred illicitly to the Soviet Union, evidence is rarely, if ever, presented on the actual level of technological capability possessed by the recipient in the particular field concerned. It is too readily assumed that the technologies are acquired because the Soviet Union is deficient in the relevant skills and knowledge, and distinction is rarely drawn between acquisitions motivated by the need to fill genuine gaps and intelligence operations designed to furnish information on the current capabilities of potential adversaries. Western countries are always interested in acquiring samples of high technology and military materiel from the USSR with the latter motive in mind, but the Soviet Union is rarely acknowledged to have similar intentions.

It also tends to be assumed that such covertly obtained technology always finds its way into the defence industry, but it could plausibly be maintained that in the last few years some of the claimed transfers of computers and other electronic equipment, not always of the latest models, have been to meet a replacement demand of civilian enterprises, as Western originals, supplied in the late 1960s and early 1970s when controls were more lax, require urgent renewal. It has been acknowledged, for example, that for imported chemical plant the least dependable element requiring earliest replacement is frequently the electronic control system, which cannot always be readily replaced by domestically-produced computer technology.[11] In general, however, covert acquisitions of Western technology can provide only episodic and marginal gains to the Soviet economy. The most substantial weakness of the economy in relation to technology is not so much its incapability of creating advanced products and processes, but its inability to produce them at high quality on a volume basis. Copying and illegal acquisitions cannot provide more than partial solutions to this cardinal problem.

The Scale of Imports of Western Technology

From Table 5.1 it can be seen that machinery and equipment imports have represented approximately one-third of total Soviet imports since 1960, with a peak of 42 per cent attained in 1978. Of the total machinery imports, two-thirds to three-quarters have been purchases from other socialist countries, predominantly other CMEA members in Eastern Europe. In purely quantitative terms, therefore, 'Eastern' technology imports have been substantially more important than Western. Imports of machinery and equipment from developed capitalist countries peaked at 41.4 per cent of all such imports in 1976, but have usually represented no more than one-third of the total. As a share of total Soviet imports, machinery and equipment from developed capitalist countries has rarely exceeded 10 per cent. Taking a long-term view, the years 1975-9 can be seen as exceptional; since 1979 the overall proportions characteristic of the early 1970s have been restored.

In order to appreciate the scale of Soviet technology imports from the West in the form of machinery and equipment, it is instructive to compare them with the equivalent flows between the Western countries themselves and with the total volume of equipment exports of these countries. These relationships are shown in

Table 5.1: Soviet Imports of Western Machinery and Equipment[a]

Year	Machinery and Equipment as a Percentage of Total Imports	Western Machinery and Equipment as a Percentage of Total Imports	Western Machinery and Equipment as a Percentage of Total Machinery and Equipment Imports
1960	29.8	7.5	25.2
1961	29.8	6.4	21.6
1962	34.8	8.6	24.6
1963	34.9	7.7	22.0
1964	34.4	8.0	23.2
1965	33.4	6.2	18.7
1966	32.4	7.0	21.7
1967	34.2	7.8	22.8
1968	36.9	9.4	25.6
1969	37.5	10.8	28.8
1970	34.5	9.5	26.7
1971	34.0	8.3	24.6
1972	34.6	8.5	24.5
1973	34.3	9.2	26.8
1974	32.4	10.3	31.9
1975	33.9	13.6	40.0
1976	36.3	15.0	41.4
1977	38.1	14.7	38.5
1978	42.0	13.8	32.8
1979	38.0	11.9	31.3
1980	33.9	10.5	30.9
1981	30.2	8.2	27.3
1982	34.4	10.4	30.3
1983	38.2	11.3	29.7

Note: a. Imports from developed capitalist countries.
Source: Calculated from *Vneshnyaya torgovlya SSSR*, various years.

Table 5.2, from which it can be seen that during the 1970s the Soviet market accounted for a mere 2 per cent or less of the total annual machinery and transport equipment exports of OECD member countries, and only 1 per cent of such exports from the US. For comparison, OECD exports of machinery and equipment to the United Kingdom represented approximately 5 per cent of all such exports; that is, the UK annually imports from other OECD members more than twice the volume of machinery and equipment that the OECD sells to the Soviet Union, despite the substantially more powerful economy of the latter. This puts the scale of Soviet acquisitions of Western technology through trade into perspective: in absolute terms the flows are really extraordinarily modest, and the question should really be not 'why so large?', but 'why so small?'

Not all Soviet purchases of technology from developed capitalist countries represent genuinely advanced technology. A study by the International Trade Administration of the US Department of Commerce indicates that of total exports to the USSR from 17 industrially developed capitalist countries, 'high' technology products represent a relatively small proportion: 16.2 per cent in 1970, 13.6 per cent in 1975, and 16.1 per cent in 1977; declining to 13.1 per cent in 1979 and 11.7 per cent in 1980.[12] During the same period, high technology as defined in that study represented approximately 40 per cent of the total machinery and equipment exports to the USSR of the same group of countries. Overall, such Western high technology (cases for which the question of Soviet capability to produce domestically could arise) accounted for barely 5 per cent of total Soviet imports. However, the methodology employed in this study is unavoidably imprecise and probably overstates the share of genuinely advanced technology in so far as entire product groups (for example, all machine tools) are so classified. This study also reveals that in many areas of high technology there are negligible imports from the West — aero-engines, nuclear reactor equipment, electronic components, bearings, X-ray equipment, etc. (Access to some of these technologies

Table 5.2: Machinery and Transport Equipment Exports to the USSR from OECD Member Countries

Year	Exports to the USSR as a Percentage of Total Machinery and Transport Equipment Exports				
	US	Japan	West Germany	UK	All OECD members
1970	0.3	1.3	1.0	1.3	1.3
1971	0.3	1.1	0.9	0.9	1.0
1972	0.3	1.4	1.6	1.0	1.1
1973	0.7	0.9	1.8	0.9	1.2
1974	0.6	0.9	2.0	0.5	1.3
1975	1.2	2.0	3.2	1.2	2.2
1976	1.2	1.9	2.9	1.1	2.1
1977	0.7	1.7	2.7	0.9	2.0
1978	0.5	2.0	2.3	1.1	1.8
1979	0.5	1.3	1.8	0.9	1.5
1980	0.3	1.1	1.8	0.9	1.2

Source: Calculated from OECD, *Bulletin of Foreign Trade*, Series C (*Trade by Commodities — Exports*) various years. Data refer to machinery and transport equipment exports, SITC-7.

has, of course, been restricted by CoCom and national export controls.) It is concluded that 'compared with exports to non-communist countries trading partners, Western exports to communist countries do not emphasise high-technology products'. Proposition (1) thus finds little support.

Western Technology and Soviet Investment

Another approach to quantification of the scale of Western technology imports is to compare them with the total volume of domestic investment in equipment. There are methodological diffi-

Table 5.3: Soviet Imports of Western Machinery and Domestic Investment

	Imports of Machinery and Equipment from Developed Capitalist Countries as a Percentage of Investment in Equipment in the Following Year	
Year	Imports in Current Prices	Imports in Constant Prices
1961	2.7	3.1
1962	3.6	4.1
1963	3.1	3.5
1964	3.3	3.7
1965	2.5	2.6
1966	2.6	2.8
1967	2.9	3.1
1968	3.7	3.9
1969	4.1	4.5
1970	3.9	4.1
1971	3.4	3.4
1972	3.8	3.8
1973	4.3	4.3
1974	5.2	5.0
1975	8.9	7.2
1976	10.0	6.5
1977	9.5	6.1
1978	9.9	6.2
1979	8.9	5.5
1980	8.7	4.9
1981	7.8	4.0
1982	10.3	4.7
1983	(11.0)	(5.3)

Note: . estimate.
Sources: Imports in current prices from *Vneshnyaya torgovlya SSSR*, various years. Investment in equipment in constant prices of 1973 from *Narodnoe khozyaistvo SSSR*, various years. Imports in constant (1970) prices calculated on basis of a price index for total Soviet imports derived from *Vneshnyaya torgovlya SSSR*, various years.

culties: the two series should be in comparable prices, account should be taken of the time-lag between importation and installation of equipment, and, if Western trade data are used, appropriate exchange rates are required. The Soviet series for gross investment in equipment, tools and inventory purports to be in constant prices of a fixed year. In reality it is a mixed series incorporating both fixed prices and elements of current pricing. Furthermore, the practice adopted to convert imported equipment prices into domestic prices probably introduces an upward bias when world prices are rising. If domestic equivalents are available, imported items of equipment are priced at the appropriate official prices of the Soviet counterparts; if no Soviet-produced equivalents are available, the price is based on the actual contract or invoice price adjusted by an appropriate coefficient approved by the State Committee for Prices. The imports of Western equipment can be valued at either their current (inflated) prices or in constant prices if a suitable deflator can be applied. As for the lag between importation and installation, a one-year period has been adopted here for illustrative purposes, although 18 months or even two years may be more appropriate for Soviet conditions. The results are shown in Table 5.3.

Measured in current prices, the share of Western machinery and equipment in total equipment investment of the following year reached 10 per cent in the late 1970s; but in constant prices just over 7 per cent in the middle of the decade, falling back to less than 5 per cent in recent years. High technology as defined by the US Department of Commerce analysts would represent a mere 2-3 per cent. Applying the same approach to imports of equipment from CMEA partners, it can be shown that they represent at least 10 per cent of total annual investment in equipment, more than twice the share for Western technology. From this it must be concluded that in quantitative terms Western technology imports make a relatively modest contribution to the growth of the Soviet capital stock and could not be considered decisive even if the embodied levels of productivity were substantially higher than those for domestically produced equipment.

Trends over Time

Has there been a tendency for the Soviet economy to become

increasingly dependent on imports of Western machinery and equipment? This question has to be asked in so far as popular discussion is often based on the assumption that such a trend exists, and that a shift to greater dependence emerged in the early 1970s. There is no doubt that the volume of Western equipment exports to the USSR rose in the early 1970s and that the share of Western equipment in total Soviet imports of machinery and equipment reached an unusually high peak in the middle of the decade, although in both cases the movement of prices exaggerated the extent of the real increases. However, a careful statistical analysis by Salter of the level of machinery imports from the West between 1955 and 1978 (based on OECD data) failed to disclose any structural break around the end of the 1960s.[13] Furthermore, examination of the long-term trend of the share of Western machinery imports in total Soviet imports reveals only a very slight tendency to rise and no discontinuity in the early 1970s. Similarly, on the basis of the evidence presented in Table 5.3, it cannot be claimed that there has been any marked shift to greater dependence on Western technology in Soviet investment in equipment.

The Structure of Imports of Western Technology

So far we have considered aggregate Soviet imports of Western technology, but in assessing their contribution to the economy it is also necessary to look at their structure and its changing pattern over time. Unfortunately, neither Soviet nor Western statistics provide a complete picture, but Table 5.4, based on the former, brings out some essential points. It can be seen that the chemical industry has been the largest recipient in recent years, during the 1970s accounting for one-fifth of all imports of machinery and equipment from the West, with a peak of 31 per cent in 1977. From Table 5.5 it can be seen that the bulk of chemical industry equipment imports have been from the West, with a peak of almost 80 per cent in 1977. Soviet writers have acknowledged that some branches of the chemical industry have been overwhelmingly dependent on technology imported from both the West and Eastern Europe. Thus, in 1973 52 per cent of all nitrogenous fertilisers were produced using imported equipment, 74 per cent of complex fertilisers, 45 per cent of calcium soda, and 84 per cent of high-pressure polyethylene.[14] For the chemical industry, employ-

ing a similar procedure to that used above for aggregate investment, it is possible to estimate the share of Western imports in the
total investment in equipment. This reveals that during the second
half of the 1960s less than one-fifth of equipment investment took
the form of Western imports, and during 1971-5 the share was
almost exactly one-fifth. The share rose in the second half of the
decade to almost half, and more recently has fallen back to its
usual level of one-fifth.[15]

Another branch which has figured prominently has been the
motor industry. The data shown in Table 5.4 understate this
industry's share in so far as the category 'machine tools' includes
machines purchased for use in the motor industry but not considered specialised production equipment for the branch. The
principal recipients during the period covered were the Toliatti
VAZ plant built with the assistance of the Italian Fiat company
and the giant KamAZ truck plant built with substantial Western
involvement. Almost all the imported special motor industry
equipment was acquired from the West. Machine tool imports
have consistently represented a quite sizeable share of Western
technology imports, although in terms of the number of machines
in physical units they have accounted for an extremely modest proportion of total Soviet installations.

Ships and equipment for ships represent a substantial item of
import, although their share has tended to decline from the high
levels of the 1960s. Finland has been the largest Western supplier.
Another branch which has consistently received large-scale
imports from the West is the timber, paper and pulp industry;
more than three-quarters of the imported equipment is acquired
from the West, notably from Finland, Germany and Sweden. The
energy sector has accounted for an increasing share of the total,
with recent substantial imports for the oil and gas industries,
including pipeline equipment. A puzzling feature of Soviet statistics on imports of Western technology is the substantial residual
element remaining after all specifically identified categories of
equipment have been accounted for. This residual share has shown
a tendency to rise over time, but even from the more detailed
OECD statistics it is difficult to account fully for its composition.
Taking the Soviet data, countries having a large residual element in
their equipment trade with the USSR include Finland (in 1982
accounting for almost one-third of the entire residual), West
Germany, France, Switzerland, Sweden and Austria. This residual

Table 5.4: Structure of Soviet Imports of Machinery and Equipment from Developed Capitalist Countries (Percentage of Total)

Imports of:	1965	1966	1967	1968	1969	1970	1971	1972	1973	1974	1975	1976	1977	1978	1979	1980	1981	1982
Machine tools	4.4	3.4	5.2	8.0	4.3	6.9	8.5	14.9	15.3	7.7	5.0	6.1	7.0	6.5	7.0	7.3	7.0	5.0
Equipment for chemical industry	21.1	26.1	26.0	22.9	13.7	8.3	14.5	19.9	16.9	13.2	10.0	18.9	30.9	27.4	28.7	17.4	10.8	7.3
Equipment for motor industry	—	.	.	—	—	16.9	6.7	4.8	7.3	15.2	6.9	4.5	3.9	2.1	3.0	2.8	2.9	2.7
Ships and ship equipment	34.8	32.0	17.9	14.6	14.1	12.9	7.2	3.7	6.5	6.7	7.2	7.8	7.2	7.7	6.7	2.7	8.5	8.1
Equipment for timber, paper-pulp and woodworking industry	7.2	6.0	8.9	9.4	10.0	6.9	4.9	9.1	7.8	6.3	3.3	4.5	5.1	4.1	3.7	3.4	2.9	3.1
Instruments and laboratory equipment	1.8	1.7	2.3	2.3	2.2	2.6	2.9	3.2	2.3	2.3	1.7	1.2	1.4	1.2	1.8	1.9	3.0	2.1
Equipment for food industry	1.4	1.7	5.0	7.0	2.8	1.7	1.6	2.5	2.3	3.1	1.8	2.0	1.3	1.0	1.3	1.0	1.1	2.0
Equipment for textile industry	4.1	5.8	9.1	14.9	7.2	2.5	2.1	2.7	2.0	2.8	3.3	3.1	1.6	1.9	1.4	1.0	1.1	1.0
Drilling equipment for oil and gas industry	—	—	—	—	—	0.7	2.2	1.1	0.2	0.3	2.4	5.3	1.7	3.4	1.2	3.5	2.5	7.6
Equipment for road building and construction	—	—	—	—	—	2.7	3.1	—	—	1.3	4.0	3.1	1.1	1.0	2.4	3.1	7.3	10.1
Total of ten categories	74.8	76.7	74.4	79.1	54.3	62.1	53.7	61.9	60.6	58.9	45.6	56.5	61.2	56.3	57.2	45.0	47.1	49.0

Source: Calculated from *Vneshnyaya torgovlya SSSR*, various years. (— negligible; . not available.)

Table 5.5: Share of Soviet Imports of Machinery and Equipment from Developed Capitalist Countries (Percentage of Total Soviet Imports for each Category)

Imports of:	1965	1966	1967	1968	1969	1970	1971	1972	1973	1974	1975	1976	1977	1978	1979	1980	1981	1982
Machine tools	16.8	15.6	30.8	38.7	26.7	37.7	36.4	47.2	54.8	45.6	40.0	47.8	44.8	45.6	37.8	37.0	28.7	27.6
Equipment for chemical industry	51.1	62.9	59.3	65.6	59.4	38.3	56.4	59.9	56.1	54.0	56.8	71.9	79.1	75.0	73.8	65.0	55.1	50.4
Equipment for motor industry	.	.	.	.	.	95.8	93.2	89.8	81.1	87.8	86.2	87.0	87.8	99.6	93.9	94.3	95.9	94.2
Ships and ship equipment	32.2	32.4	24.1	23.1	27.0	22.6	18.2	12.7	20.6	22.6	24.0	36.7	34.7	32.1	24.5	10.1	29.7	35.4
Equipment for timber, paper-pulp and woodworking industry	88.7	81.7	53.1	76.2	84.4	76.0	71.8	88.4	86.6	87.6	79.7	90.7	89.6	86.1	77.9	75.8	75.7	82.0
Instruments and laboratory equipment	13.4	14.2	30.6	24.3	24.2	25.2	21.6	25.0	23.9	42.6	32.4	23.7	23.9	21.7	25.9	26.4	32.3	24.6
Equipment for food industry	6.2	8.5	26.1	31.0	18.2	13.9	16.5	23.5	20.9	30.7	28.8	38.1	24.2	17.9	18.2	34.0	19.1	22.4
Equipment for textile industry	21.3	31.0	54.3	60.7	48.5	33.4	30.8	29.1	23.0	34.1	43.4	42.8	23.1	14.6	16.6	11.4	11.2	10.7
Drilling equipment for oil and gas industry	—	—	—	—	—	24.1	51.1	34.6	10.4	.	.	68.4	60.7	65.5	38.6	65.3	54.2	67.2
Equipment for road building and construction	—	—	—	—	—	37.2	39.4	—	—	14.5	66.6	76.1	32.2	48.4	48.0	51.4	67.2	74.7
Total of ten categories	18.7	21.7	22.8	25.6	28.8	26.7	24.6	24.5	26.8	31.9	40.0	41.4	38.5	32.8	31.3	30.9	27.3	30.3

Source: Calculated from *Vneshnyaya torgovlya SSSR*, various years. (— negligible; . not available.)

probably includes such categories as office equipment, computers and radio, electronic and communications equipment.

Having identified Soviet economic activities which regularly draw on Western machinery and equipment, it is worth considering those which do not. This dimension is frequently absent from discussion of the role of Western technology but is important if a correct assessment is to be made. Looking first at non-industrial sectors, it is apparent that agriculture, construction and transport, with certain important exceptions, depend to a considerable degree on domestically produced technology supplemented by imports within the framework of CMEA. The mechanical inputs to agriculture are almost exclusively Soviet and East European and the enterprises building tractors and agricultural machinery appear to rely heavily on domestically produced equipment. In the agricultural sector the principal exception is technology for the production of fertilisers and other chemicals. In building and construction most equipment is domestically produced except for certain types of specialised and heavy-duty machinery and some equipment for use in the inhospitable Northern and Eastern regions of the country. In the transport sector, reference was made above to imports of ships, but the railway system is relatively independent of Western supplies. Similarly, there is a high level of self-reliance in aviation, partly enforced by CoCom and national export control regulations. While large-diameter pipelines for oil and gas have been built with substantial inputs of Western-supplied pipe, compressor units and pipelaying equipment, it is often overlooked that Soviet pipeline building has been on a very considerable scale for many years with many smaller-diameter networks playing an important economic role. It has been claimed that only 8 per cent of the country's gas pipeline compressor stations are equipped with foreign-made units and only 9 per cent of the total length of pipeline consists of pipe imported from capitalist countries.[16]

Turning to industry, one can identify certain branches which have little resort to imports from the West, or which import on a selective basis to meet certain specific requirements. Thus in conventional and nuclear electric power generation and transmission the USSR is largely self-sufficient, and can justly claim many technological firsts. The same is substantially true for basic processes in the ferrous and non-ferrous metals industries, although there has been a tendency for increasing resort to imports to secure higher quality end products, for example, rolling mill equipment and the large direct-reduction electric steel-making complex at Oskol being built with West German assistance. Western technology inputs have not played a significant role in the building materials industry, and, until recently, the mining and extractive industries. Detailed study of the light and food industries would probably reveal a mixed picture, with whole sectors based almost exclusively on domestically produced or East European technology, but others with substantial Western inputs in recent years, for example, the soft drinks and tobacco and cigarette industries.

Classifying Imported Technology

Examination of the volume and structure of Soviet imports of machinery and equipment from the West over time suggests that distinction should be drawn between 'normal', 'structural', 'conjunctural' and 'non-discretional' imports. These categories cannot be rigidly defined and inevitably shade into one another, but they may be useful in analysing the economic significance of Western technology. As indicated above, the overall branch structure of imported equipment is relatively stable. Certain branches regularly import a proportion of their equipment, from either the West or other CMEA members, for example, ships, railway rolling stock, agricultural machinery, timber, paper and pulp-making machinery, metallurgical equipment, and machinery for the light and food industries. These are well established patterns indicating an accepted international division of labour. It would be reasonable to conclude that in such cases, generally not having strategic significance, the USSR sees no strong grounds for expanding its own production capacities, preferring to reap the benefits of international specialisation. Such 'normal' imports probably represent a quite substantial proportion of total Western technology transfers. In other cases one can identify shifts in the pattern of imports associated with attempts to quickly pull up lagging sectors of the economy: the motor and chemical industries have been the most prominent recipients of such 'structural' imports, and, more recently, the oil and gas industries. In these cases the relevant domestic industries simply do not possess the capacity to secure the volume of inputs required in a short period of time, and expansion to meet the demands of rapid structural change would lead to the creation of excess capacity in the future (and would itself probably require large-scale imports, for example, of equipment to produce large-diameter pipe). Such structural imports may be linked with attempts not only to meet pent up domestic demand, but also to increase export earnings. It is claimed that the hard currency outlays on the VAZ plant were rapidly recouped through exports of 'Lada' cars.[17]

At certain times favourable international conditions or other advantageous circumstances permit the Soviet Union to increase Western technology imports above the normal trend. Such 'conjunctural' imports were a notable feature of the period 1974-7: imports of Western technology rose as a proportion of total imports and as a share of total machinery and equipment imports. Furthermore, if individual categories of equipment are examined, it is found that the Western share rose in almost all cases, falling back to the normal trend in 1979-81. It is difficult to determine the scale of these 'conjunctural' imports with any precision because of the complex relative price movements of the period, but analysis indicates that there was a sizeable peak above trend. It is likely that a large share of these conjunctural imports took the form of deliveries of plant for turn-key projects built under the terms of compensation agreements, although the precise value of such deliveries cannot be determined from Soviet statistics. According to one Soviet source, large-scale buy-back agreements accounted for 9 per cent of Soviet trade turnover with the West in 1976, rising to 15 per cent in 1978.[18] By the early 1980s, 65 major compensation projects were under construction, the majority in the chemicals and petrochemicals industries.[19] The crucial factor here was probably the availability of Western credit on favourable terms. Not only was Western technology acquired, but, as Soviet writers stress, domestic sources of investment were supplemented by foreign credit.[20]

For many 'normal', 'structural' and 'conjunctural' imports of technology, the question of the Soviet Union's technological capability is not an issue. If, as a matter of policy, it were decided to produce the equivalent technology using domestic R&D and production resources the task could be fulfilled within a reasonable period of time at an acceptable technological level, quality and cost. However, this will not be true of all imports from the West: in some cases the domestic capability may not be adequate to the task with the consequence that imports are for practical purposes 'non-discretional'. This inadequate capability could stem from a variety of factors, including a lack of appropriate technological knowledge and experience, structural weaknesses of the economy, deep-rooted problems of the system of planning and management, etc. Some of the 'structural' and 'conjunctural' imports could be of a 'non-discretional' character, and some 'normal' imports may shade into the 'non-discretional' category. Similarly, 'non-discretional' imports can become 'normal' (or eliminated altogether) as the domestic capability is enhanced.

An interesting case study of the fluidity of 'normal' and 'non-discretional' imports is provided by the Soviet paper and pulp industry. This is a branch which has traditionally satisfied part of its equipment needs on a regular basis through imports from Finland, other Scandinavian countries and West Germany. The Ministry of Chemical and Oil Engineering has a specialised industrial association, Soyuzbummash, for the development and production of paper and pulp-making equipment, with its own R&D organisations. This industry has substantial capacity, but, as an article in 1977 explained, it is devoted in the main to repair activities and the making of spares rather than the building of complete sets of equipment. A substantial proportion of the repair work and spares production is for maintaining and modernising imported plant. (In 1977 80 per cent of paper-making machines in use in the paper industry were of foreign manufacture.) The ministry places orders for such work with domestic enterprises because it is not prepared to engage the foreign supplying firms on grounds of expense. As the equipment-making enterprises are fully occupied, orders for new production equipment are placed abroad. A vicious circle has evolved: the domestic industry is increasingly unable to make modern paper-making machinery because it receives insufficient orders to gain experience and keep up with world standards. 'Normal' imports have thus become 'non-discretional'. As the article correctly observes, this situation is reversible given an appropriate ordering policy and a more rational system of maintenance and modernisation of the existing capital stock.[21] Paradoxically, in this and similar cases one gains the impression that denial of access to imports would provide the external stimulus required for decisive action to raise the capability of the domestic industry, and that this could be achieved without substantial resource diversion.[22]

Licences

During the post-war period some countries, notably Japan, have reaped substantial benefit from technology acquisition in the form of licence purchases. The Soviet Union was a latecomer in the licence market. The specialised agency, Litsenzintorg, was created in 1962, but during the 1960s most Soviet licence purchases were directly associated with the importation of machinery and equipment and outlays on their acquisition were included in the total value of such imports.[23] Only in the late 1960s did 'pure' licence purchases expand: by 1972 payments for pure licences represented one-third of total annual payments for licences.[24] However, Litsenzintorg has since sold more pure licences than it has purchased. During the period 1971-5, 233 foreign licences were acquired compared with 350 sold, leading to the domestic assimilation in the same period of 48 new technological processes and manufacture of 77 new types of products.[25] There is no evidence of any subsequent marked expansion of pure licence purchases, but there does appear to have been a determined effort to promote Soviet licence sales. By 1983, over a 20-year period, a total of 700 licences had been acquired, compared with licence sales of 720 during the five years, 1976-80.[26] In 1980 licence purchases amounted to a mere 64 million dollars, compared with West Germany's licence imports in the same year of 1,300 million dollars and Japan's 1,200 million.[27] By international standards the Soviet Union's use of foreign licences as a means of technology transfer is extremely modest: if its need for Western technology were really as great as often claimed, one would have expected much greater participation in world licence trade.

A sample of 51 licences acquired between 1972 and 1976[28] indicates that the chemical industry was the principal recipient, accounting for one-third of the total, compared with one-quarter for the engineering industry. An interesting feature of licence purchases has been the willingness to buy them for the consumer goods industry, which accounted for 16 per cent of the sample. These licences often relate to precision components crucial to the successful functioning of products otherwise built domestically; for example, motors and magnetic heads for cassette tape recorders, and styluses for record players. They have been used to initiate the production of consumer goods with which the domestic industry has little familiarity; for example, automatic washing machines are now being built to an Italian licence.[29]

Advocates of greater use of foreign licences have acknowledged that there is opposition and lack of enthusiasm on the part of some Soviet agencies. As Efimov has observed, considerations of prestige sometimes take precedence over economic wisdom, as leaders and specialists of some research organisations regard a decision to purchase a licence as an affront to their honour and competence.[30] Supporters of resort to licences stress the benefits in terms of reduced R&D costs and saved time, and also the potential for reducing foreign exchange outlays on imports of the licenced products. In 1973, for example, it was reported that the purchase of the licence for the building of 'Burmeister & Wain' diesel engines had resulted in a hard currency saving of 30 million rubles over a six-year period.[31] But it is also acknowledged that even the purchase of pure licences often involves additional hard currency expenditure in so far as Soviet industry does not make various types of special equipment and complementary products required for their rapid assimilation. Such equipment purchases were tending to rise as a proportion of the value of pure licence purchases during the 1970s: in 1974 import agencies other than Litsenzintorg accounted for approximately 35 per cent of total outlays on 'pure' licences.[32] Overall, it can be concluded that the Soviet economy has derived benefit from the acquisition and assimilation of Western technologies through licence purchases, but the scale of such transfers has been modest and the transfer process has not been trouble-free.

The Benefits and Problems of the Acquisition of Western Technology

Some of the benefits derived from the use of Western technology have been outlined above. Such acquisitions assist in raising the technological level of the Soviet economy, compensate for weaknesses of the domestic technological capability, and facilitate the realisation of desired structural transformations. The imported technology may permit the production of goods of higher quality than their existing domestic equivalents, thereby opening up possibilities of expanding export sales. Overall, the use of Western technology could be expected to contribute to the rates of growth of output and productivity, although attempts to quantify the impact of imports of Western machinery and equipment are fraught with methodological and data problems. Green and Levine concluded that Western machinery imports accounted for almost 1.2 per cent of an annual average industrial output growth of 6.6 per cent over the period 1960-74, while an alternative approach adopted by Hanson indicated a more modest 0.2-0.5 per cent annual increment during the 1970s.[33] The latter is based on an assumption as to the size of the productivity differential between imported Western equipment and its domestically produced equivalent, but even if such a differential could be measured with accuracy, there could still be a considerable gap between theoretically attainable productivity levels and actual performance in the conditions of the Soviet economy. Indeed, one econometric study by Weitzman arrived at the surprising conclusion that there was effectively no difference between the marginal productivity of imported Western capital and capital of non-Western origin.[34] These global estimates of the contribution of Western technology to Soviet economic performance must be treated with caution, and they all suffer the substantial limitation that they attempt to measure only the direct impact of imports of Western machinery rather than the overall contribution, direct and indirect, of all forms of Western technology acquisition.

In principle, some of the large-scale projects built with substantial resort to Western technology should have provided substantial gains in productivity. The giant KamAZ truck building complex was planned for a level of output per worker 1.5 times that achieved at the VAZ car plant, and more than twice the level at the older Gor'kii truck plant.[35] These benefits were to be achieved from both economies of scale and the very advanced technology employed. The KamAZ works is the world's largest truck producing facility, and in purchasing Western chemical industry plant there has been a preference for installations of an unusually large scale. However, there is much evidence to indicate that the theoretically attainable productivity gains have proved difficult to realise in practice. Problems have included delays in construction, supply bottlenecks, inadequate managerial and worker skills, and difficulties in providing material inputs of the requisite quality. Furthermore, the manning levels of the new chemical plants and other Western-technology based enterprises appear to be higher than typical for their equivalents in the West, reflecting characteristic Soviet organisational and managerial practices.[36]

This does not necessarily mean that the potential productivity gains cannot be realised, but rather that they are usually achieved much later than originally planned.

So far we have considered only the direct impact of Western technology, that is, the specific benefits derived from the use of a new plant built on the basis of imported technology or the use of equipment from the West at an existing enterprise. But the economic gains may take less direct forms and it is possible that in the long run they may be quite as significant as the primary benefits. For purposes of analysis, I distinguish here between secondary benefits associated with the creation of the conditions for the effective use of Western technology, and tertiary benefits achieved later on the basis of the successful assimilation of Western technology. The VAZ plant provides a good illustration. The primary effect of the building of the VAZ works was the achievement of large-volume, high-productivity manufacture of modern passenger cars capable of being sold in Western markets. The assimilation of this facility led to a substantial growth of domestic car ownership.[37] However, this success was achieved through the modernisation and upgrading of production at many other enterprises supplying material inputs to VAZ. This secondary effect is difficult to measure, but it has been claimed that enterprises supplying materials, bearings, electrical equipment and other components had to adapt their production to meet quality levels significantly higher than provided by Soviet state standards — more than 90 per cent of the materials and components supplied to VAZ were made to special technical specifications.[38] It can be assumed that the experience gained in meeting these enhanced quality standards has been gradually passed on to other enterprises of the motor industry. Thus, the original Western-technology based enterprise has served as a lever for raising the general technical standards of many other producers throughout Soviet industry.

Finally, once the VAZ plant had been successfully assimilated, attempts were made to diffuse its experience both within the motor industry and more widely. The factory has now become a leading centre of progressive production organisation and management. Training facilities have been created and specialists of VAZ act as consultants to other enterprises. Particular attention has been paid to the diffusion of organisational arrangements, managerial practices and systems of work organisation and payment. The role of VAZ as an example of best practice for Soviet industry as a whole was acknowledged in a 1979 decree of the USSR Council of Ministers, which set out measures to facilitate the adoption of the VAZ experience at other enterprises.[39] One dimension of this tertiary impact of Western technology is the fact that a number of managerial personnel of both VAZ and KamAZ have now risen to leading positions in Soviet industry: the current minister of the motor industry, V.N. Polyakov, is a former general director of VAZ, and a former director of KamAZ, L.B. Vasil'ev, is now the minister responsible for the production of domestic consumer durables and equipment for the light and food industries. The example of VAZ demonstrates that the impact of Western technology on Soviet economic performance has to be viewed from a long-term perspective: individual large-scale projects may exert a positive influence many years after their primary assimilation.

It would be a mistake to conclude that the impact of Western technology on the Soviet economy is always positive. There is evidence that the expansion of imports during the 1970s, when world market machinery prices exhibited a substantial upward movement, gave rise to some internal economic problems which may have been a factor promoting the more cautious approach to imports of Western technology apparent since the end of the decade. In principle, the state monopoly of foreign trade, central planning and a highly centralised system of price fixing should permit some degree of protection from external inflationary pressure. In practice, the position is not so simple. The official methodology for translating prices of imported equipment into internal prices was established at a time when inflation in the West was at a relatively modest level. As noted above, according to the rules, the 'estimate' price (prices employed for investment projects) of an item of imported equipment is determined according to the official price of an equivalent item of domestically produced equipment. If no domestic equivalent is available, the estimate price of the imported item is fixed according to the price established in the contract concluded with the foreign supplying firm or in the invoice of the foreign trade organisation concerned, converted into an internal price according to the official exchange rate fixed by the State Bank, and adjusted using a coefficient appropriate to the given type of equipment. These coefficients, differentiated for specific categories of equipment, are set and approved by the State Committee for Prices and undergo periodic review; for equipment imported during the 1970s the relevant editions of these lists of coefficients were those approved in 1967 and 1974. If the cost of imported equipment increases by more than 10 per cent as against the original estimate prices incorporated in the investment project, the coefficients can be reviewed by the State Committee on an *ad hoc* basis. For those items of equipment for which no coefficients have been established a standard coefficient of 0.9 is applied. Finally, for individual items of equipment purchased as specific one-off examples of new technology no coefficients are applied, that is, their internal prices are simply their foreign contract prices converted at the official exchange rate.[40]

These pricing rules have implications for the investment process in the Soviet economy. During a period of rapid inflation in the Western supplying countries it is likely that there will be upward price movements between the time when projects for construction are first drawn up (in estimate prices then appropriate) and the time of actual acquisition of the ordered foreign equipment or material inputs. To the extent that this occurs, it will be necessary to increase project cost estimates with consequent additional pressure on investment resources: for a given volume of planned investment fewer projects can be realised and, without corresponding reductions in the number of planned projects, there will be a tendency for projects to overrun their time schedules. In either case, less new capacity will be introduced than originally planned, with negative implications for economic gowth. If Western equipment is concentrated in a few branches of the economy, disproportions may arise leading to further economic difficulties. The reality of these problems has been acknowledged by Soviet authors. Fal'tsman has observed that the overall cost appreciation of domestic and imported equipment during 1976-80 amounted to 32 per cent, with consequent absolute reductions in commissioned new capacities compared with the preceding five-year period.[41] An analysis of 54 chemical industry projects revealed that investment costs per unit of output showed a 28 per cent increase over similar plants already in operation; the most important factor accounting for this cost appreciation was the growth of prices of imported equipment.[42] Thus, the importation of Western technology during a time of inflation has a direct disruptive influence on the Soviet planned investment process.

Another economic problem arises from the secondary impact of Western technology discussed above. In so far as new enterprises built on the basis of imported technology require inputs of a higher

quality than usual for Soviet industry, the overall investment outlays required for a given expansion of capacity may be substantially larger than if domestic technology is employed. The
chemical industry provides an example. According to specialists of
the industry, for each ruble of imported equipment on average an
additional 2-3 rubles of capital investment is required, much more
than for Soviet equipment of a similar purpose. The cost of the
eventual product is usually lower than when domestic equipment is
installed, but in conditions of overstrained investment resources
the additional burden is seen as a real problem. This helps to
explain the interest in compensation agreements in some capital-
intensive sectors of the economy.[43]

It is often assumed that Soviet purchases of technology from its
CMEA partners represents a second-best solution; that if more
hard currency were available and political considerations permitted there would be a substantial switch to Western sources of
supply. This is surely mistaken. First, the Soviet Union obtains
much technology of a respectable technological level and quality
from Eastern Europe, probably at lower prices than for Western
equivalents and with more stable and predictable conditions of
acquisition. Second, the conditions of the creation and use of this
technology are similar in many respects to those encountered in
the USSR. It is probably easier and quicker to reap the potential
economic benefit of such technology than it is for much Western
technology. Direct interchange of personnel is easier and conditions are more favourable for an ongoing sharing of knowledge
and experience. While from a purely engineering point of view
Western technology may often be superior and offer higher potential
productivity than 'Eastern' technology, the difference in actual performance in Soviet conditions may well be much smaller. The
question of the acquisition and use of East European technology in
the USSR has received very little attention in the West.

Another relatively neglected issue is that of Soviet technology
exports to the West. If we are considering technology transfer and
Soviet economic power, this dimension should not be overlooked.
Given that the Soviet Union experiences many problems in producing high quality and reliable engineering products on a large
scale, this dimension may be quite as important as the direct
acquisition of Western technology. Feedback from Western
markets is, I suspect, a far more significant mechanism for
improving Soviet economic performance than is generally realised.

Soviet machinery and equipment exports in general, and to the West in particular, have grown substantially in recent years. The extent of the growth has been concealed by relative price movements. According to Soviet current-price statistics, the share of machinery exports in total exports has declined, from 21.5 per cent in 1970 to 15.8 per cent in 1980. In the latter year machinery exports to developed capitalist countries represented only 4.4 per cent of total exports. However, in constant prices the overall share of machinery exports is estimated to have risen to 26.3 per cent in 1980.[44] Again the experience of the VAZ association has been important: the 'Lada' and 'Niva' are sold in many developed capitalist countries and there are now well developed channels for relaying this market experience back to Soviet industry.

Conclusion

It is ironic that discussion of the role of Western technology in the Soviet economy has been raging at a time when the conjunctural wave of the 1970s has broken. Soviet acquisition of Western technology has now returned to its modest long-term trend. At only one period of Soviet history could Western technology be truly considered decisive for economic development — during the First Five Year Plan, 50 years ago. In recent years Western technology has made an important supplementary contribution to Soviet economic power; it has by no means been the decisive factor. The available evidence does not support the six propositions presented at the beginning of the chapter. Considering its overall economic strength, it could be argued that the USSR has consistently undertraded in advanced technology and that even the peak of imports during the mid-1970s represented a very modest resort to the latest technology of the capitalist world. The recent one-sided attention to Western technology has led to some neglect of research into the state of the Soviet economy and its internal potential for development. It is time to renounce Western Technology fetishism.

Notes

1. Thus a major study in which the author participated concluded, 'In most of the technologies we have studied there is no evidence of a substantial diminution of

the technological gap between the USSR and the West in the past 15-20 years ...'
(R. Amann, J. Cooper and R.W. Davies (eds), *The Technological Level of Soviet Industry* (Yale University Press, London and New Haven, 1977), p. 66). The attendant reservations and qualifications to this baldly stated conclusion inevitably received less attention, and five years elapsed before the authors were able to present their detailed analysis of the intricate web of factors and circumstances accounting for the patterns of technological performance set out in the earlier study (R. Amann, J. Cooper (eds), *Industrial Innovation in the Soviet Union* (Yale University Press, London and New Haven, 1982)).

2. See, for example, V. Shemyatenkov, *Mirovaya Ekonomika i Mezhdunarodnaya Otnosheniya*, no. 3 (1983), p. 34.

3. In the case of the United States it may well be that technological chauvinism has been fuelled by mounting anxiety over the Japanese challenge in many advanced technologies. 'Most people in the electronics business are aware of the Soviet and Japanese threats', one US writer has revealingly observed (*Defense Electronics*, October 1983, p. 12).

4. These issues are discussed by the author in an unpublished paper, 'Technology and the Transition from Capitalism to Communism' (prepared for the Second World Congress for Soviet and East European Studies, Garmisch-Partenkirchen, Federal Republic of Germany, September-October 1980; available from the author on request).

5. The distinction between active and passive transfer mechanisms is a central feature of the Bucy Report on technology transfer prepared for the US Department of Defense in 1976 (Office of the Director of Defense Research and Engineering, *An Analysis of Export Control of US Technology — A DOD Perspective*, A Report of the Defense Science Board Task Force on US Technology, Washington, DC, 4 February 1976).

6. See B. Parrott, *Information Transfer in Soviet Science and Engineering — A Study of Documentary Channels*, RAND Report R-2667-ARPA (Rand, Santa Monica, CA, November 1981).

7. See *Electronics*, 15 March 1979, pp. 42, 44; and 27 January 1981, pp. 39-40.

8. E.P. Balashov and D.V. Puzankov, *Mikroprotsessory i mikroprotsessornye sistemy* (Radio i svyaz', Moscow, 1981), p. 292.

9. Central Intelligence Agency, 'Soviet Acquisition of Western Technology' (April 1982) in G.K. Bertsch and J.R. McIntyre (eds), *National Security and Technology Transfer* (Westview, Boulder, CO, 1983), p. 102.

10. U.M. Kruse-Vaucienne and J.M. Logsdon, *Science and Technology in the Soviet Union — A Profile*, George Washington University, Washington, DC, 1979, p. 74.

11. *Khimicheskaya Promyshlennost'*, no. 11 (1983), pp. 56-7.

12. J.A. Martens, *Quantification of Western Exports of High Technology to Communist Countries*, Office of East-West Trade Policy and Planning, International Trade Administration, US Department of Commerce, Washington, DC, January 1981, pp. 8-9; and January 1982 update.

13. J.B. Salter, 'Trends in Soviet Imports of Technology', *Economics of Planning*, vol. 18, no. 1 (1982), pp. 43-50.

14. *Vneshnyaya Torgovlya*, no. 10 (1974), p. 45.

15. Imports of Western chemical equipment from *Vneshnyaya Torgovlya SSSR*, various years; investment in the chemical industry from *Narodnoe Khozyaistvo SSSR*, various years; share of investment in equipment in chemical industry from *Statisticheskii ezhegodnik stran — chlenov SEV*, various years. No account has been taken of the time-lag between importation and installation. If the share of Western equipment is calculated in current prices, we obtain 18, 22 and

60 per cent for the five-year periods and 44 and 25 per cent for 1980 and 1981. If imports are deflated using the index employed in Table 5.1, we obtain 18, 20 and 48 per cent, and 33 and 18 per cent respectively. The former inflate the share, the latter probably understate it; therefore, I have rather arbitrarily taken the mean of the two figures in each case.

16. BBC Summary of World Broadcasts, SU/W1200/A/7, 27 August 1982 (G. Sudobin, Deputy Minister for the Construction of Oil and Gas Industry Enterprises).

17. *Vneshnyaya Torgovlya SSSR: itogi devyatoi pyatiletki i perspektivy* (Mezhdunarodnye otnosheniya, Moscow, 1977), p. 14.

18. Cited in *Economic Bulletin for Europe*, vol. 34 (June 1982), p. 181.

19. *Vneshnyaya Torgovlya*, no. 8 (1981), p. 36.

20. V. Savin, *Vneshnyaya Torgovlya*, no. 4 (1980), pp. 17-18. Savin points out that the majority of compensation agreements relate to capital-intensive industries. From one listing of compensation agreements concluded between 1969 and 1977, it can be calculated that 60 per cent were related to the chemical and petrochemicals industry, 12 per cent the oil and gas industry, and 8 per cent the timber, paper and pulp industry (E. Zaleski and H. Wienert, *Technology Transfer Between East and West* (OECD, Paris, 1980), pp. 364-9).

21. *Sotsialisticheskaya Industriya*, 22 February 1977.

22. Cf. the reported observation of Academician A.P. Aleksandrov, President of the USSR Academy of Sciences, in October 1982: 'US economic sanctions, on balance, benefited the Soviet Union by speeding improvement of domestic technology. In retrospect, I am glad about the limitation on technology, in that it provided practical backing for my own wish that we should develop our own computer technology further ... It was this US move which facilitated a speeding up of our work' (cited in M.S. Daoudi and M.S. Dajani, *Economic Sanctions: Ideals and Experience* (Routledge and Kegan Paul, London, 1983), p. 188).

23. *Voprosy Ekonomiki*, no.3 (1975), p. 71. Unfortunately, there is virtually no information on the scale of such 'tied' licence purchases, although it is known that for the building of the VAZ car plant 380 licences were acquired (*Trud*, 24 July 1981).

24. *Novyi etap eknomicheskogo sotrudnichestva SSSR s ravitymi kapitalisticheskimi stranami* (Nauka, Moscow, 1978), p. 198.

25. *Ekonomika i Organizatsiya Promyshlennogo Proizvodstva*, no. 1 (1979), p. 58; *Voprosy Izobretatel'stva*, no. 11 (1979), p. 12; *Vneshekonomicheskie svyazi Sovetskogo Soyuza na novom etape*, (Mezhdunarodnye otnosheniya, Moscow, 1977), p. 51.

26. *Vneshnyaya Torgovlya*, no. 9 (1983), p. 31; G. Marchuk in *XXVI CPSU Congress: Press Centre Dialogues* (Novosti, Moscow, 1981), p. 67.

27. *Trud*, 24 July 1981.

28. Zaleski and Wienert, *Technology Transfer*, pp. 344-6.

29. *Kommercheskii Vestnik*, no. 3 (1981), pp. 6-7 and no. 13 (1983), p. 11.

30. *Vsesoyuznaya nauchno-tekhnicheskaya konferentsiya 'Metody uskoreniya nauchnykh issledovanii i proektnykh razrabotok v proizvodstvo' (tezisy dokladov)*, Part 1, Voronezh, 1976, p. 7.

31. *Materialy nauchnoi konferentsii Akademii Obshchestvennykh Nauk pri TsK KPSS, 'Sotsial'no-ekonomicheskie i ideologicheskie problemy organicheskogo soedineniya dostizheniya nauchno-tekhnicheskoi revolyutsii s preimushestvami sotsialisticheskoi sistemy khozyaistva', 19-20 Dekabrya 1973*, Section 2, Moscow, 1974, p. 397.

32. *Novyi etap eknomicheskogo sotrudnichestva SSSR s razvitymi kapitalisticheskimi stranami* (Nauka, Moscow, 1978), p. 198.

33. See P. Hanson, *Trade and Technology in Soviet-Western Relations*

110   *Western Technology and Soviet Economic Power*

(Macmillan, London, 1981), pp. 146-55 for a useful discussion of this issue.

34. M. Weitzman, *Journal of Comparative Economics*, vol. 3, no. 2 (1979), pp. 167-77.

35. *Zakonomernosti sozdaniya material'no-tekhnicheskoi bazy kommunizma* (Mys, Moscow, 1976), p. 309.

36. For a sample of chemical plants supplied by British firms it was found that manning levels were on average 50-70 per cent above normal West European levels (Hanson, *Trade and Technology*, p. 192).

37. Car ownership is still low by West European standards: by 1982 there were ten million privately owned cars, or 40 per 1,000 population (*Izvestiya*, 10 May 1982), compared with a stock of 16 million in Britain, 285 per 1,000 population.

38. *Ekonomika avtomobil'noi promyshlennost' i traktorostroeniya* (Vysshaya Shkola, Moscow, 1978), p. 129.

39. See *Pravda*, 6 May 1976; *Avtomobil'naya Promyshlennost'*, no. 1 (1979), pp. 2-3; and E.A. Afitov, *Sistema VAZ na deistvuyushchikh predpriyatiyakh* (Belarus', Minsk, 1981).

40. E.D. Kachurin and G.L. Gershevich, *Smety na oborudovanie i montazh promyshlennykh predpriyatii* (Metallurgiya, Moscow, 1976), pp. 103-4.

41. *Ekonomika i Organizatsiya Promyshlennogo Proizvodstva*, no. 7 (1983), p. 16.

42. *Zhurnal Vsesoyuznogo Khimicheskogo Obshchestva im. D.I. Mendeleeva*, vol. 26, no. 1 (1981), p. 29.

43. *Ekonomicheskie problemy nauchno-tekhnicheskogo progressa v khimicheskoi promyshlennosti* (NIITEKhIM, Moscow, 1976), p. 61.

44. *Vneshnyaya Torgovlya*, no. 5 (1982), p. 37.

6 WESTERN COMPANIES AND TRADE AND TECHNOLOGY TRANSFER WITH THE EAST*

Malcolm R. Hill

Introduction

This chapter is concerned with trade and transfer of technology between West and East from the perspective of the Western company. Consideration of this perspective is important because companies are the main agents for these activities in the decentralised Western economies. I will pay particular attention to the role played by Western companies in East-West trade and technology transfer and their attitudes towards the Soviet and East European markets, and to the effect of government policies on their East-West business activities.

I will first discuss the experiences of Western companies during the period of rapid increase in East-West trade in the 1960s and 1970s. I will then discuss the recent policies and actions of Western governments towards East-West trade, and the effects of these actions on US and West European companies in the 1980s. The chapter concludes with recommendations for further research on East-West trade and technology transfer, pressing the case for more consistent policy-making, and more informed and open debate.

Western Companies' Commercial Activities in Soviet and East European Markets in the 1960s and 1970s

During the 1960s and 1970s the Soviet Union and Eastern Europe presented Western companies with important market opportunities. These countries were also convenient suppliers of particular technologies, and of certain, especially labour-intensive, commodities and components.

The main commercial activities between Western companies and Soviet and Eastern European foreign trade organisations (or enterprises having the legal competence to engage in foreign trade

111

activities) can be classified as follows:

(1) import and export activities;
(2) licensing;
(3) inter-firm industrial co-operation;
(4) technical co-operation.

Each of these categories, together with the relevant experiences of Western companies, is described in more detail below.

Export and Import Activities

The majority of trade between the socialist countries of Eastern Europe and the industrially developed Western market economies is in the form of commercial export and import transactions between Western companies and authorised foreign trade organisations based in the socialist countries. A great deal of technology embodied in many types of exported machinery, processing plant and other types of engineering products has been transferred through these trading channels.[1] The socialist countries were a growing market for Western products, particularly engineering goods[2] during the 1960s and 1970s, with Western exports to the socialist countries increasing by more than 300 per cent from 1960 to 1972, and by the same figure during the shorter time interval from 1972 to 1979.[3] These figures were higher than the increases in total world exports, and also higher than the increase in exports of the developed market economies to the world as a whole (248 per cent from 1960 to 1972, and 262 per cent from 1972 to 1979); though much of the accredited growth in exports from the Western countries was due to inflation in Western prices, particularly after 1972.[4]

Prior to 1970, it was usually the case that the socialist countries had a surplus in their trading relations with the West. The post-1970 increase in East-West trade turnover, however, was associated with a deficit on the part of the socialist countries reaching some 16 per cent of total East-West trade turnover in 1975.[5] These growing Eastern deficits in the 1970s were caused partly by increasing real demands for Western products and technology to update, refurbish and expand certain industrial sectors as shown by the large and widening Eastern trade deficit in engineering products;[6] but post-1972 Western price inflation was clearly a crucial factor in the overall trade deficit.

Although the socialist countries were growth markets for Western goods during the 1960s and 1970s, the proportion of total Western developed market economy exports delivered to the Soviet Union and Eastern Europe was generally low: 2.9 per cent in 1960, 3.1 per cent in 1970 and 3.8 per cent in 1979.[7] At the level of the individual industrial sector or company, however, the picture has frequently been different, because of the tendency for Soviet and East European import requirements to come in large discrete quantities as specific industrial sectors are earmarked for priority expansion. For example, as a consequence of the expansion of the Soviet motor industry in the 1970s, and the demand for equipment imports, the USSR accounted for some 20 per cent of total exports of British special purpose machine tools in certain years; similar patterns were also apparent for other OECD supplier countries.[8] For certain individual companies, Soviet and East European exports in certain years accounted for almost all exports and up to 50 per cent of total sales.[9]

The Western economies, on the other hand, have been import-ant markets for Soviet and East European goods, receiving more than 20 per cent of the socialist countries' total exports during most years between 1960 and 1979.[10] For food, beverages and tobacco this proportion was some 30 per cent, and 45 to 50 per cent for crude materials and mineral fuels.[11] In view of the importance of Western markets in aggregate terms and as sources of hard currency to help pay for import requirements, socialist foreign trade organisations have always paid attention to the potential for increasing their volume of exports to the West. Many export and import transactions have conventionally been carried out independently, with Western companies selling either to the competent foreign trade organisation, or to another Western company acting as a project leader; and the foreign trade organisations in their turn exporting their products to Western import specialists who have acted as distributors. To assist in the payment of their imports, however, foreign trade organisations have also developed methods of 'countertrading', 'compensation trading' and 'industrial co-operation', which link their exports to Western companies to a proportion of their imports from those same firms.[12] In addition, during recent years, socialist foreign trade organisations have increased their ownership of Western companies which have traded as distributors of products exported by that same foreign trade organisation, as a means to develop appropriate marketing methods for exports to the market economies.[13]

Research results[14] suggest that most of those Western engineering and chemical companies which have been successful in obtaining, and subsequently fulfilling, capital goods export contracts with the socialist countries of Eastern Europe have possessed six major technological, commercial, and managerial capabilities, as outlined below.

(1) The ability to draft technical and commercial proposals in a meticulous manner, to submit repeated but modified versions of these proposals over comparatively short periods, and to sustain long and highly contended technical and commercial negotiations over a lengthy pre-contract time cycle. This is a result of repeated and extended discussions which take place between user factories and foreign trade organisations in the socialist countries and which are punctuated by long time intervals, and also a result of the frequent wish of socialist buyers to acquire equipment which match their needs exactly, at the most competitive price.

(2) The ability to design, manufacture and install products embodying comparatively advanced, but proven, technology, frequently as an integral part of a complex manufacturing system.

(3) The ability to co-ordinate the timely manufacture, construction and installation of complex plant over quite lengthy time periods, particularly when the volume of orders from the customer may consume a substantial proportion of the company's total resources for that period. Soviet orders especially have usually been large when they arrived, as a consequence of the frequent Soviet practice of designating an entire factory or industry for priority expansion, and also because of the large absolute size of that country's industry.

(4) The willingness to purchase articles manufactured in the country of the socialist trading partner, a condition to trade advanced by the latter in order to reduce the outlay of scarce foreign currency reserves. The conditions of 'countertrade' and 'counterpurchasing' are themselves frequently the subject of hard negotiation.

(5) In the case of large companies, a willingness to act as a project leader. This latter activity has been related to the export of other suppliers' items as well as the company's own products

and technology, and to the formation of framework contracts to co-ordinate the counterpurchase activities of various principals.

(6) The ability to estimate costs accurately for fixed-price contracts, particularly during the conditions of rapid price inflation in the 1970s. This is especially important because of the long lead-times between submission of proposals and completion of contracts which are frequently found when exporting to the socialist countries of Eastern Europe.

At first sight many Western companies often viewed the USSR and Eastern Europe as 'markets of last resort', as a consequence of:[15]

(1) the extended pre-contract negotiation times, and associated high costs of tendering;
(2) the possibility that too much technological know-how would be transferred at the pre-contract stages, with no associated guarantee of business;
(3) the high degree of price competitiveness;
(4) the stringent inspection requirements:
(5) extended installation times;
(6) the necessity of compensation trading.

In spite of these difficulties, however, Soviet and East European enquiries and orders frequently moved from positions of last resort to those of first priority as a consequence of their size and the general inactivity in other international markets. This was certainly the case with many machinery orders in the late 1960s and 1970s when the Soviet Union began an ambitious investment programme in its engineering and chemical industries. In addition, prior to the recent economic crises in Poland and to a lesser extent in Romania, Soviet and East European foreign trade organisations were generally viewed by Western exporters and their bankers as reliable payers of outstanding debts once delivery contractual requirements had been met.[16]

Licensing

It is difficult to obtain accurate data on East-West trade in licences and associated payments because of the lack of detail on this topic in published official statistics, and because the sale of a piece of processing plant may also include a licence which is not usually itemised as a separate payment. The estimates that have been made on this topic, however, suggest a predominantly eastward flow of licences and associated technological know-how, and a predominantly westward flow of payments, either in hard currency or in goods produced under the licence. This latter form of payment has frequently formed part of an inter-firm industrial co-operation agreement.

Wilczynski[17] estimated in 1976 that the total number of licences sold by Western companies to organisations in the socialist countries of Eastern Europe, had exceeded 2,400 (including 500 to Yugoslavia), of which more had been sold during 1970 to 1975 than during the entire period prior to 1970. The entire proceeds to the West from the sale of these licences were estimated to be some $300 million, or some $240 million if Yugoslavian royalties are excluded on a *pro rata* basis.[18] The main purchasers of these licences were apparently the USSR and Poland (about 450 licences each) followed by Czechoslovakia and Hungary (250 to 300 licences each). The socialist countries, on the other hand, were estimated to have sold approximately 700 licences to the West, 'mostly involving minor specialised (but not necessarily of low sophistication) inventions, not in the same class as those purchased from the West'. Czechoslovakia was claimed to be the largest single exporter of socialist licences to the West (approximately 350), followed by the USSR, Hungary, the GDR and Poland. These licences were also generally of a lower unit value than those bought by the East from the West: during the 1960s the payment per licence by the West to the East was estimated to have been only one-eleventh of the payment per licence by the East to the West. By the early 1970s this ratio had increased to one-quarter, although the sale of socialist licences to the West still only amounted to $40 million by the mid-1970s.[19]

In general, those Western companies which have sold product and process licences to the socialist countries of Eastern Europe have done so to secure income from both initial and royalty payments. Particular care was usually necessary to establish the detailed manner in which the relevant technology was to be transferred, including the scope of documentation to be delivered and the support services to be provided; but once these had been clarified and agreed upon, the contracts were usually executed to the satisfaction of both parties.[20] In addition, a study[21] of a sample of

British purchasers of socialist licences revealed that the technical information provided was quite adequate, although the socialist licensor was sometimes slow in operation, with a lack of sensitivity towards the licensee's problems of operating in a market economy. These complaints were comparatively rare, however, and should be seen in the context of the influence of bureaucracy as a fact of commercial life in the planned economies, and against a background in which the licensee himself was sometimes slow to move until he felt convinced of the business viability of the technology to be transferred. In spite of problems sometimes arising from differences in political and economic structure, most companies found the business arrangements to be satisfactory. In conclusion, therefore, it appears that parties on both sides of the eastward and westward sales of industrial licences found the agreements to work adequately.

Inter-firm Industrial Co-operation

East-West inter-firm industrial co-operation agreements have been shown usually to display the following characteristics.[22]

(1) Technology is transferred from one partner of the agreement to the other, for the design, development and/or manufacture of a particular finished product. The technology transfer may also include the sale of appropriate licences, manufacturing equipment, or components; and the training of personnel.
(2) The time interval of the industrial co-operation agreement is usually longer than that associated with a one-off sale.
(3) If appropriate, payment for the technology transferred is made partly in items related to the finished product.
(4) The flow of technology via these agreements has been predominantly from West to East.

The number of existing industrial co-operation agreements increased rapidly from the mid-1960s to the mid-1970s, apparently by more than four times (from 180 to 1,000). Such an estimate is very tenuous, however, since all Western compilers of the quantity of industrial co-operation agreements sound a note of caution over the accuracy of their estimates.[23] Furthermore, it is difficult to ascertain the degree to which these estimates are independent, and the extent to which the frequently cited figure of '1,000 industrial co-operation agreements' was selected as a convenient rounded figure for publicity purposes for 1975. Although the rate of growth of the signing of industrial co-operation agreements was probably quite rapid over the decade considered, in my opinion the total quantity of these agreements is probably quite small when compared with the total number of East-West business arrangements.

It is still more difficult, however, to obtain reliable estimates of the total financial value of East-West co-operation agreements. A publication by Wilczynski in 1976[24] estimated such trading activities to have been worth some $1 billion (presumably in 1974 and 1975), but this figure may include some co-operation activities between Western companies and Yugoslavian organisations. Comparing this estimate with total foreign trade between socialist countries of Eastern Europe and the developed market economies, it appears that industrial co-operation activity accounted for approximately 2 per cent of total East-West trade.[25] Other data available for Hungary and Poland suggest that their proportions of exports through industrial co-operation agreements may be much higher for certain products and markets, notably machinery exports to Western Europe in general, and to the Federal Republic of Germany in particular.[26]

A typical industrial co-operation agreement between a Western company and a socialist foreign trade organisation consists of the sale of a licence with the provision of associated know-how, together with the sale of relevant critical components, especially during the start-up phase. Part of the value of the sale to the socialist country frequently has been compensated by the purchase of related components; but these have usually been arranged through separate, although linked, contracts. Furthermore, there has frequently been a marketing agreement to protect the licensor from unwanted competition and attempts have been made to carry out quality control, although on-site difficulties usually have reduced this to a pass/fail decision at the component purchase stage.

The main motives for Western companies entering into the industrial co-operation agreement have been the following:[27]

(1) income from the sale of a licence and particularly from the sale of associated components, and sometimes income from the sale of related manufacturing equipment;
(2) possibilities for cheaper sourcing, particularly of less-

sophisticated or labour-intensive components;
(3) keeping a presence in the Eastern European market, and maintaining good working relationships with the relevant East European foreign trade organisations. This has been particularly important since, as in the case of counter-purchasing discussed above, industrial co-operation has been viewed favourably by socialist foreign trade organisations as a means of obtaining Western technological know-how and manufacturing plant, with a comparatively lower outlay of foreign exchange.

In the majority of cases, these anticipated advantages which have motivated the signing of the industrial co-operation agreement have been borne out in practice, although certain problems have been frequently encountered, namely:[28]

(1) inconsistent product quality from the East European partner, especially during start-up;
(2) a lack of breadth in the range of products offered for counter-purchase by the socialist foreign trade organisation;
(3) inconsistencies in the meeting of delivery schedules by the East European partner;
(4) cumbersome business relationships caused by the bureaucratic methods of industrial management in Eastern Europe.

In most cases, however, these problems were reduced through determined management by both partners to the industrial co-operation agreement.

Technical Co-operation

Many Western companies have signed agreements to cover joint research and development, and the exchange of technical information, with industrial and scientific organistions of the socialist countries of Eastern Europe. These arrangements have sometimes been referred to as 'umbrella agreements' since they have covered a wide range of technologies, particularly when the larger multinational organisations were involved; or as 'framework agreements' since they have sometimes been viewed by Western companies as a means to carry out joint discussions on a range of selected topics within a defined framework. This author prefers to use the term 'technical co-operation agreement', however, since the use of this term denotes that the main objective of the agreement is technologically determined. An umbrella agreement may, in practice, have trade in licences, components or machinery as its final objective; whilst the use of the term 'framework agreement' may be confused with the term 'framework contract', which is a business arrangement used to link together temporarily several principals to separate contracts within a defined counter-trading framework.

Two surveys of American businessmen conducted in the mid-1970s[29] showed that a frequent motivation for US companies to sign technical co-operation agreements with the Soviet State Committee for Science and Technology was to use the agreement as a means of entry into the potentially large Soviet market. One American businessman cited felt that the State Committee for Science and Technology was 'the appropriate vehicle for big deals'; but this enthusiastic response has to be balanced by the view of another observer, who claimed that 'those businessmen who signed [technical co-operation] agreements are usually not those who sign contracts'. Uncertainty about the commercial value of such agreements was further illustrated by the view of another observer that only travel had resulted from the signing of his technical co-operation agreement, although frequent travel for associated discussions was usually a prerequisite for trade with the USSR. It is my view, however, that some of the pessimistic comments by those American businessmen have to be viewed in relation to the stated objectives of technical co-operation agreements, which are not usually trade, but joint technical development and the exchange of information. Furthermore, it should be borne in mind that the main role of the State Committee for Science and Technology in the Soviet economy has not been one of foreign trade, but the co-ordination of scientific and technical development.

The surveys also evinced a similar range of opinions on the transfer of scientific and technical information. One firm expressed concern that the Soviets were surreptitiously obtaining technology through visits to US plants by State Committee personnel, whilst on the other hand another observed that 'we are gaining information at a far greater rate than we are giving it'. Another, more pragmatic, observer considered the technical co-operation agreement to offer a 'preliminary opportunity to assess Soviet technical potential and marketing opportunities'. A further apparent realist observed that the main opportunity for his multinational company

lay in the trade-off of US technology for research and development results from Soviet scientific research institutes, project-
technological institutes, or pilot plants.

Research by McMillan[30] strongly suggests that the Soviet State
Committee for Science and Technology is more likely than its
counterparts in other socialist countries to favour this kind of
agreement. Using this information in the course of some recent
research,[31] I looked for announcements of British companies that
had signed technical co-operation agreements with that organisation. A survey of various publications followed by discussions with
British trade officials in 1977 revealed that some eleven British
companies had signed co-operation agreements with the Soviet
State Committee for Science and Technology between 1972 and
1977.[32] Through personal contacts, I also located two other British
companies that had signed technical co-operation agreements,
thereby increasing the total to 13; it is possible that still other cases
may exist that have not been recorded. From this population, I was
able to interview executives from seven companies.

From this survey it was apparent that all of those companies
which expected the signing of the co-operation agreement to lead
directly to trade had been disappointed, as the subsequent volume
of trade had been generally quite low. In hindsight, this is not surprising, since the activities relevant to the technical co-operation
agreement were carried out with either a state committee for
science and technology or with an industrial ministry, the majority
of which do not possess the right to engage in foreign trade activities on a large scale. It is likely that officials within these organisations were far more interested in obtaining information which
related to long-term and medium-term technical policies and production strategies, rather than short- to medium-term plant purchasing decisions. In addition, some companies entered these
agreements when Anglo-Soviet inter-governmental relations were
at their most friendly during the late 1960s and mid-1970s, raising
the question as to whether the agreements may have been signed
primarily to assist both governments' political objectives.

However, the marketing effort put into technical co-operation
agreements by Western companies should not necessarily be
regarded as wasted; some companies considered the signing and
operation of the technical co-operation agreements to be
extremely beneficial. In the first place, companies built up channels
of communication and points of contact with several officials in

industrial ministries and foreign trade organisations in the socialist countries. This can be an important benefit when trying to sell to this market, because the end-user is frequently organisationally separated from the purchaser. Secondly, the establishment of a technical co-operation agreement can be viewed by a Western firm as a medium- to long-term promotion exercise. Finally, Western firms have benefited from technical co-operation agreements particularly when the objectives of agreements were clearly technological and related to the exchange of information, and not necessarily when objectives were commercial and related to the purchase and sale of products.

Government Policies on East-West Trade and Technology Transfer[33]

The policies of individual Western governments had a significant effect on their domestic companies' commercial relations during the increase in trading activity with the socialist countries of Eastern Europe in the 1960s and 1970s. In the first place, inter-governmental agreements provided a statement of intent of trading between the respective countries, and also provided a framework in which business, scientific and technical contacts could be created and strengthened. Secondly, many Western governments were prepared to support lines of credit to socialist countries by meeting the difference between the rate of interest charged to the particular socialist buyer, and the commercial rate. In addition, policy guidelines were set by export credit guarantee agencies regarding the category of credit risk into which particular socialist countries should be placed, and the proportion of the value of the export contract which could be covered by credit facilities. These policy guidelines were regarded as generous by some Western observers, but the socialist countries had generally shown themselves to be good credit risks at that time. Thirdly, Western governments helped to increase the volume of imports from the respective socialist country by the modification of quota levels over a wide range of imported products. Finally, most Western governments were prepared to permit the export of many products to the socialist countries, which had previously been embargoed.[34] In general, the West European countries removed a proportionately larger number of products from their embargo lists than did their US ally.[35]

The policies listed above were followed by Western governments to meet particular sets of objectives, which can be generalised into two main categories, namely:

(1) a desire to obtain economic and financial benefits through the development of foreign trade, particularly from exports of those products for which the respective Western governments' domestic industries were considered to have a competitive edge;
(2) a desire to obtain geopolitical benefits through the use of trading activity as a lever to modify both the domestic and foreign policies of the socialist countries.

These objectives rested on a series of assumptions regarding:

(a) government/industry interaction;
(b) the economic and geopolitical objectives of the socialist countries;
(c) the degree to which these objectives could be modified through East-West trading activity;
(d) the extent to which Western countries could act in a coordinated manner with their major trading partners and military allies.

Each of the above merit further discussion.

Concerning government/industry interaction first, it appears that in most of the decentralised Western economies (particularly those in Europe) industry has generally been in advance of government in attempting to develop trading links with the socialist countries of Eastern Europe.[36] Industrial and financial executives were developing trading opportunities with socialist foreign trade organisations in the 1950s before the signing of intergovernmental agreements in the 1960s and the granting of associated lines of credit; but these latter actions certainly acted as a further impetus to the subsequent rapid growth of East-West trade. During most of the 1960s and 1970s, therefore, it would appear that the broad policies of Western governments and companies ran in parallel, although different in objective and time scale of operation. Companies were enthusiastic to obtain orders to generate income and subsequent profits, frequently over a business planning cycle of some five years between receipt of order and completion of contract; whilst governments were keen to achieve economic and geopolitical objectives.

These economic and geopolitical objectives in their turn rested on certain assumptions by the West concerning the objectives of the governments of Eastern Europe. The first assumption was economic, namely that the socialist countries required Western-manufactured products to a far greater extent than Western countries required socialist-manufactured articles.[37] The second set of assumptions were based on the degree to which the socialist countries appeared to be prepared to modify their domestic and geopolitical objectives as a consequence of the policy of detente initiated in the early 1970s and formalised at the 1975 Helsinki Conference on Security and Co-operation in Europe. As a result of these assumptions, therefore, it was considered that a certain amount of leverage could be exerted on the socialist countries to influence their geo-political behaviour; as will be shown later, however, these expected objectives were not always achieved at a satisfactory level in practice.

The final point which has influenced government policies and procedures in this field has been the relationships between military allies, and those between economic partners. The former relationships have included the degree to which a government should use export licences to restrict the sale of products and technological know-how to the socialist countries because of perceived national security risks or economic and political objectives. These policies have been frequently modified by the perceived reactions of allies, and the degree to which these allies have been prepared to act in a concerted fashion (usually through the framework of CoCom).[38] The latter relationships have included the degree to which governments have acted in line either with their partners within the EEC, or within a credit consensus established by the OECD.[39]

Since the mid-1970s, however, with the changing state of East-West relations have come new developments in government policies on East-West trade and technology transfer. I will discuss in turn the particular issues of leverage, legal Western sales and Soviet military capability, illegal Western sales, and the differing views within NATO, all of which have now presented themselves as important topics for study in this field of commercial activity.

Leverage

Several Western governments, but particularly the US, have questioned for some time whether the policy of leverage (that is, the use of trade as a lever to influence the behaviour of the socialist countries) has been a success, and have claimed that the socialist countries have merely secured technology from Western sources for their economic and military advancement without any concessions on their side. This concern was recently exacerbated in the late 1970s and early 1980s as a consequence of a lack of any apparent improvement in civil liberties in the USSR, the Soviet intervention in Afghanistan, and the introduction of martial law in Poland. Indeed, the only successes for the leverage policy would appear to have been the increase in flow of Jewish emigrants from the USSR and Romania.[40]

This concern of Western governments is understandable, but it is not unreasonable to question whether the advocates of 'leverage' may not have been over-optimistic in their hopes. The USSR is well known to move at a slow pace over most internal reforms, has always been wary at the possibilities of outside interference in its own internal affairs, and has always been concerned over the security of its borders. Furthermore, the scope for Soviet influence in Poland has been limited by the recent social and economic conditions within that country. Nevertheless, the normal Western, and particularly US, government reaction has been to prevent the sale of specific products in retaliation against certain Soviet and East European government actions. These cancellations have included a Sperry-Univac computer system for TASS in 1978 following Soviet actions against dissidents; grain, and oil extraction equipment in 1980 following the Soviet intervention in Afghanistan; and gas pipeline equipment in 1982 following the introduction of martial law in Poland.[41] It is not clear whether these actions were meant only to show extreme disapproval, or to act as a lever to modify subsequent Soviet and East European behaviour. It is certainly the case, however, that trading conditions became surrounded by uncertainty as a result of these actions.

Legal Western Sales and Soviet Military Capability

In addition to the general concern about the lack of leverage apparently provided by foreign trade, and a general disenchantment with detente, several Western government agencies, and particularly those in the US, have claimed that technology purchased from the West has substantially increased the military capability of the USSR in four ways,[42] namely:

(1) direct absorption of relevant Western technologies into the military supply industries, thereby improving the quality of Soviet weaponry and the pace of innovation;
(2) the absorption of Western technologies ostensibly to produce non-military products, but which were subsequently put to use in the military sphere (that is, 'dual-use' technologies);
(3) the use of Western supplies to provide products required for civilian application, whilst using Soviet domestic capacity thereby released to produce military equipment;
(4) the use of Western technology to improve the general economic efficiency of Soviet industry, and thereby generate additional resources which can be devoted to military spending.

This section of the chapter will only discuss material relating to direct absorption of Western technologies into the military supply industries, and the dual use of Western technologies in both the civilian and military sectors. It is particularly difficult to discuss the other issues relating to the expansion of Soviet capacity for military use, without assuming certain patterns of allocation and priority among Soviet policy-makers. A discussion of such issues is beyond the terms of reference of the present chapter.

The concerns related to the Soviet military application of Western-supplied technology are well summarised by one American senator who claimed that increased Western military expenditure needed to compensate for Soviet military advances gained from the use of Western technology 'far outweigh the West's earnings from the legal sales to the Soviets of its equipment and technology'.[43] It is my opinion, however, that more substantive evidence is necessary before such statements alone can justify the introduction of significant extensions to Western product and technology export embargoes. There may be other interpretations to the Soviet use of Western exports than those advanced by individuals who wish to constrain that trade.

The reasons for this opinion are illustrated by the sale of a large number of Bryant Centralign high precision grinding machines by their American suppliers to the USSR in the 1970s.[44] After a certain time interval following the sale, the accuracy of Soviet missiles improved considerably, as a consequence of improvements in the precision of the bearings in the gyroscopic guiding mechanism; and it was subsequently claimed that the Bryant machines were used, or the know-how copied, to produce these components.[45] These claims, however, make certain assumptions, some of which are certainly open to question.

First, it is assumed that the 'critical components' were produced using Centralign technology, but to my knowledge there has been no definite proof of this presented in open publications. Even if such proof is presented, however, it is also important to note that Gustafson states that the US intelligence community believes that the Bryant machines arrived in the USSR 'too late to have played a crucial gap filling role in the development of the Soviet fourth generation missiles'.[46]

Second, it is assumed that Soviet-produced machine tools were inherently less capable of producing to the required accuracy and output rate than those built by Bryant. Although Soviet machines may have been less precise and productive than their American counterparts, this does not necessarily mean that they were incapable, as the requisite quantity and quality might have been obtained by rigorous product screening and the willingness to reject high volumes of scrap to obtain the requisite volume of acceptable items.[47] Alternatively, if the USSR was attempting to buy these machines over a period of eleven years as claimed,[48] it is also difficult to believe that substitute machines or methods could not have been developed by Soviet engineers given the project's supposed priority.

Consequently, the question of the supply of advanced Western technology is worthy of more serious study to test the relatively simple assumption that such know-how is automatically used by the Soviet Union to obtain a significant military advantage.

The questions to be considered which relate to 'dual-use' technology are the degree to which technology and equipment purchased from the West may be put to direct or indirect military application by the USSR, and whether such application could have been reasonably foreseen at the time of sale. An example which demonstrated these issues is provided by the sale of technology and machinery by Western companies for installation in Soviet truck plants at Kama, Moscow, Minsk and Gor'kii in the 1970s. Some of the vehicles produced in those factories (presumably using

Western-supplied machinery), were subsequently found to be used by Red Army units stationed in both Eastern Europe and Afghanistan; and associated criticisms were then made by US politicians concerning the permitted delivery of these machines.[49] In my view, however, the main questions to be asked relate not just to the existence of these trucks in the Red Army vehicle stock but the proportion of that stock accounted for by those vehicles, the proportion of their designs and manufacture achieved using Western technology, the proportions of output of these vehicles being put to either civilian or military uses, and the timing of implementation of these dual-use products using Western technology. This latter question becomes particularly relevant when it is recalled that the designs of the trucks in all of the factories mentioned above were Soviet[50] and that the trucks could have been manufactured using Soviet-built machinery, although possibly over a longer project-implementation cycle and at reduced levels of product quality and reliability and plant labour productivity. If attempts are made to answer such questions, it will then be possible to judge more accurately whether Western companies should be forbidden to sell machinery, and lose the concomitant benefits of sales income, profits and provision of employment, when the machinery may be used to manufacture a civilian product which may conceivably have a dual military application, no matter how basic.

The provision of such an estimate is clearly a difficult matter and worthy of further research, when it is borne in mind that at the time of the sales of the machines and technology referred to in the previous paragraph, there was ample evidence to suggest that the Soviet truck fleet was in urgent need of refurbishment to meet the civilian transport demands to be placed upon it.[51] Furthermore, according to the evidence of a US government official responsible for approving the sale of these machine tools to the USSR, at the time of the sale it was considered that this machinery would not have any military effect, since the vehicles to be manufactured by these machines were not believed to meet the criteria used to indicate a military specification.[52]

The above points are important issues for debate, bearing in mind the recent strong criticism of the West European NATO allies for their exports of equipment and technology to the USSR and the other socialist countries; one US senator has suggested that leverage should be exerted on Western Europe to prevent 'damage [to] our national security by selling vital technology to the

Soviets'.[53] There is a definite need for further study of such issues, in order to establish clearly the boundaries within which such trade can be carried out by Western companies, without damage to national security. To implement further trade restrictions without such a debate would probably have a marginal effect both on Soviet and East European behaviour and possibly a comparatively small effect on Western security. The consequences for income and profitability of many Western companies could be considerable, however, with subsequent effects on Western employment levels.

Illegal Western Sales

In addition to restriction of trade in technological items carried out in a legal framework, claims are also frequently made that a large volume of such trade takes place illegally. In 1982, the Deputy Director of the CIA, Admiral B.R. Inman, stated that 70 per cent of militarily useful technology transferred to the USSR is gathered by intelligence agencies,[54] although the validity of such estimates must clearly be open to doubt when the full range of trade activities is probably unknown. If this estimate is accurate, however, there is a clear necessity for the NATO governments to agree and implement procedures which prevent or limit illegal activity, to allocate the necessary resources for monitoring, and to establish adequate penalties for deterrence.

In June 1981, the US Office of Export Administration had approximately 30 administrative cases pending in various states, some of which were awaiting the completion of investigations relating to potentially serious violations.[55] In addition to these administrative cases, a US Customs Commissioner claimed that up to the spring of 1982 his agency 'had made more than 200 seizures in its crackdown on overseas shipments of high technology equipment'.[56] This 'crackdown' has become known as 'Operation Exodus' and has continued apace with evidence of success and co-operation from customs services in other CoCom countries.[57]

Concerning the criminal magnitude of these offences, when replying to a senator's question on administrative sanctions, Mr Lawrence Brady, Assistant Secretary for Trade Administration of the US Department of Commerce, stated that a variety of factors had to be reviewed in any given case. Many of the cases involved only technical violations such as overshipment, and in some of the cases only a warning letter was justified. In other cases, a civil penalty and/or denial of export privileges may have been warranted.[58] In practice, however, there appears to have been a wide range of penalties imposed upon those persons found to be involved in illegal technology sales activities. For example, one radar engineer received a sentence of eight years imprisonment for espionage for passing radar secrets to a 'highly trained Polish intelligence officer', who received a life sentence for the same charge. On the other hand, the owner of a company manufacturing laser mirrors falsified statements on export documents in order to sell a range of such mirrors to the USSR. The penalty in this case was ten years' imprisonment; but the sentence was suspended except for the first six months, and appended with 500 hours of voluntary work for a charitable organisation plus a company fine of $100,000. In a third case, a Belgian executive, who repeatedly tried to secure an American software system for the USSR without a valid licence, received only a four month imprisonment when charges against him were reduced from felonies to misdemeanours.[59]

A narrower and more relevant range of sentences for this type of illegal activity might enhance the facility of such penalties to deter potentially profitable illegal action. Under new US law enacted in December 1981, firms found guilty of national security violations can now be fined up to five times the value of the export or $1 million, whichever is the greater.[60] It appears, therefore, that steps are being taken to tighten illegal transfers from the US, and it would seem to be appropriate to observe the efficacy of these changes rather than proceed further along avenues which may substantially reduce the volume of legal trade between the East and West with disadvantages to both sides.

It is frequently the case, though, that this issue of illegal activity becomes associated with a view that the CoCom list of embargoed exports should be tightened. In this author's opinion the two issues are completely separate, the first relating to illegal activity which needs to be halted, and the second relating to legal activity which may require a closer definition. There is no advantage to be gained by confusing these two issues; but the prevention of illegal activity is clearly worthy of further attention.

It should be noted that most Western companies would probably not run the risks of illegal trade because of a number of possible dangers: their reputations may be harmed, export licences may be refused after expensive long-term negotiations, and their far more important Western customers may view them with suspicion[61] and consequently place orders elsewhere. Those companies that are less responsible, and are willing to risk their reputations by illegal exporting, run the risk of court action, its associated publicity and penalties, and subsequent loss of business.

Views Within the NATO Alliance

A final, but highly significant, factor which influences Western government policy on East-West trade is the difference between the various partners of the NATO alliance. On this issue, the Alliance partners have generally been divided into the West Europeans, who have advocated a more flexible approach to trading with the socialist countries with embargoes placed only on goods having a military application; and the US, which has generally followed a more restrictive approach, attempting to use trade as one of a range of strategic and economic levers.[62] In addition, the West European governments have differed from their US allies by keeping a lower profile of rhetoric on East-West relations generally.

This West European approach has caused a certain amount of concern in the US, concern which became even more vocal in 1981 and 1982 over the supply of West European equipment for use in the Urengoy pipeline, with associated Western credit and subsequent counterpurchase to finance Soviet equipment purchases. It was considered by American policy-makers that such transactions would not only provide further investment and hard currency for Soviet economic development and associated military expansion, but would also make West European countries dependent upon Soviet energy supplies and more vulnerable to Soviet diplomatic pressure. Furthermore, there has also been some American concern that West European companies were becoming too dependent upon Soviet and East European orders for their continued business existence and workforce employment, and that in a time of recession this dependence may turn into vulnerability (although there is alternative evidence from Treml[63] to suggest that certain Soviet purchasing industries may be just as dependent on Western suppliers as Western companies are on Soviet markets). One senator became so disenchanted with the attitudes of West European companies and their governments towards American concerns that he stated '... there are a lot of us that are quite impatient with our NATO allies ... the people that we have been protecting being so uncooperative at crucial moments'.[64]

Recent West European policy has generally been one of attempting to create the conditions for East-West trade to continue at the highest level possible, commensurate with a satisfactorily high interest rate on credits and with no military technology being exported to the USSR. For example, there has been some European concern for over-generous credit terms, with one British government minister on record as saying that

> ... indiscriminate trade-orientated export credit policy can lead to the absurdity of the United Kingdom providing capital equipment to regimes in, say, the centrally planned economies which are opposed to all we stand for and ... [providing] capital equipment on financial terms which are far more agreeable than those that are available to our own domestic buyers ... So overall our main concern in devising and implementing export credit policy is the interest subsidy involved and the extent to which that subsidy is worthwhile. A sense of proportion, we believe, is a primary need.[65]

This European approach is likely to continue without major changes, unless there is more substantive evidence to show that such trade is overtly harmful to Western national security, or unless further economic and political pressure is exerted by the US.

Before finishing this section of the chapter, it is important to note that differences in trading policies towards the socialist countries that are clearly evident between the US and West European partners of the NATO alliance may have come about as a consequence of differences in commercial relations with the socialist countries of Eastern Europe, and/or differences in industrial structure, the US military-industrial complex being stronger than in Western Europe. Senator Heinz has noted that 'in 1979, US high technology exports to the USSR amounted to $183 million, or about 1/10th the level of Soviet imports of advanced machinery and equipment from just three countries — West Germany, France and Japan — combined'.[66] It is still an open question whether and how much these differences in performance between American and other Western companies are due to comparative expertise and energy in marketing to the socialist countries, to differences in trading culture, history and geographical location, or to recent government policy. It has been suggested to this author, for example, that the attitudes and experiences in Western Europe and the US may have differed quite substantially in relation to business and government interest in the Soviet and East European markets. There were probably far more West European than American business entrepreneurs interested in the Soviet and East European markets, prior to the more trade-oriented policies of their respective governments, whereas a higher proportion of American business leaders were probably led by their governments to explore the Soviet and East European markets. Consequently, West European business gradually built up more experience than its American counterpart in the socialist markets, and was probably less vulnerable to changing government policies.

Finally it is important to note, however, that the oft-quoted statement of Senator Heinz cited above cannot be used to justify a contention that the Western European allies are in any way more responsible than the US for the sale of military-applicable technology. All Western countries have been involved in the export to the East of machinery and equipment for a wide range of civilian industries; and I know of no substantive evidence to demonstrate that reputable West European companies, which carry out the majority of this trade, have been involved knowingly and continuously in security-sensitive or illegal trade. Nor would these companies be likely to run such risks, for reasons noted earlier.

Company Experiences in the 1980s

It is this author's view that Western companies and banks will continue to view the Soviet and East European markets in a similar fashion to previously, comparing the opportunities for sales income, profits and reliable payment from that region with those available from elsewhere. It is clear, though, that price competition in this market will probably become more keen if the present recession continues in Western markets; and that pressures for counterpurchase will also increase, particularly as many advantageous Western government-backed credit facilities to the socialist countries have now ceased. Consequently, most companies will probably need to plan their marketing resources in this region with even more care than previously, and will prefer the absence of avoidable instabilities which only serve to complicate this planning task. Several recent Western government policies and actions from 1978 onwards, however, have acted as a brake to developments of further reliable East-West commercial relations.

American Companies

Considering American companies first, in addition to the 1978 Sperry-Univac computer sale to TASS referred to above, an export licence was also withdrawn in 1978 from Dresser Inc. to provide plant and know-how to the USSR for a $150 million drill-bit plant, as a result of Soviet treatment of certain of its dissidents and the consequent American decision to restrict oil drilling technology and equipment deliveries to the USSR. In early 1980, an export licence was withdrawn from Armco Inc. for the supply of equipment for a steel mill, because the equipment was viewed as improving the capability of the Soviet military infrastructure, and as contravening the post-Afghanistan American embargoes. More recently, following the imposition of martial law in Poland in December 1981 and the American implementation of the 1979 Export Administration Act to embargo equipment for the Urengoy pipeline, export licences were withheld from Caterpillar Tractor Limited for the supply of pipelayers; but the most publicised case has been the ban on the sale of rotors, stator blades and nozzles worth some $175 million by General Electric for use in turbines to be installed in the Urengoy pipeline. In the Sperry-Univac case, the cancelled computer contract was reportedly taken up by a consortium of French companies (CII-Honeywell, Bull SA, Thomson CSF SA, and Steria).[67] Armco's lost business was reportedly secured by a joint Japanese-French consortium headed by Nippon Steel and Creusot-Loire, whilst Caterpillar's lost business was reportedly secured by Komatsu of Japan at a time when the American company was facing severe problems of sales volume and profitability.[68]

West European Companies

It is only recently that West European companies have been exposed to the same problems as their American counterparts. As a result of the implementation of the American export legislation in December 1981, the John Brown Engineering Company at Clydebank, Scotland,[69] and other companies in Western Europe (AEG-Kanis, Nuovo Pignone, Alsthom-Atlantique) delivering turbines and component sets containing General Electric-sourced components, were finding it almost impossible to meet contractual delivery requirements to their Soviet customer during 1982. These problems resulted from component supply difficulties caused by the US government ban on General Electric components referred to above. The situation was exacerbated in June 1982 by further implementation of the US Export Administration Act when the above-mentioned European companies were expected to conform to US requirements for embargoes to specified third markets even when the companies had stocks of previously sourced American components and technology; in other words, to observe retroactive implementation of American legislation. Most of these companies were then ordered by their own domestic government to disobey the American requirements, thereby laying themselves open to possible loss of US markets and legal penalties on their US assets and personnel. Although these extra territorial sanctions were withdrawn in late 1982, it is apparent that because of the uncertainties during that year, many companies found it extremely difficult to operate.

Another West European company which was affected by the 1981 American sanctions was Fiatallis, part of the Fiat group of companies based in Turin. This company has a marketing and commercial organisation in Europe and manufacturing facilities throughout the world including factories in the US and Canada which are managed by a subsidiary company, Fiatallis North America Inc. Just prior to the imposition of the sanctions, Fiatallis Europe had in progress two transactions for sales to the Soviet Union by Fiatallis North America: one for the transfer of design data and associated kits of parts for a large bulldozer of proven design and application which had originally been designed in 1965 and updated in the 1970s; and another for the sale of almost 200 sideboom tractors which had been specially modified to meet Soviet specifications for pipelayers. The value of the designs of the bulldozer was some $110 million and the kits of parts to establish Soviet manufacture were expected to be worth some $360 million over a four-year period; there was furthermore a high probability that orders for another $960 million would be received for other models of assembled bulldozers. In addition, it was expected that the pipelayer sales would be worth approximately $280 million over a five-year period, with an additional $50 million for spare parts.

An application for a validated licence to supply the Soviet customer with design data for the bulldozer had been filed with the US Department of Commerce on 4 November 1981, but this application was returned to the company without comment in January 1982 following the Department's General Order suspending the processing of all licensing for exports to the Soviet Union. In addition, the company lost all of its potential sales for pipe-layers, as these products were specifically listed in the President's sanctions on the American export of oil and gas equipment. The company was of the view that the General Order suspending all licensing was inconsistent with the President's 29 December 1981 statement on sanctions which referred primarily to high technology products, and therefore felt that it had been unfairly treated in the first instance. Furthermore, it had lost two large orders in a period of grave recession in the construction machinery industry. This was even more disappointing in view of both Fiatallis North America's status as an American subsidiary of an Italian company, and the fact that when the sanctions were lifted in November 1982, Fiatallis North America had lost almost $2 billion worth of business whilst its Japanese competitors (Komatsu) had sold over 900 machines to the USSR during the period of the sanctions, at an average price of $400,000 per machine.[70]

To sum up, it is apparent that the recent differences in policies between the US government and its Western allies, and the quite sudden changes in direction of US policy as a result of certain actions of the Soviet and East European governments, have significantly affected the business activities of several American and West European companies. Consequently, in view of the contribution of such companies to Western economic activity and employment, it is important to consider whether such problems may be reduced in future years. This is discussed further in the final section of this chapter.

Future Research in East-West Trade

The information contained in the previous sections of this chapter suggests that governments should attempt to make their East-West policies more stable and consistent and base them on more accurate and reliable information, in order that the business community can plan and allocate its resources more effectively. Government policies and actions operate over a wide range of political, economic and financial issues, and these policies and actions attempt to achieve a wide range of political, economic and financial results; they may also change substantially over the time interval of a business planning cycle, and sometimes with unpredictable results. Furthermore, government actions may need to be implemented at very short notice as a result of unwelcome actions by a political adversary, and consequently it is important that the influence of these actions be clearly weighed and balanced.

It is this author's view, therefore, that the area of government/ industry interaction is worthy of further clarification and research. For example, there have been few detailed studies carried out to examine the mechanisms of interaction between government and industry in this area, particularly with regard to specific trade deals. This is especially important both in the light of current changes in government policy, with some differences of view evident between the US and its West European allies, and in the light of the claim that decision-making over export licences is frequently a lengthy procedure sometimes taking up to three years.[71]

Now is also an appropriate time to arrive at a more specific consensus on those military critical technologies which have recently been suggested by two US sources as crucial to the Soviet military effort.[72] There is, as well, a need for further substantial research to assess accurately the degree to which the legal sale of Western technology to the socialist countries has affected Western security. Such research should investigate the mechanisms and the degree to which this Western technology is adopted to a point where it can be militarily offensive, its subsequent diffusion throughout the Soviet economy, the additional Western military expenditure required to counter this specific threat, and the direct and indirect[73] economic benefits to the Western economy arising from the relevant sale. It may be useful to compare the transfer of such technologies to the USSR to the transfer to the other socialist countries of Eastern Europe. Some earlier research by Philip Hanson (University of Birmingham) and myself[74] on absorption of Western technology in the Soviet chemical and automotive industries, found that the imported technology was mainly restricted to the factory for which the relevant plant was purchased as a means to meet a capacity constraint; it would be useful to extend this research into other industries and technologies.

In particular, more research is needed on Soviet acquisition of Western microelectronic technology. It is claimed, for example, that many Soviet microelectronic components used in military applications are direct copies of their Western counterparts,[75] that components used in many consumer goods can be transferred to Soviet military application[76] and are being obtained illegally by Soviet diplomatic officials, and that processing know-how and equipment is being illegally obtained from the US through West European companies.[77] If these claims have some validity, then it is important to study both the manner and degree to which the Soviet electronics industry can acquire and assimilate these design and production technologies, including legal and illegal channels of transfer, and the extent to which these technologies can be put to military application.[78] In addition the problems of attempting to control the sale of very widely used electronic components, having application in a broad range of consumer goods, should be thoroughly studied and appropriate policies proposed. Illegal transfers of equipment, however, are clearly a matter for customs officials and require co-operation on the detection of illegal activities by the NATO allies. There is clear evidence that such co-operation is now being more actively and vigorously pursued, particularly by the United Kingdom.[79]

Any restriction of legal exports must be seen to be founded on well-researched information, and any changes in CoCom lists must be felt to be fair by all parties, something which has not always been the case in the past.[80] More recently, a certain amount of concern has been reported in Europe, for example, over the removal of cheap home computers from duty-free airport outlets, and the seizure in Britain of computers of 14-year-old design designated for Czechoslovakia.[81] Furthermore, export control decisions should be based not only on evidence from military specialists, but also, where possible, on corroboratory evidence from commercial sources, to retain a sense of balance. At present, for example, British decisions are made by the Department of Trade, following advice from the Ministry of Defence and consultation with the Foreign Office;[82] it would be useful to study how this structure obtains relevant information and arrives at final decisions.

One reason that some Western governments have argued for a stronger contribution from national defence organisations in export control[83] is the fear that today the development of civilian technology with military application has slipped from the control of security organisations to that of civilian companies.[84] Furthermore, there is also a view that a better basis for multilateral trade stability will be created by paying more attention to the defence aspects of East-West trade. Many believe, for example, that the establishment of a 'militarily critical technologies list' can be used as an agreed basis for a revised CoCom list.[85] Though I am sympathetic towards such a view, I am also of the opinion that such reviews should be held in an atmosphere as open as possible consistent with adequate national security, to enable companies likely to be affected to state their case in a more informed manner. At the time of writing this chapter, discussion on this topic has so far been held in an atmosphere clouded by perceived security constraints, and the quality of debate has suffered accordingly.

There is certainly scope to investigate and discuss these issues more widely and rigorously, with more attention paid to open evidence and less to rhetoric. The experience and policies of the US have generally been different from those of the West European allies. It would seem to be appropriate, therefore, for the members of the NATO alliance to arrive at a range of policies to be developed to take account of these differences, and to let commerce develop to mutual economic benefit, with the minimum of security and political risks.

Notes

*The author wishes to acknowledge the financial assistance provided by the Foundation for Management Education, London, to support a visit to Washington, DC, in September 1983. The visit enabled research to be carried out in American libraries, and discussions to be held with US specialists.

The author also wishes to record the assistance of various individuals during the preparation of this chapter, particularly Tony Burkett, David Buswell, Don Cowell, Tony Mason, Stanley Nollen, John Rogers and Mark Schaffer. Any errors in fact or interpretation, however, rest with the author himself.

1. See P. Hanson, *Trade and Technology in Soviet-Western Relations* (Macmillan, London 1981), pp. 128-208; M.R. Hill, *East-West Trade, Industrial Co-operation and Technology Transfer* (Gower Press, Aldershot, 1983), pp. 49-74; E. Zaleski and H. Wienert, *Technology Transfer Between East and West* (OECD, Paris, 1980), pp. 67-91, 139-62, 197-240.

2. Engineering products accounted for some 28 per cent of developed market economies' exports to the socialist countries of Eastern Europe in 1960, 35 per cent in 1970, and 37 per cent in 1978. (See Hill, *East-West Trade*, pp. 18-25.)

3. Western ('developed market economy') exports to the socialist countries of Eastern Europe are given as follows in the 1969 and 1979 editions of the *UN Yearbook of International Trade Statistics* (vol. 1, Table B): 1960 — $2,520 million; 1972 — $10,199 million; 1979 — $41,192 million. From these figures, therefore, Western exports to the socialist countries increased by 305 per cent from 1960 to 1972, and 304 per cent from 1972 to 1979.

4. Total world exports for the developed market economies were as follows for 1960, 1972 and 1979 respectively: $85 billion, $298 billion, $1,079 billion.

140   *Western Companies, Trade and Technology Transfer*

(See the 1969 and 1979 editions of the *UN Yearbook of International Trade Statistics*, vol. 1, Table B.)

The January 1981 *UN Monthly Bulletin of Statistics*, Special Table B, provides the following information on the Unit Value (Price) Index (in US dollars) for World Exports from the Developed Market Economies: 1960 — 45; 1972 — 59; 1979 — 140. From these figures. it can be estimated that the Unit Value (Price) Index increased by 31 per cent from 1960 to 1972, but by 137 per cent from 1972 to 1979.

5. In 1975, developed market economies' exports to the socialist countries of Eastern Europe are listed as $27.9 billion, and their imports as $20.2 billion. (See *UN Yearbook of International Trade Statistics 1979*, vol. 1, Table B.)

6. For 1960, 1972 and 1978, trade in engineering products between the two systems was as follows:

Year	Exports of the Developed Market Economies to the Socialist Countries of Eastern Europe	Exports from the Socialist Countries of Eastern Europe to the Developed Market Economies
1960	$710 million	$205 million
1972	$3,309 million	$947 million
1978	$12,670 million	$3,131 million

(Data abstracted from *UN Monthly Bulletin of Statistics*, March 1965, Special Table E; *UN Yearbook of International Statistics 1974*, Table B; *UN Yearbook of International Trade Statistics 1979*, Table B.)

7. Calculated from export data presented in notes (3) and (4) above.

8. M.R. Hill, 'Desk Research for the Soviet Capital Goods Market', *European Journal of Marketing*, vol. 13, no. 8 (1979), pp. 271-83.

9. Hill, *Export Marketing of Capital Goods to the Socialist Countries of Eastern Europe* (Wilton House Publications, Farnborough, 1978), p. 111.

10. Hill, *East-West Trade*, pp. 15-20.

11. Ibid., p. 27.

12. Ibid., pp. 1-7.

13. See C.H. McMillan, 'Growth of External Investments by Comecon Countries', *The World Economy*, vol. 2, no. 3 (September 1979), pp. 363-86, and M.R. Hill, 'Soviet and East European Multinational Activity in the United Kingdom and Republic of Ireland' and 'Soviet and East European Multinational Activity in Sweden'. These latter papers were completed in 1983 for a forthcoming publication by the Institute for Research and Information on Multinationals, Geneva.

14. See Hill, *Export Marketing*, pp. 67-178; Hill, *East-West Trade*, pp. 49-74; Business International, *Doing Business with Eastern Europe* (Business International Publications, New York, 1972); and K. Ch. Rotlingshofer and H. Vogel, *Soviet Absorption of Western Technology: Report on the Experiences of West German Exporters*, report submitted to Stanford Research Institute, Menlo Park, CA, 1979.

15. See Hill, *Export Marketing*, pp. 85-135 and Hill, *East-West Trade*, pp. 49-74.

16. Ibid.

17. J. Wilczynski, 'Licences in the West-East-West Transfer of Technology', *Journal of World Trade Law*, vol. 11, no. 2 (March/April 1977), pp. 121-36.

18. I.e., $300 million × (2,400 − 500)/2,400.

19. Wilczynski, *Licences*, pp. 121-36.
20. Hill, *East-West Trade*, pp. 75-132.
21. Ibid., pp. 133-47.
22. See: (a) Hill, *East-West Trade*, pp. 5-7, 37-9, 75-132, 163-79; (b) C.H. McMillan, 'East-West Industrial Co-operation' in United States Congress, Joint Economic Committee, *East European Economies Post-Helsinki* (US Government Printing Office, Washington, DC, 1977), pp. 1175-224; (c) F. Levcik and J. Stankovsky, *Industrial Co-ope'ation between East and West* (M.E. Sharpe Inc., White Plains, NY, 1979); and (d) J. Wilczynski, *The Multinationals and East-West Relations* (Macmillan, London, 1976).
23. See estimates by: (a) Levcik and Stankovsky, *Industrial Co-operation*, p. 173; (b) Economic Commission for Europe (ECE), *A Statistical Outline of Recent Trends in Industrial Co-operation* (Trade/AC.3.R8, Geneva, 1976); (c) McMillan, 'East-West Industrial Co-operation'; (d) A. Bykov, 'Perspectives of East-West Relations in Technology Transfer and Related Problems of Dependence' in C.T. Saunders (ed.), *East-West Co-operation in Business: Inter-firm Studies* (Springer-Verlag, Vienna and New York, 1977), pp. 165-78.
24. Wilczynski, *Multinationals*, p. 80.
25. This was some $43 billion in 1976 according to the *United Nations Yearbook of International Trade Statistics 1979*.
26. See data quoted in: (a) J. Szita, *Perspectives for All-European Economic Co-operation* (A.W. Sijthoff, Leyden, 1977), p. 174; (b) McMillan, 'East-West Industrial Co-operation', p. 1210; (c) E. Tabaczynski, *Revue de l'Est*, no. 3 (1974), pp. 27-35; (d) J. Olszynski, *Zeszyty naukowe*, no. 4 (1973); (e) Levcik and Stankovsky, *Industrial Co-operation*, p. 176.
27. Hill, *East-West Trade*, pp. 73-132.
28. Ibid.
29. L.H. Theriot, 'US Governmental and Private Industry Co-operation with the Soviet Union in the Fields of Science and Technology' in United States Congress, Joint Economic Committee, *Soviet Economy in a New Perspective* (US Government Printing Office, Washington, DC, 1976), pp. 739-66.
30. See McMillan, 'East-West Industrial Co-operation', p. 1186.
31. See Hill, *East-West Trade*, pp. 148-59.
32. The fields covered by these reported agreements included antibiotics, car tyres, aerospace technology, agrochemicals, fibres, paints, oil drilling, computer systems, electronics, electrical engineering and precision instruments.
33. The following publications discuss various Western government policies and procedures relating to East-West trade which have been summarised in this section of the chapter: (a) Hill, *East-West Trade*, pp. 7-10; (b) United States Congress, Office of Technology Assessment, *Technology and East-West Trade* (Allanheld Osmun, Montclair, NJ, and Gower, Farnborough, 1981); (c) A.S. Yergin, *East-West Technology Transfer: European Perspectives*, The Washington Papers, vol. 8, no. 75 (Sage Publications, Beverly Hills and London, 1980); (d) Zaleski and Wienert, *Technology Transfer*; (e) S. Sternheimer, *East-West Technology Transfer: Japan and the Communist Bloc*, The Washington Papers, vol. 8, no. 76 (Sage Publications, Beverly Hills and London, 1980).
34. See A.C. Sutton, *Western Technology and Soviet Economic Development 1945-65* (Hoover Institution Press, Stanford, CA, 1973) for a discussion of this topic, listing some of those items removed from various embargo lists during the 1960s. Also see Office of Technology Assessment, *Technology*, p. 156, for the number of items on the CoCom embargo list between 1949 and 1976. According to this source, most of the liberalisation of CoCom controls occurred in the mid-1950s. (NB: this latter source quotes R.T. Cupitt and J.R. McIntyre, 'CoCom: East-West Trade Relations, The List Review Process', a paper presented to the

International Studies Association Convention, Toronto, 1979, p. 23.)

35. Zaleski and Wienert, *Technology Transfer*, p. 46 indicate that the West European countries revised their international lists for the second time in 1975, reducing the embargo list to some 100 items. The US, however, in 1964 had some 1,303 separate entries on its 'positive' list. During the 1970s, the US removed a large number of items from its embargo list, but it still controlled more products than its West European allies — at least another 33 categories, but shorter than the 494 categories of 1971. See 'US Still Bears Burden of Soviet Embargo', *Financial Times*, 13 May 1981.

36. It is worthy of note, however, that the United Kingdom signed a series of 'Trade Agreements' with most of the socialist countries during the mid-1950s to early 1960s, and signed a Long Term Trade Agreement with the USSR in 1959. Long Term Trade Agreements were subsequently signed with the other socialist countries during the early 1970s (see Hill, *East-West Trade*, pp. 7-10). It is difficult to examine the degree to which British businessmen were signing contracts prior to the signing of inter-governmental agreements, but it is useful to note that British exports to the socialist countries were apparently quite static (and possibly in decline) between 1948 and 1953, but rapidly increased between 1953 and 1958 by 190 per cent, and also between 1958 and 1963 by 176 per cent. The rates of increase were particularly high for British exports to the USSR, which had declined from $22 million to $9 million from 1948 to 1953, but then increased to $65 million in 1958 and $155 million in 1963 (600 per cent increase from 1953 to 1958, and 138 per cent increase from 1958 to 1963) although, clearly, care has to be taken not to conclude too much from sample year data. West European and British exports to the socialist countries of Eastern Europe for the same years were as follows (UK exports shown in brackets): 1948 — $890 m. ($76 m.), 1953 — $880 m. ($43 m.), 1958 — $1,515 m. ($125 m.), 1963 — $2,540 m. ($345 m.) See *UN Yearbook of International Trade Statistics 1963*, p. 22. West European exports to the USSR were as follows: 1948 — $305 m., 1953 — $310 m., 1958 — $565 m., 1963 — $1,010 m. Consequently the British share of West European exports to the socialist countries, but particularly to the USSR, appeared to increase following the signing of the 1959 Long Term Trade Agreement with the USSR.

37. See also B. Askansas, G. Fink and F. Levcik, *East-West Trade and CMEA Indebtedness in the Seventies and Eighties* (Zentralsparkasse and Kommerzbank, Vienna, 1979) for an account of various options for management of the Eastern deficit.

38. A further discussion of these issues will be found in Yergin, *East-West Technology Transfer*, Sternheimer, *East-West Technology Transfer*, and Stephen Woolcock's chapter in this volume.

39. See J. Pinder and P. Pinder, *The European Community's Policy Towards Eastern Europe* (RIIA/PRP, London 1975).

40. See statements of D.V. Simes and K.B. Jenkins in United States, Committee on Foreign Relations, and Congressional Research Service, *The Premises of East-West Commercial Relations — A Workshop*, December 1982 (US Government Printing Office, Washington, 1983), pp. 18-24, 75.

41. See Office of Technology Assessment, *Technology*, p. 81, for a note on the suspension of the sale of a computer to TASS in 1978; United States Senate, Committee on Banking, Housing and Urban Affairs, *Suspension of United States Exports of High Technology and Grain to the Soviet Union*, Hearings 19 & 20 August 1980 (US Government Printing Office, Washington, DC, 1980), for discussion on grain and oil equipment embargoes; and S.D. Nollen, 'Commercial Ties with Political Adversaries: The Case of John Brown Engineering and the Soviet Gas Pipeline', unpublished paper, February 1983 for an account of the post-1981 sanctions following the imposition of martial law in Poland. Professor

Nollen's paper was subsequently presented at the conference on *Export Controls: Building Reasonable Commercial Ties with Political Adversaries*, organised by the National Center for Export-Import Studies, Georgetown University, Washington, DC, on 21 September 1983. The proceedings of this conference were published in 1984 — M.R. Czinkota (ed.), *Export Controls* (Praeger Publishers, NY, 1984).

42. These four categories are summarised from Office of Technology Assessment, *Technology*, pp. 85-96, and M.M. Costick, *The Strategic Dimension of East-West Trade*, ACWF Task Force on Strategic Trade, Washington, DC, 1978, *passim.*

43. United States Senate, Committee on Banking, Housing and Urban Affairs, *East-West Trade and Technology Transfer*, Hearings before the Subcommittee on International Finance and Monetary Policy (US Government Printing Office, Washington, DC, April 1982), p. 5. (Opening statement of Senator J. Garn.)

44. Ibid. The case of American grinding machine exports and Soviet missile development has also been quoted as recently as April 1984 in a British newspaper editorial 'The High-Tech Trail', *The Economist*, 21 April 1984.

45. US Senate, Committee on Banking, *East-West Trade*, pp. 7,8.

46. See T. Gustafson, *Selling the Russians the Rope? Soviet Technology Policy and US Export Controls*, Rand Report R-2649-ARPA (Rand, Santa Monica, CA, April 1981), pp. 10-14.

47. Gustafson cites Soviet sources to illustrate the priority being given to precision grinding techniques and machinery during the early 1970s, using the design and performance of the Bryant machines as bases for comparison. Furthermore, acceptable bearing quality was apparently achieved in Soviet factories by means of rigorous inspection procedures and associated high rejection rates. See Gustafson, *Selling the Russians the Rope?* pp. 10-14. The CIA study 'Soviet Acquisition of Western Technology' also notes, 'The Soviets probably could have used indigenous grinding machines and produced the required quality of bearings over a long period by having an abnormally high rejection rate.' Central Intelligence Agency, 'Soviet Acquisition of Western Technology' (April 1982) in G.K. Bertsch and J.R. McIntyre (eds), *National Security and Technology Transfer: The Strategic Dimensions of East-West Trade* (Westview, Boulder, CO, 1983), p. 101.

48. US Senate, Committee on Banking, *East-West Trade*, pp. 8, 9.

49. Ibid., pp. 11, 25.

50. See Chase World Information Corporation, *KamAZ: The Million Beginning* (CWIC, New York 1974), and CIA National Foreign Assessment Center, *USSR: Role of Foreign Technology in the Development of the Motor Vehicle Industry* (US Government Printing Office, Washington, DC, 1979), pp. 13-19.

51. M.R. Hill, 'Two Case Studies of Soviet Industrial Technology — Machine Tools and Motor Vehicles', discussion paper, Loughborough University of Technology, July 1975.

52. United States Senate, Committee on Armed Services, *Soviet Defense Expenditure and Related Programs*, Hearings before the Subcommittee on General Procurements, 1 November 1979 and 4 February 1980 (US Government Printing Office, Washington, DC, 1980), pp. 167, 168.

53. US Senate, Committee on Banking, *East-West Trade*, p. 110.

54. See David Holloway's chapter (p. 179) in the present volume.

55. See US Senate, Committee on Banking, *East-West Trade*, p. 82.

56. Ibid., p. 86 quoted by Senator Heinz from the *New York Times* of 14 April 1982.

57. See: *International Herald Tribune*, 21 May 1984, p.1 ('US Agents Track High Tech Smugglers along Shadowy Trail to Russia'); *International Herald*

Tribune, 22 May 1984, p. 1 ('In High-Tech Smuggling, Rewards are Great, Risks are Slight'); and *International Herald Tribune*, 23 May 1984, p. 6 ('Even Friends will be Watched Closely as US Guards its High Tech').

58. US Senate, Committee on Banking, *East-West Trade*, p. 78.

59. These convictions occurred in 1980 and 1981, and are recorded along with others in United States Senate, Committee on Governmental Affairs, Permanent Subcommittee on Investigations, *Transfer of United States High Technology to the Soviet Union and Soviet Bloc Nations* (US Government Printing Office, Washington, DC, 1982), pp. 9-33.

60. US Senate, Committee on Banking, *East-West Trade*, p. 84.

61. See Hill, *Export Marketing*, pp. 209-211, and Hill, *East-West Trade*, p. 157.

62. See S. Woolcock, 'East-West Trade after Williamsburg', *World Today*, vol. 39, no. 7 (July-August 1983), pp. 291-6.

63. See V. Treml in US Senate, Committee on Foreign Affairs and Congressional Research Service, *Premises of East-West Commercial Relations*, pp. 103, 104. Treml quotes 60 per cent of Soviet merchant fleet capacity as being produced in the West (whilst, it is claimed, some domestic shipbuilding capacity was converted to military vessel production), 50 per cent of chemical industry equipment, 20 per cent of woodworking and textile equipment, and 70 per cent of measuring instruments.

64. See US Senate, Committee on Banking, *East-West Trade*, p. 124.

65. Cecil Parkinson, MP, Minister for Trade, 'Export Credit: the Government's View' in *Export Credit: The Next Phase*, Chatham House Briefing, 28 January 1981 (Royal Institute of International Affairs, London, 1981), p. 4.

66. See US Senate, Committee on Banking, *East-West Trade*, p. 109.

67. See Office of Technology Assessment, *Technology*, p. 187.

68. See statement of H.A. Lewis in US Senate, Committee on Governmental Affairs, *Transfer of United States High Technology*; *Financial Times*, 24 February 1982; and *International Herald Tribune*, 11 February 1982.

69. See Nollen, 'Commercial Ties'; *International Herald Tribune*, 24 June 1982; and *Financial Times*, 28 June 1982.

70. The information for this application of the sanctions to Fiatallis North America was obtained from a paper presented by D.H. Buswell, Director of Government Affairs, Fiatallis North America Inc., at a conference on *Export Controls: Building Reasonable Commercial Ties with Political Adversaries*, National Center for Export-Import Studies, Georgetown University, Washington, DC, 21 September 1983. The proceedings of this conference were published in 1984 (see note 41 above).

71. See 'British Firms Face Customs Probe Over Exports Ban', *Observer*, 25 January 1981.

72. The list is roughly: computers; microelectronics; semiconductors; propulsion, engine and turbine technology; laser and optics; nuclear physics, fibre optics; advanced structural materials (materials precision and batch machine tools); microbiology; acoustical sensors; electro-optical sensors; radars; navigation and control; robotics; communications and switching equipment; and precision instruments. See US Senate, Committee on Banking, *East-West Trade*, p. 38, and Office of Technology Assessment, *Technology*, p. 93. There are slight differences in the topics listed between the 1981 and 1982 publications. The 1981 publication relies heavily on the Bucy Report (Office of the Director of Defense Research and Engineering, *An Analysis of Export Control of US Technology — A DOD Perspective*, A Report of the Defence Science Board Task Force on Export of US Technology, Washington, DC, 4 February 1976), and subsequent discussions. The 1982 publication relies heavily on the Central Intelligence Agency document of

April 1982 entitled 'Soviet Acquisition of Western Technology' included in US
Senate, Committee on Banking, *East-West Trade*, pp. 23-37, and reprinted in
Bertsch and McIntyre, *National Security*, pp. 92-112.

73. For example, many companies need to engage in a certain amount of
product innovation and managerial development to be successful in the competitive
Soviet export market, and these changes can consequently make them more
effective in other markets.

74. See: (a) P. Hanson and M.R. Hill, 'Soviet Assimilation of Western
Technology: A Survey of UK Exporters' Experiences' in United States Congress,
Joint Economic Committee, *Soviet Economy in a Time of Change*, vol. 2 (US
Government Printing Office, Washington, DC, 1979), pp. 582-604; (b) Hanson,
Trade and Technology, pp. 128-210 (especially pp. 186-210); (c) Hill, *East-West
Trade*, pp. 49-74.

75. 'Russians "Planted" Sonobuoy', *Guardian*, 23 June 1983, p. 4. It is also
claimed that SS-18 missiles are guided by microprocessors taken from an American
stand at a trade fair (see *Daily Telegraph*, 25 January 1982).

76. 'Why Design If You Can Pinch It?', *Daily Telegraph*, 30 May 1983, p. 8.

77. M. Cockerell, 'The Hi-tech Trail to Moscow', *The Listener*, 24 February
1983, pp. 2-4, 18.

78. A useful framework for approaching this problem is provided by Office of
Technology Assessment, *Technology*, pp. 85-107, and T.J. Eckert, 'The Transfer
of US Technology to Other Countries: An Analysis of Export Control Policy and
Some Recommendations', Woodrow Wilson School of International Affairs,
Princeton University, June 1981, pp. 46-50.

79. See 'US Knows Chips are Down', *Guardian*, 13 December 1983, p. 2, and
'How West Controls High-tech Exports', *The Times*, 14 December 1983, p. 2.

80. See Yergin, *East-West Technology Transfer*, and Hill, *East-West Trade*,
pp. 151, 152.

81. 'High-tech Rules for Computers Anger Europeans', *Observer*, 18
December 1983, p. 2. The computers were DEC PDP models 11/34 and 11/44.

82. 'How West Controls High-tech Exports', *The Times*, 14 December 1983,
p.2.

83. See United States Congress, Joint Economic Committee, *East-West
Commercial Policy: A Congressional Dialogue with the Reagan Administration*
(US Government Printing Office, Washington, DC, 1982), pp. 26-8.

84. Ibid., pp. 8, 9.

85. United States Congress, Office of Technology Assessment, *Technology and
East-West Trade: An Update* (US Government Printing Office, Washington, DC,
1983), p. 37.

7 LEGAL ASPECTS OF TECHNOLOGY TRANSFER TO EASTERN EUROPE AND THE SOVIET UNION

Neville March Hunnings

The industrial revolution broke the old method of transferring technology from master to apprentice as part of a more or less secret mystery. The new techniques were too public to be controlled in such a manner and yet innovation itself became more valuable. So by the mid-nineteenth century a new device was developed based on the letters patent used by post-renaissance monarchs to grant industrial and commercial monopolies to their subjects. Patents enabled inventors to accept that knowledge of their inventions would become public in return for a legally protected but temporary monopoly right in their exploitation.

That did not replace entirely the old ways. Secret recipes and secret methods are still to be found, their owners relying for protection on their own ability to prevent knowledge reaching unauthorised persons. A more modern variant of this is 'know-how', a word which covers such unquantifiable possessions as skill and experience, knowledge of how to make machines give the best results, strategic overviews of particular industrial processes. In a very real sense, know-how brings the wheel full circle and relates to the skills of the old master-craftsmen. Now, however, the law takes note of its economic value and, while not applying to it the procedures of the patent system, enforces to a certain extent — by means of its rules on contract, tort and property — the exclusive rights of the enterprise which develops such know-how.

Thus, although patented processes must by definition be workable by any normally skilled industrial engineer working from the information contained in the patent specification, in order to exploit the invention profitably it may in practice be desirable, even necessary, to have access as well to the accompanying know-how. Trade in patents — through the grant of exclusive or non-exclusive licences — thus often includes know-how as well, both being treated as a semi-property right which is capable of transfer either completely or partially.

146

Technology is also transferred in other ways, however, where legal controls have a smaller part to play or may be avoided altogether. The information may be published in a scientific journal (which disqualifies it from patent protection). The skill which a person acquires while working for an enterprise remains part of his own personality which he may use when he works for another enterprise or on his own account. In this way some elements of know-how may migrate outside the control of its originators. And by means of 'reverse engineering' the possessors of a machine may discover how to make others like it, a process which, however, in most circumstances would be an infringement of the patent.

The great mass of industrial innovation takes place within the OECD countries and there is a considerable net outward flow of technology to both the third world and the second world (the state-trading countries). With regard to the former group, the legal transfer under the international patent system has the consequence that the Western transferor enterprise retains control and profits through the payment of royalties. As the recipient countries are mostly politically weak and economically poor, there is little chance of acquiring technology through the non-legal methods without suffering damaging reprisals. Negotiations have therefore been pursued for many years through UNCTAD to find methods for transfer of technology to developing countries which are less onerous for the recipients.

The state-trading countries, because of their political and economic solidarity, have greater power and although they form part of the international patent system there are several additional ways in which its strict application can be avoided, in particular through the use of 'public interest' or 'eminent domain' concepts. In addition, the almost hermetically sealed legal systems of the Eastern countries often make it difficult to enforce remedies against patent infringements if the resultant products are not traded in the West. This is particularly so, of course, in relation to military or public service equipment.[1]

When therefore the United States wished to restrict the transfer of technology to the state-trading countries it was not able to rely wholly on direct politico-economic pressure. Its own negative power was not sufficient. It needed the co-operation of its fellow members of OECD to provide a collective boycott as and when necessary.

Collective Boycotts

CoCom

The main instrument for applying such collective restrictions on exports originated from post-war discussions between the US, the UK and France. In November 1949 an organisation was created to co-ordinate its members' national controls over the export of strategic materials and technology to the Communist world.[2] This body, the Co-ordinating Committee for Multilateral Export Controls (abbreviated to CoCom) began operations on 1 January 1950 with 7 members: the US, the UK, France, Italy and the Benelux countries (the same membership as the Western European Union formed in 1948 but with the US instead of Germany). Now its membership comprises all the member states of NATO (except Iceland and Spain) plus Japan; but the European neutrals and the Asian NICs such as Taiwan and South Korea are not members. Sweden and Switzerland, recognised as major alternative sources of some products and technologies controlled by CoCom, follow an informal albeit somewhat unpredictable co-operation, neither being desirous of allowing a sale that would push its relations with CoCom members to a serious confrontation but neither being particularly interested in formalising its co-operation. The target countries, export of goods to which is subject to the CoCom rules, are: the USSR, the other Eastern European countries except Yugoslavia, China and other Asian communist countries. CoCom thus does not apply to African or American countries such as Cuba.

CoCom has no official existence. There is no treaty or written constitutive document and some of its members do not even admit publicly that they are members. Instead it is a gentleman's agreement, taking decisions by unanimity, each member possessing a veto. It occupies offices in Paris (in an annexe of the US Embassy which it shares with the US Internal Revenue Service, the legal attaché, FBI agents and the Marines[3]) where it meets in continuous session, its member countries being represented by middle-ranking diplomats and technical specialists who deal with the day-to-day problems of its export control system, none of which activity is made public. The representatives, with a permanent clerical staff of about 15, engage in three types of activity: developing lists of products and technologies to be embargoed, controlled or monitored; weekly consultations on exceptions to the lists; and consultation on enforcement.

The Lists. There are three lists: (1) a munitions list, which includes all military items; (2) an atomic list; (3) an industrial/ commercial list. The first two cause little difficulty, and it is the third which provides most of the work for the Committee, since it contains dual-use items which, although primarily civilian in character and normal use, also have military potential. This concept is not restricted to high technology. When during the 1970s Sweden restricted the import of footwear from the EEC contrary to its Free Trade Agreement with the Community it justified its action on public security grounds, claiming that maintaining a viable domestic footwear industry was a military necessity to ensure the supply of boots for the armed forces in the event of war. Boots are not on the CoCom list.

The Industrial List is subdivided into three categories: International Lists I (embargoed items), II (quantitatively controlled items) and III (items which may be sold but the end-use of which must be monitored). These lists are not published but conform closely to the US Commodity Control List (see below). They had not been up-dated since the mid-1970s, but on 12 July 1984 a major revision of them was all but completed and this was widely reported in the press.[4] Most of the 100 major proposals for change, mostly from the US, fell into the three linked areas of computer hardware, software and telecommunications, and only a few issues of substance, e.g. robotics and aero engines, remained to be settled.[5]

The new rules permit most eight-bit home computers to be freely exported (previously even the Sinclair ZX81 had been banned[6]) as well as some business machines like the Apple II. More far-reaching, however, is the new inclusion of specially written software (albeit only military software and programs that can be used to develop otherwise banned technologies[7]) in the embargo. Hitherto, CoCom has dealt with the export of goods. Software, however, may not only be goods but also a service and it can be transferred through the public telephone network or even over the air by radio. The EEC is already experiencing the greatest conceptual difficulty in finding an appropriate legal category to cover the free movement of television signals.[8] While a disk or tape containing software is clearly covered by CoCom controls over

exports, it is not at all clear that an English programmer who contracts to write a program for an East German client and who trans-
mits it over the telephone (rather than by courier) can be brought
within the export legislation at all. The same could apply to the
transfer of an existing program by the same means.

Application of the lists is carried out by the participating states
through their ordinary customs laws. Normally no distinction is
there made between CoCom export restrictions and export controls for other reasons. However, individuals who have the opportunity to sell a product which is on the CoCom lists may always ask
for an *ad hoc* exemption.

Exceptions. Requests for exception are considered at weekly
meetings of representatives. Each request is considered by all the
member governments and must be approved unanimously. A
decision is supposed to be given within 18 days of the request, with
certain possibilities for extension of time; but largely owing to
rather complex internal reviewing procedures within the US
administration (through the Economic Defense Advisory
Committee structure) and power battles between the Departments
of Defense and Commerce, US approval is frequently seriously
delayed, giving rise to accusations of bad faith by exasperated
Europeans.

The vast majority of exception requests (some 1,000 each year)
are approved and in the mid-1970s only between 1 per cent and
3½ per cent were rejected. Of these, nearly all had been objected
to by the US, while no US requests for exceptions were refused.
Nearly half of all exception requests were made by US firms, and a
majority of such requests pertained to computers and computer-
related technology.

Enforcement. If a firm exports a product embargoed by CoCom
the only remedy lies in the relevant national law. Inter-state disputes about compliance are dealt with, if at all, in private at high
diplomatic level. Little is known and less is published about
instances of either of these. States may, however, decide to pro-
ceed with a particular export through use of a 'national interest'
exception, but these cases are very rare (about one every two and a
half years). It is far more common for problematic cases never to
appear before CoCom at all, either because the government determines that there is no need to submit them or because it prefers to

deal with other governments directly at the highest political levels. This happened, for instance, when the UK first proposed selling *Harrier* jump jet aircraft to China.

The US Export Administration Act

CoCom provides a framework for joint international action to restrict exports to the Soviet bloc. Parallel to it and providing the legal basis for implementing the CoCom rules are the national laws to control exports generally. These are normally concerned with a broader range of export controls than CoCom. Of them, by far the most important is that of the United States, both because it is the driving force behind CoCom and because it had developed its legislation as a means of compelling other countries to follow its lead.

Since the end of the Second World War the US had maintained controls on exports for the purpose of pursuing national security, foreign policy or domestic economic objectives, most frequently the former.[9] The first major post-war control legislation — the Export Control Act of 1949 — established controls on all exports to communist countries. These were gradually relaxed throughout the 1960s, the Act itself being amended and extended several times until it was replaced in 1969 by the Export Administration Act. This maintained export controls but required removal of constraints on goods and technology which were already readily available to communist countries from non-US sources and on items of marginal military value. Whereas the main bias of the earlier Act 'had been to limit East-West trade, the 1969 Act was designed to foster such trade'.[10] The new Act was amended three times before being replaced in turn by the Export Administration Act of 1979. Under this, the US Department of Commerce, through its Office of Export Administration, has jurisdiction over most non-classified[11] exports from the US, its territories and possessions. Goods or technical data exported to any country except Canada are required to be licensed. Most US exports are made under a general licence; goods and technical data of a more sensitive nature which may not be exported freely require a 'validated licence' which identifies the type, quantity and destination of the particular export.

The Act sets out three objects for its export controls (s. 3(2)):

(1) to restrict the export of goods and technology which would

make a significant contribution to the military potential of
any other country or combination of countries which would
prove detrimental to the national security of the United
States ('national security');

(2) to restrict the export of goods and technology where necessary to further significantly the foreign policy of the United
States or to fulfill its declared international obligations
('foreign policy');

(3) to restrict the export of goods where necessary to protect
the domestic economy from the excessive drain of scarce
materials and to reduce the serious inflationary impact of
foreign demand ('short supply').

Each of the following three sections of the Act which correspond
to these three objects authorises the President to 'prohibit or cur-
tail the export of any goods or technology[12] subject to the jurisdiction of the United States or exported by any person subject to
such jurisdiction' and a 'commodity control list' is kept of any
goods or technology which are subject to export controls under the
Act.

These controls may be applied to any country of destination,
unlike the CoCom rules. In applying the national security criteria,
the Act (s. 5(b)) requires that 'United States policy toward individual countries shall not be determined exclusively on the basis of a
country's Communist or non-Communist status but shall take into
account such factors as the country's present and potential relationship to the United States, its present and potential relationship
to countries friendly or hostile to the United States, its ability and
willingness to control retransfers of United States exports in
accordance with United States policy, and such other factors as the
President considers appropriate'. The criteria for foreign policy
controls (s. 6(b)) include the following:

(1) the probability that such controls will achieve the intended
foreign policy purpose, in light of other factors, including
the availability from other countries of the goods or technology proposed for such controls;

(2) the compatibility of the proposed controls with the foreign
policy objectives of the United States, including the effort to
counter international terrorism, and with overall United

States policy toward the country which is the proposed target of the controls;

(3) the reaction of other countries to the imposition or expansion of such export controls by the United States;

(4) the foreign policy consequences of not imposing controls.

Section 7(a) on short supply controls requires the President to allocate some of the export licences on the basis of such factors as 'the extent to which a country engages in equitable trade practices with respect to United States goods and treats the United States equitably in times of short supply'.

In March 1982, foreign policy export controls were being applied as follows:[13] (1) Vietnam, North Korea, Kampuchea and Cuba — almost total trade embargoes as 'an integral part of our overall policies towards these countries'; (2) South Africa — 'to support the UN arms embargo of South Africa, to distance ourselves from the practice of apartheid, and to promote racial justice in southern Africa'; (3) Libya — which has 'departed in major ways from international norms of behavior' including 'the extraordinary Libyan support for international terrorism and its efforts to destabilize its moderate neighbors'; (4) human rights — controls on the export of crime control and detection instruments 'to distance the United States from governments with poor human rights records and to encourage improvements in the respect of human rights'; (5) antiterrorism — 'to underscore our strong opposition to governmental support for international terrorism'; (6) USSR — 'in response to the Soviet invasion of Afghanistan and to answer to the Soviet role in the current Polish crisis'.

The Act should have expired in October 1983,[14] but because of delays in the passage of its replacement bill it is still effectively in operation. This was done by Presidential decree. The 1969 Act had been 'continued' in a similar manner in 1976. Then, the President used powers under the Trading With the Enemy Act (TWEA) to maintain in force the regulations issued under the 1969 Act. Since this could only be done in relation to a state of 'national emergency', the President announced a continuation of both the emergency declared in 1950 during the Korean War and that declared during the international monetary crisis of 1971. The artificiality of these 'emergency' bases was tested when an American company, Spawr Optical Research Inc., refused to submit to the denial of an export licence on national security grounds in 1977 and shipped laser mirrors to Switzerland for onward for-warding to the USSR in violation of the preserved regulations. The Ninth Circuit Court of Appeals affirmed the resultant convictions, holding that the 1976 controls did have a rational relationship with the Korean War emergency![15] Use of the TWEA in this way was no longer possible after June 1977. But when the 1979 Act expired, President Reagan was able similarly to extend its regu-lations by relying this time on the International Economic Emergency Powers Act. This authorises the President to regulate exports if he has declared a national emergency with respect to any unusual and extraordinary threat. By Executive Order 12,444 effective 14 October 1983 (when the 1979 Act expired) the Presi-dent declared a national economic emergency and maintained the Export Administration Act regulations under it because 'the unrestricted access of foreign parties to United States commercial goods, technology and technical data and the existence of certain boycott practices of foreign nations constitute, in light of the expiration of the [Act] of 1979, an unusual and extraordinary threat to the national security, foreign policy and economy of the United States'.[16]

In the meanwhile discussion on the replacement legislation con-tinued, and on 8 March 1984 the two mutually inconsistent bills of the Senate and House of Representatives respectively (S 979 and HR 3213) were sent to a joint Senate-House conference. A com-promise acceptable to both the Senate and the House could not be achieved before Congress adjourned in October 1984, leaving the regulations of the 1979 Act maintained by the economic emer-gency declaration.[17]

At present, the Act is administered[18] by the Commerce Depart-ment through its Office of Export Administration (OEA), with the exception of munitions (State Department), nuclear materials (Nuclear Regulatory Commission), and gold and foreign currency (Treasury Department). In doing so the Commerce Department works in co-operation with three other departments.

The State Department advises on foreign policy implications (for example, US national security, UN sanctions, human rights, regional stability, nuclear non-proliferation, hazardous sub-stances); it also assumes the leading role in implementing multi-lateral export controls and represents the US in all CoCom sessions; finally, under the Battle Act it has primary responsibility for the development of a list of items completely embargoed to the communist world, the Mutual Defense Assistance Control List, which includes arms, ammunition, implements of war, atomic energy materials and certain dual-use items.[19]

The Department of Energy advises on energy-related exports, e.g. oil-extracting equipment, and it reviews all cases involving nuclear materials.

The Department of Defense (DoD) has been heavily involved with the export control system from the beginning. Its task is to evaluate the military and strategic potential of items under review, a process which entails a complex internal consultation system involving the technical and intelligence arms of the armed services as well as several other offices and agencies.

Other agencies with pertinent expertise may be asked to contribute technical advice on individual applications, such as the Treasury Department, the CIA, NASA and the National Bureau of Standards.

The Senate's Permanent Subcommittee on Investigations was somewhat critical of the way in which the Commerce Department applied the Act and it was suggested by some members that enforcement should be carried out instead by the Customs Service (which has stronger police powers). A stronger involvement by the DoD was also encouraged, and the lack of it in other countries was regretted: 'The US Defense Department is encouraging these nations to include their own military officials in the writing of export policy and regulations ... It is an unwise course for any of America's Allies and friends to develop export policy without advice from their own ministries.'[20] In late March 1984 the DoD's authority to review licence applications for exports to the communist countries was extended by the President (as the Senate bill would also have done) to exports to a dozen other countries which are believed to include Sweden, Switzerland and Austria, following recent cases of illegal traffic in advanced US electronics to the Soviet bloc.

In addition, Commerce Department regulations proposed in January 1984 would have prevented a new range of high technology goods (for example, lasers, electron beam recorders and some compact computers), from being exported under a 'distribution licence' (which enables an exporter to make a series of shipments over a period of time without needing a separate licence for each specific shipment) to destinations other than CoCom countries (plus Australia and New Zealand). Furthermore, buyers of US goods outside those 'CoCom plus' countries would have had to supply to the US information every three months on all their final customers. This resulted in a strongly worded protest note to the US from the Swedish government complaining that the new rules would in effect discriminate against Swedish companies.[21] There were also widespread protests from US businesses. In the face of strong criticism from home and abroad the Commerce Department announced in September 1984 that it had relaxed these proposed regulations, due to go into effect in January 1985.[22]

Export controls can have unexpected effects on occasion, as when Marconi Avionics tried to send from its plant in Atlanta, Georgia, to its head office in England a high technology product (a 'head-up display' for use in a pilot's cockpit) which had in fact been made in England and then exported to the US: it took six weeks for the Customs Service to release it and allow it to return to its country of origin, a CoCom country at that![23]

Export controls are not, however, the only technique used by the US authorities to prevent sensitive (but unclassified) information reaching other countries. Other restrictions have included pressure on the directors of a private company, Global Analytics (manufacturers of 'stealth technology' which makes war vehicles invisible to radar), to refrain from seeking a public quotation on the stock exchange for fear that by going public it would present a bigger target for industrial espionage.[24] University scientists supported by US government funds are often required to submit research papers for government comment and approval prior to publication. 'Scientific and engineering societies have had their conventions and symposia derailed by last-minute government demands for the suppression of unclassified papers. Meetings open to invitees from communist countries have been put under surveillance.'[25]

The European Communities

The EEC Treaty contains as one of its central principles the free movement of goods. Customs controls in the member States are therefore of special interest to Community law. They are relevant in two ways: intra-Community trade, and trade across the common external customs border.

Intra-Community Trade.   Controls on exports from one member

State to another are governed by art. 34 of the EEC Treaty which prohibits 'quantitative restrictions on exports and all measures having equivalent effect' — meaning in practice all non-tariff barriers to exports as well as outright bans whether absolute or limited. This would certainly cover CoCom-type situations. Thus any restrictions on the export of dual-use items from, say, Britain to Germany would be prohibited by art. 34. The action of the UK Customs in banning the sale of Sinclair home computers in the duty-free shops at Heathrow Airport was undoubtedly illegal in so far as it related to travellers flying to other EEC countries.

There are, however, two provisions which might attenuate this prohibition. Art. 36 allows restrictions which are 'justified on grounds of public policy or public security'. Hitherto this has only been applied to imports, so it is difficult to forecast how it would operate in the case of exports. The US Defense Department would doubtless argue that all CoCom restrictions are by definition aimed at protecting public security. However, the European Court of Justice has always interpreted art. 36 strictly, as befits an exception clause derogating from a fundamental Community principle. It is probable, therefore, that dual-use items would have to be very close to the armaments end of the spectrum to benefit from the 'public security' exception. 'Public policy' is more vague and has not been glossed very clearly as yet. Whether the Court would allow it to justify export bans under CoCom is an open question.

More to the point is art. 223. 'Any member State may take such measures as it considers necessary for the protection of the essential interests of its security which are connected with the production of or trade in arms, munitions and war material; such measures shall not adversely affect the conditions of competition in the Common Market regarding products which are not intended for specifically military purposes' (para. 1(b)). This would probably permit CoCom restrictions on war matériel, so long as it appears on the list referred to in para. (2). But the meaning of the second sentence as regards dual-use items is very vague: it would seem to have in mind the possibility that arms control measures might spill over on to goods which are not specifically military, and to be trying to shield them from such side-effects. Para. (2) of the Article requires the EC Council to draw up a list of 'products to which the provisions of para. (1) shall apply', which it did by a decision of 15 April 1958. It never published it, but nationals of member States who can show a sufficient interest may obtain a copy of the list from their government.

There is no doctrine of 'continuous voyage' in Community law. It is therefore unlikely that the art. 34 principle could be evaded by arguing that the export from Britain to Germany was really intended for forwarding to Poland. That ultimate movement from Germany to Poland would be a matter for Germany and the EEC external border.

Extra-Community Trade. The power of the member States to control exports to countries outside the Community territory is confused, and they frequently act as though their old legislative powers remain. Art. 113 EEC, however, provides for a 'common commercial policy', a term which refers to external trade, and it makes specific mention of 'export policy'. For the most part, this Article relates to commercial treaties and customs duties. However, it is also the legal basis for the common external tariff. In its opinion on the *OECD Understanding on a Local Cost Standard* (1/75)[26] the European Court held that the common commercial policy as expressed in arts. 113 and 114 pre-empted the powers to enter into treaties on export credits, as part of 'export policy', the member States retaining no concurrent powers in the matter. 'It cannot therefore be accepted that, in a field such as that governed by the Understanding in question, which is covered by export policy and more generally by the common commercial policy, the member States should exercise a power concurrent to that of the Community, in the Community sphere and in the international sphere' (at para. 31). This, like the other pre-emption decisions on external trade, relates to treaty power. It is still uncertain therefore whether such pre-emption of export controls applies also to unilateral action by a member State.

The main uncertainty here is whether the Community has occupied the particular field of arms exports. The European Parliament, adopting the Fergusson Report in 1983, proposed a direct Community involvement which would probably result, if adopted, in replacement of the current national powers exercised by the member States.[27]

Compelled Boycotts

If the phenomenon described here consisted purely of voluntary restriction of exports by States acting within their territorial sovereignty and practically unrestrained by international treaty law, the implications for the free flow of world trade would be significant enough. Some aspects of this will be mentioned in the final section of this chapter.

But the situation does not stop there, and a far more active phase of inter-State interference has developed which has serious consequences for the world legal order. In classical international law States had exclusive power to control activities within their territory. Outside that area their direct relations were with other States and not with the latter's citizens. The protective envelope of the foreign State could be broken, of course, through intervention, by a forcible irruption into direct contact with the foreign citizens. But even then, the intervening State was, as it were, partially replacing the territorial sovereign and the basic international structure remained intact.

The new practice is much more subversive, for it puts in question the very notion of State sovereignty by diluting its territorial basis. It consists in States, either individually or in concert, exercising State power directly but from a distance over foreign citizens living and acting in foreign countries. The nexus of allegiance which each citizen owes to his State is thus fractured and his public obligations are refracted. This phenomenon is called 'extraterritoriality'.

Extraterritorial Jurisdiction

This concept has been developed by the American courts and more recently by the legislature and the executive. Its origin can probably be found in the federal nature of the United States and particularly in the 'full faith and credit' clause in its Constitution. A New York resident can easily drive into New Jersey. A New Jersey court must enforce a New York judgment *ipso facto*. It does not seem a very great step for the New Jersey court to try a case against the New Yorker even if he does not move out of his state, particularly if what he does in New York has an effect in New Jersey. From there it is only a short step to apply the same thinking to Canada, another state bordering on New York. The difference is that Canada is a foreign country. In the *Alcoa* case in 1945[28] this was done: US antitrust law was applied to a Canadian company related to a US company for conduct in Canada which affected imports into the US. The US court, in the course of its judgment, held it to be settled law 'that any state may impose liabilities, even upon persons not within its allegiance, for conduct outside its borders that has consequences within its borders which the state reprehends; and these liabilities other states will ordinarily recognize'.[29]

The next step was even easier: to extend the trans-border exercise of its judicial power to countries outside the Western hemisphere altogether. In the *Swiss Watchmakers* case (1962)[30] US antitrust law was applied to an agreement made in Switzerland between Swiss enterprises established in Switzerland and having no links with American companies, the link being the fact that they sold their goods in the US. The court clearly set out the basis for all future developments: 'A United States court may exercise its jurisdiction as to acts and contracts abroad, if ... such acts and contracts have a substantial and material effect upon our foreign and domestic commerce.' The fact that the defendants were complying with their government's policy was no defence; and only if their conduct had been actually *required* under their domestic law would the jurisdiction of the US courts be stopped. 'An American court would have under such circumstances no right to condemn the governmental activity of another sovereign nation.' Even this limitation was reduced to almost nothing in the Siberian pipeline affair, when compliance with a peremptory domestic government's order was held by the US authorities to be no excuse for disobeying a US governmental order. But by then, the development of extraterritorial jurisdiction had moved from the courts to the executive, where even fewer legal restraints operate.

Alcoa and *Swiss Watchmakers* and their successors were concerned with antitrust law and hence with a particularly strong area of public policy. It was not merely a question of which courts should be entitled to try the case but involved the direct application of US law to the conflict abroad (the US courts never in these cases asserted jurisdiction and then proceeded to apply a foreign, for example, Canadian or Swiss, law).

Another parallel line of cases did, however, follow more traditional conflict of law rules. These were concerned with ordinary issues of tortious damage, that is, no US public policy was involved. But because American law on manufacturers' liability is very powerful and consumers injured by products have very strong rights to damages, any tendency in the American courts to extend their jurisdiction (and frequently but not always their law) to situations which were essentially foreign was bound to cause unease.

That is precisely what did happen. Again, influenced by the full faith and credit ethic, little distinction was made between acts performed in the 'foreign' state of Illinois and in the foreign State of Belgium. Thus a midwestern court could claim jurisdiction in an action by a local citizen against a French tyre manufacturer who had no connection whatever with the US and did not even sell its tyres there, because it must expect that they would in fact be exported by some independent middleman. This purely judicial approach was taken up by many state legislatures which passed 'long-arm' statutes enabling their courts to reach out to events beyond the state boundaries.

Both types of long-arm claim (the antitrust and the tort) gave rise to protective counter-measures by other States which felt threatened. Many of these were aimed at blocking attempts by US agencies and courts to obtain information or evidence, particularly in connection with shipping cartels. The UK Protection of Trading Interests Act 1980 went further than this and not only enabled the government to ban compliance with foreign orders but also provided that where a foreign court exercised jurisdiction abusively the defendant might claim repayment of excess damages. In response to this and to proposals by the EEC to impose reporting obligations on foreign parent companies of EEC subsidiaries (in the Vredeling Directive), a number of bills were introduced in the US Congress to protect US enterprises from the exercise of long-arm and extra territorial jurisdiction abroad.

None of these has been pushed through to enactment. But the Arab boycott of firms trading with Israel was taken more seriously and a series of US statutory provisions has been passed forbidding US persons to comply with foreign boycott requirements, including the furnishing of boycott-related information.[31]

The Export Administration Acts represented a new stage in the escalation of extraterritorial jurisdiction. While the 1979 Act does not itself provide any startling powers in this respect, the regulations issued under it have done so. For instance, on 22 June 1982 revised regulations were issued[32] relating to controls on the export of oil and gas equipment to the USSR. This prohibited *inter alia* any unlicensed export or re-export to the USSR or Afghanistan of 'any foreign produced direct products of US technical data, or any commodity produced by any plant or major component thereof that is [such a direct product]' if '(i) a written assurance was required under these regulations when the data were exported from the US; or (ii) the US technical data are the subject of a licensing agreement with, or the use of the data is contingent upon royalty payments or other compensation to, any person subject to the jurisdiction of the United States ... regardless of when the data were exported from the US; or (iii) the US technical data are the subject of a licensing agreement, or other contract, whereby the recipient of the technical data has agreed to abide by US export control regulations' (s. 379.8(a)(4)).

The consequence of this type of provision is that non-US companies may require a US licence to export from their own country not only US goods which were originally imported from the US but also goods which they have themselves manufactured but using US technology. Furthermore, the requirement for a US licence may be imposed upon them at any time at the whim of the US government even if there was no such requirement at the time of acquisition of the technology or at the time of manufacture; and the requirement may be imposed to further the foreign policy of the US irrespective of the foreign policy of the country from which the export is sought to be made. It is hardly surprising, therefore, that the European Community, in its protest note[33] to the US government, complained that the new provisions could not be validly based on any of the generally accepted bases of jurisdiction in international law and constituted 'an unacceptable interference in the independent commercial policy of the European Communities'.

The situation is exacerbated by the fact that the controls apply not only when the goods themselves have some sort of link with the US but also, irrespective of the goods, when the exporter has such a link, however tenuous. Section 385.2(c) applies to an exporter who is '(i) Any person, wherever located, who is a citizen or resident of the United States; (ii) Any person actually within the United States; (iii) Any corporation organized under the laws of the United States or of any state, territory, possession or district of the United States; or (iv) Any partnership, association, corporation, or other organization, wherever organized or doing business, that is owned or controlled by persons specified in paragraphs (i), (ii) or (iii) of this section'.

Thus a French company that is a subsidiary of a US company could be prevented from exporting a French product made using French technology. Worse, the same would apply if the French company was merely *de facto* controlled by a minority of

American nationals resident in France or by Frenchmen resident in the US, whatever the interests of its majority shareholders might be.

The highest point of such jurisdictional claims was probably reached in connection with the Siberian pipeline (see below), but none of the techniques has been abandoned. Other less crude devices are also used, relying on the operation of ordinary domestic law. One of these is the 'submission clause' in private contracts. An English company, contracting with an American licensee to use an American patent (in spite of the fact that technically it is a UK patent since patent rights do not run beyond the borders of the country in which it is registered), would agree as a term of the contract to submit 'voluntarily' to the US export regulations.[34] The theory here is that the US rules are incorporated into the contract and will thereupon be enforced by the host State under its law of contract. This in fact ignores two major difficulties: enforcement of a contract is always subject to national public policy which may make such a term illegal or unenforceable; and contracts cannot be enforced by third parties. The US government could not therefore use this device to exercise its power directly on the foreign licensee; it could only act through the American licensor, which has to be persuaded, or compelled, to bring a private action for breach of contract.

Another more alarming proposal was made by the Senate's Permanent Subcommittee on Investigations in its report on the Transfer of United States High Technology. This would make foreign nationals directly liable to US criminal law:

Volker Nast of Hamburg, Werner J. Bruchhausen of Dusseldorf and Dietmar Ulrichshofer of Vienna have in common the fact that each was indicted in the United States on charges that they conspired to ship militarily critical high technology to the Soviet Union. None of the men was prosecuted, however, because they remained in their native lands free from American justice. In Nast's case, he was indicted twice — in California in 1976, in Maryland in 1981 — and, regarding Bruchhausen and Ulrichshofer, their alleged crimes constituted one of the most serious diversions ever perpetrated.

Bringing reported criminals like Nast, Bruchhausen and Ulrichshofer to justice is a difficult task. Most nations are very hesitant to allow extradition of their own citizens. West

Germany, for example, has a constitutional prohibition against extradition of German nationals. Moreover, as European law experts have pointed out, criminal sanctions in the German export control system are exceptional, in view of the free trade orientation of German foreign economic relations legislation, and most infractions of it are punishable merely by administrative fines. Similarly, few nations treat export violations as serious offenses, as the United States does.[35]

It then went on to suggest that there might be an obligation on NATO countries to protect their mutual security by adopting laws to enforce the US export controls.

The Siberian Pipeline.   On 30 December 1981 the US government tightened its controls on exports to the USSR in reaction to the latter's involvement in the Polish governmental crisis. On 22 June 1982 these were extended still further and aimed particularly at the contracts which many Western companies had concluded to supply equipment for the construction of the Siberian pipeline. The regulations of that date, summarised in part above, extended jurisdictional claims to a hitherto unheard of extent and gave rise to a storm of protest from governments and lawyers.[36] The UK government made an order[37] on 30 June applying the Protection of Trading Interests Act 1980 to the relevant sections of the Export Administration Regulations; and when a British company, John Brown Engineering Ltd, was threatened with US enforcement measures it issued an order requiring the company to defy them and to deliver to the USSR the contracted gas turbines which it made under licence from General Electric and which incorporated US-origin rotors and technology. Notwithstanding the peremptory intervention of the UK government, the US government penalised the company by denying it 'export privileges' by an order of 9 September 1982.[38] A similar fate befell companies in Germany (Mannesmann Anlagenbau AG and AEG-Kanis Turbinenfabrik GmbH), Italy (Nuovo Pignone SpA) and France (Creusot-Loire SA and Dresser France SA).[39] The latter was a French subsidiary of a US parent but the French government took strong measures to ensure that it fulfilled its contract. In Holland the courts were involved and the President of the District Court of The Hague ordered specific performance of a contract for supply by a Dutch subsidiary of a US parent to a

French company of geophones intended for the USSR. Under Dutch private international law the contract was not subject to the US export ban.[40]

Corporate Veil

In the course of his judgment in *Sensor Nederland* the Dutch judge held that the US had no nationality jurisdiction over the company since it was Dutch, even though it was owned by an American company. He thus directly controverted the claims by the US Department of Commerce in its rules of 22 June that enterprises controlled by Americans could be assimilated to Americans.

This is an issue which is much wider than the US export rules. Traditionally companies, being given legal personality, are regarded as independent persons and the courts have not looked behind that personality to the shareholders who own them. That purity of concept is being increasingly sullied, and the corporate veil is now frequently pierced, first to identify enemy-controlled enterprises, then to protect creditors, and now to try to control multinationals. Often a country which objects to its subsidiaries being subject to another country's laws through their foreign parents will itself be applying similar pressures, for instance to force South African subsidiaries of Swedish parents to follow certain employment policies promoted by Swedish legislation.

Trading with the Enemy

Behind most of the US legislation on export controls can be discerned a sense of enmity, albeit in peacetime. The Cold War is exactly what its name implies. This is, of course, seen in the emphasis on military material. It can also be found in an otherwise troublesome concept embodied in the export administration practice. In wartime, trading with the enemy is strictly controlled and detailed rules govern the proper commercial conduct of neutrals. As part of this, a principle of 'continuous voyage' developed, whereby a belligerent could treat goods shipped to a neutral or friendly State as enemy goods if it could be established that they would continue on their journey and end in enemy hands. The increasing US insistence on controlling end customers has much in common with this principle.

Information and Free Trade

The implications of the practices described in this chapter are very
deep indeed. Their fundamental impact on international law has
already been indicated. There are at least three other areas in
which they have similarly important consequences.

Free Trade.   Hitherto the main effort of free traders has been to
promote the freedom of goods to enter a country as imports. If
restrictions on imports could be removed international trade would
be free.

Now we are seeing another side of this. Restrictions on exports
introduce another element into the equation, because commer-
cially they aim to protect the know-how and prevent other countries acquiring the knowledge to compete.

Information.   Even though much of the export restrictions
applies to goods, the purpose is to protect knowledge and information. As States move into the tertiary (service) stage, information
becomes more central. The old ideas linked to freedom of the
press, academic freedom and scientific comradeship are facing tre-
mendous strains from the interests which wish to exploit information as a property right and therefore to restrict its circulation.

Freedom of Commerce.   The coming dominance of copyright and
patents in advanced legal systems risks introducing as the norm the
concept of continuous control of goods and ideas. No longer will it
be sufficient to make an article and sell it, the sale price being
sufficient remuneration and the purchaser having full power to use
it for whatever purposes he chooses, whether to earn money or
not. The copyright mentality would retain an economic interest in
the article, taking a percentage from any income it subsequently
earned: a taxi driver, for instance, would have to pay a proportion
of his fare income to the manufacturer of his cab. The US
approach to export controls shows a very similar attitude, but
expressed in terms of power rather than economic interest —
although there are some who claim to see an economic benefit
behind the political policy.

The legal techniques used by the US in this economic cold war
are part of a much wider phenomenon, of which East-West trade

is only one, perhaps minor, part. But there is no doubt that it is raising issues of the very greatest importance.

Notes

1. There is a flourishing patent Bar in the East European countries but it is small and scattered, with only one or two specialised lawyers in each capital city. Although a few West German patent lawyers such as Alexander von Führner are connected with it, information about its activities is not easily accessible except through the grapevine. For a few years the European Law Centre published *I.P. [Intellectual Property] Reports from Socialist Countries*, but this was discontinued in 1981.

2. For the whole of this section, see in particular United States Congress, Office of Technology Assessment, *Technology and East-West Trade* (US Government Printing Office, Washington, DC, 1979). See also National Academy of Sciences, *Scientific Communication and National Security* (National Academy Press, Washington, DC, 1982) and William Schneider, Jr (Under Secretary of State for Security Assistance, Science and Technology), 'Export Control of High Technology', *State Department Bulletin*, June 1983, p. 71.

3. See David Marsh, 'Boost for CoCom's Shoestring Technology Patrol', *Financial Times*, 30 December 1983.

4. See, for example, David Buchan, 'The West Plugs the Hi-Tech Drain', *Financial Times*, 25 July 1984; 'CoCom Compromises', *The Economist*, 21 July 1984, p. 68; 'US Relaxes Proposals on Soviet Bloc Computer Sales', *Financial Times*, 5 May 1984; 'CoCom Deal on Computer Trade with Soviet Bloc', *Financial Times*, 16 July 1984.

5. As the UK government (Mr Paul Channon) said on 20 July 1984:

Representatives of the member States of CoCom reached agreement in principle on software and telecommunications switching equipment. This brings to a satisfactory conclusion the current review of the lists of goods subject to export control for strategic reasons. The Government will accordingly be able to bring British export controls on computers into line with up-to-date strategic and commercial circumstances.

These arrangements will require the formal assent in due course of the Governments concerned: this is expected in the autumn of this year. I hope shortly thereafter to make the necessary Statutory Instrument, implementing them in United Kingdom law. In the meantime, I am exploring ways of introducing the maximum degree of flexibility in the existing export control framework to reflect the future arrangement.

When the new arrangements are in force low-powered computers of no strategic significance will be freed from export control, while substantial flexibility will be introduced into the export control arrangements for computers and related equipment of higher levels of performance. Certain strategic categories of software and stored programme controlled telecommunications equipment of strategic concern (including terminal and transit switches) will be brought under export control. All CoCom countries have agreed to respect the agreement on stored programme telecommunications switching as from 12 July 1984.

My Department will make guidance available to British companies as soon as possible.

168   *Legal Aspects of Technology Transfer*

Hansard Commons c. 370-1 W.A. The promised statutory instrument had still not been made by May 1985!

6. See '"High-Tech" Rules for Home Computers Anger Europeans', *Observer*, 18 December 1983.

7. *The Economist*, 21 July 1984, p. 69.

8. See for instance *Sacchi* (155/73) in *European Court Reports* (1974), p. 409 and *Common Market Law Review*, vol. 2 (1974), p. 177, *Procureur du Roi* v. *Debauve* (52/79) in *European Court Reports* (1980), p. 833 and *Common Market Law Reports*, vol. 2 (1981), p. 362, and case note on the latter by N. Hunnings in *Common Market Law Review*, vol. 17 (1980), p. 564.

9. See United States Senate, Committee on Governmental Affairs, Permanent Subcommittee on Investigations, *Transfer of United States High Technology to the Soviet Union and Soviet Bloc Nations* (US Government Printing Office, Washington, DC, 1982).

10. Congressisonal Research Service, Library of Congress, *Foreign Espionage and US Technology*, Report for the US Senate Permanent Subcommittee on Investigations, Washington, DC, 1980.

11. There is also a parallel statute, the Arms Export Control Act, which is administered by the State Department.

12. This relates to national security controls (s. 5). Foreign policy controls apply to goods, technology *or other information*; short supply controls apply only to goods.

13. Ernest B. Johnson, Jr, Statement before the Subcommittee on Near East and South Asian Affairs of the Senate Foreign Relations Committee, 18 March 1982; see *Department of State Bulletin*, June 1982, p. 55.

14. Originally intended to expire on 30 September 1983, it was temporarily maintained by Congress for two weeks to allow amendments to be considered but was allowed to lapse on 14 October. It was later temporarily re-extended.

15. *US* v. *Spawr Optical Research Inc.* 685 F.2d 1076 (1982). See also the note on that decision in *Texas International Law Journal*, vol. 18 (1983), p. 614, for the background.

16. In addition Congress has passed a series of short-term extensions of the Act.

17. See 'Capitol Hill Dissent Over Technology Export Law', *Financial Times*, 8 May 1984; Nancy Dunne, 'Plan for Tighter US Export Control Draws Widespread Criticism', *Financial Times*, 24 April 1984; 'Last Phase in Battle over Soviet Export Curb', *The Times*, 26 April 1984, and 'South Africa Loan Ban Kills Export Control Bill', *New York Times*, 12 October 1984.

18. See generally Office of Technology Assessment, *Technology*, Ch. 8.

19. Ibid. See also Schneider, 'Export Control of High Technology', p. 73.

20. US Senate, Permanent Subcommittee on Investigations, *Transfer of United States High Technology*, p. 64. See also Christopher Madison, 'Commerce Department Feels the Heat Over Diversion of High-Tech Exports', *National Journal*, 10 March 1984, p. 465.

21. 'Sweden Protests at Tighter Computer Shipment Rules', *Financial Times*, 28 March 1984.

22. See Dunne, 'Plan for Tighter US Export Control', and Nancy Dunne, 'US Softens Stance over Hi-Tech Import Restrictions', *Financial Times*, 12 September 1984.

23. See 'Marconi Falls Foul of US Customs', *Financial Times*, 31 May 1983.

24. *Guardian*, 22 November 1983.

25. William Carey, 'High Tech Export Controls: Why the US Must Not Go Overboard', *Financial Times*, 25 April 1984.

26. *European Court Reports* (1975), p. 1355; *Common Market Law Reports*,

vol. 1 (1976), p. 85.

27. See Reimund Seidelmann, 'European Security and the European Communities', *Journal of European Integration*, vol. 7 (1984), p. 221.

28. *United States* v. *Aluminum Co. of America* 148 F.2d 416 (2nd Circuit).

29. Ibid., p. 443.

30. *United States* v. *Watchmakers of Switzerland Information Center Inc.*, *Commerce Clearing House Trade Cases* no. 70,600 (SDNY).

31. Beginning with the Export Administration Act of 1969 and developed in s. 8 of the 1979 Act, and also including the Tax Reform Act of 1976 which denied certain tax credits to persons co-operating with an international boycott during the tax year.

32. *Federal Register*, vol. 47 (24 June 1982), p. 27250.

33. *International Legal Materials*, vol. 21 (1982), p. 891.

34. See in particular A.V. Lowe's perceptive article, 'Public International Law and the Conflict of Laws: The European Response to the United States Export Administration Regulations', *International and Comparative Law Quarterly*, vol. 37 (1984), p. 515.

35. US Senate, Permanent Subcommittee on Investigations, *Transfer of United States High Technology*, p. 63 (recommendation no. 12).

36. See, for example, J.W. Bridge, 'The Law and Policy of United States Foreign Policy Export Controls', *Legal Studies*, vol. 4 (1984), p. 2; R.B. Ferguson, 'British Companies and America's Pipeline Embargo', *Scots Law Times*, 29 October 1982, p. 281.

37. Statutory Instrument 1982/885 Protection of Trading Interests (US Re-export Control) Order 1982.

38. *Department of Commerce* v. *John Brown Engineering Ltd.*, *European Commercial Cases* (1983), p. 257.

39. All promulgated in *Federal Register*, vol. 47 (1982), pp. 39708-10. For an analysis of the French position see Geric Lebedoff and Caroline Raievski, 'A French Perspective on the United States Ban on the Soviet Gas Pipeline Equipment', *Texas International Law Journal*, vol. 18 (1983), p. 483.

40. *Compagnie Européenne des Pétroles* v. *Sensor Nederland BV*, *European Commercial Cases* (1983), p. 532.

8 WESTERN TECHNOLOGY AND SOVIET MILITARY POWER

David Holloway

One of the fruits of detente was an increase in East-West trade. Between 1967 and 1978 Soviet imports of machinery and transport equipment from the West grew from 499 million to 2,254 million roubles (in 1969 investment estimate prices).[1] As disillusionment with detente began to mount in the United States in the mid-1970s, so too did opposition to trade with the Soviet Union and Eastern Europe. The fear that exports of Western technology might be enabling the Soviet Union to increase its military power was a particular cause of anxiety.[2]

As East-West relations have continued to worsen in the 1980s, so the concern about the transfer of technology to the Soviet Union has grown. In March 1981, shortly after the Reagan administration took office, the CIA began a study of the military benefits the Soviet Union had gained through its acquisition of Western technology. A sanitised version of the final report was published in April 1982. This defines the central issue as follows:

> The United States and its Allies traditionally have relied on the technological superiority of their weapons to preserve a credible counterforce to the quantitative superiority of the Warsaw Pact. But that technical superiority is eroding as the Soviet Union and its Allies introduce more and more sophisticated weaponry — weapons that all too often are manufactured with the direct help of Western technology. Stopping the Soviets' extensive acquisition of military-related Western technology — in ways that are both effective and appropriate in our open society — is one of the most complex and urgent issues facing the Free World today.[3]

The CIA concluded that 'the Soviets have acquired militarily significant technologies and critically important industrial Western technologies that have benefited every major Soviet industry

170

engaged in the research, development and production of weapon systems'.[4]

Admiral Bobby R. Inman, Deputy Director of the CIA, said that the results of the CIA's study were 'startling to those of us inside the intelligence community'.[5] Inman has spoken of a 'haemorrhage' of American technology, and other officials have used similarly vivid language to describe what is happening.[6] This understanding of the contribution of Western technology to Soviet military power has underpinned the efforts of the Reagan administration to tighten up the control of technology exports to the Soviet Union. These efforts have caused considerable controversy in the United States and between the United States and its allies.

The export of weapons is not at issue. No one argues that the West ought to sell military equipment to the Soviet Union. The difficulties are caused by 'dual-use' technologies that have both military and civilian applications. The Kama River Truck Plant is often quoted as an example of dual-use technology. It was built with the help of more than $1 billion worth of production equipment and technology purchased from the West, and has produced military-specification trucks that are now being used in Afghanistan and Eastern Europe.[7]

The Kama River Truck Plant points to some of the problems raised by dual-use technologies. Where, for example, should the line be drawn in imposing export controls? Many technologies have both civilian and military uses: should all technologies with potential military use be embargoed? This case illustrates another problem, too. Most of the Western technology used in the Kama River Truck Plant was purchased not from the United States, but from other Western countries. What should United States policy be in such cases — should it try to make other countries adopt tight restrictions on technology exports, or should it accept that such controls are impossible? It is issues like these that have given rise to disagreement inside the Western alliance.[8]

Further complications arise from the fact that there is ambiguity about the purposes that controls on technology transfer should serve. The primary aim of the strategic embargo co-ordinated by CoCom is to deny the Soviet Union technologies that would enable it to improve the performance of its weapon systems, or to produce better systems.[9] Some critics of the Reagan administration's efforts to tighten the controls on technology exports have accused it of using the argument about dual-use technologies as a cover for economic warfare. This criticism has come from the American business community, which is worried about the effect of the administration's policy on access to overseas markets.[10]

The Reagan administration has said that it does not advocate trade warfare, and that it supports trade as long as the benefits are mutual and specific transactions do not contribute to the strategic advantage of the Soviet Union.[11] At the same time, however, it is evident that at least some people in the administration believe that economic and technological pressure on the Soviet Union should form part of United States policy. The Pentagon's 'Fiscal Year 1984-1988 Defense Guidance', for example, recommended the development of weapons that 'are difficult for the Soviets to counter, impose disproportionate costs, open up new areas for major military competition and obsolesce previous Soviet investment'.[12]

The Reagan administration's case about the relationship between Western technology and Soviet military power raises some important questions: Does the Soviet Union lag behind the West in technology? Does this technological lag harm Soviet security and enhance Western security? How important has foreign technology been to the Soviet military-technological effort? It may seem foolish to try to answer these questions, since much of the relevant information is classified, but there is enough evidence to make at least partial answers possible. In this chapter I shall look chiefly at the transfer of technology from the United States.

The Level of Soviet Technology

The whole argument about technology transfer rests on the premise that the West enjoys a technological lead over the Soviet Union. If that were not so, there would be little for the West to fear from the transfer of technology.

There is in fact almost universal agreement in the West that the technological level of Soviet industry is significantly lower than that of Western, and particularly of American, industry. The most comprehensive non-governmental attempt to assess the technological level of Soviet industry concluded, on the basis of a series of case studies covering the period from the early 1950s to the early 1970s, that 'in most of the technologies ... studied there is no evidence of a substantial diminution of the technological gap between the USSR and the West in the past 15-20 years'.[13]

This assessment is supported by estimates published by the United States Department of Defense, which stated in 1980 that the United States led the Soviet Union in 15 of 'the twenty most important basic technology areas', and was equal in the other five.[14] In 1982 the United States was estimated to lead in 14 of these areas, to tie in four, and to lag in two (neither of these two — conventional warhead technology and mobile power sources — were included in the 1980 assessment).[15]

This poor performance does not result from neglect on the part of the Soviet authorities. Ever since the First Five Year Plan (1928-32), they have given high priority to the development of science and technology. In the mid-1930s the Soviet Union appears to have spent a higher proportion of its GNP on research and development than the United States.[16] After the war the Soviet R&D effort grew rapidly, especially in the years from 1955 to 1975. The Soviet Union now has more scientists and engineers engaged in R&D than any other country in the world.[17] In spite of this effort, however, the poor performance of Soviet industry in technological innovation remains a major worry for the Soviet leaders.

The causes of this poor performance are both historical and systemic. In the 1930s the Party leaders created a 'command economy' in order to enforce their priorities in their drive to overcome the country's economic and technological backwardness. The planning system enabled the Soviet Union to build up its industry and its military power by concentrating high levels of investment in key sectors. Now the opportunities for increasing the labour force and capital investment have diminished, and so economic growth has come to depend more on technological innovation. But the 'command economy', which remains unchanged in its basic outlines, provides few incentives for innovation, and in fact hampers the transfers of scientific knowledge into industrial production.[18]

It is important, however, not to exaggerate the obstacles to innovation, or the backwardness of Soviet technology. The Soviet Union has not closed the technological gap with the West, but neither has it fallen much further behind in an age of rapid technological change. Moreover, innovation has been more successful in some sectors than in others, as a result of political priority. This is particularly true of the defence sector, where pressure from the Party leaders and management by the military have helped to

overcome many of the obstacles to innovation to be found elsewhere in the economy.[19]

Two case studies I did of innovation in the defence industry
suggested that although the processes of innovation are more
effective in the defence sector than in civilian industry, this is
because of the operation of the priority system, and not because
the two sectors operate in fundamentally different ways. Moreover, although the case studies suggested that the defence sector is
more effective at innovation than civilian industry, they also indicated that the level of Soviet military technology is not as high as
that in the West when measured in terms of major technological
innovations and the diffusion of those innovations through stocks
of weapons.[20]

Two case studies cannot give a picture of the whole field of
military technology: in 1980 the Soviet Union is reported to have
had 112 types of weapon in production.[21] But the results of the
two studies are compatible with the conclusions of analyses done
by US government agencies. In 1976 the CIA stated in a report to
Congress that 'although some Soviet weapons systems have capabilities that exceed those of US systems in such things as range,
these are the result of design choices and do not reflect a higher
state of technology'.[22] In the following year the Director of the
CIA testified that 'while virtually all of the Soviet inventory
weapons fall within US production technology, the Soviets simply
do not have the technology required to produce many of the US
weapons nor could they produce close substitutes'.[23]

A similar picture emerges from the Department of Defense
assessment of the relative US/USSR technological level in
deployed military systems. Here the United States enjoys a general
lead, although a smaller one than in the comparison of basic technology areas. In 1980 the United States was held to be superior in
14 systems, to be equal in 9, and to lag in 7; in 1982 the United
States was estimated to lead in 12 systems, to be equal in 14, and
to lag in 6.[24] These studies suggest that the Soviet Union has had
some success in creating effective weapons on the basis of a generally lower technological level in industry.

The defence sector, in spite of its special features, is not an isolated realm within the Soviet economy, and cannot be completely
protected from failings elsewhere in the economy. The distinction
between the civilian and defence sectors was never absolute, and is
becoming less sharp than it once was. This suggests that Soviet

military technology may be increasingly affected by the low technological level of Soviet industry as a whole, and particularly of the electronics industry. In the United States the civilian market has led the defence sector in applications of microelectronics, software and instrumentation, and has thus generated new technological possibilities for military application; but this has not happened in the Soviet Union.

The Soviet lag in technology creates an incentive to acquire technology from abroad, but the obstacles to indigenous innovation are likely also to hamper the assimilation and diffusion of foreign technology. A policy of acquiring foreign technology cannot wholly circumvent these obstacles.

The Military Significance of the Soviet Lag in Technology

The military significance of the Western technological lead is not self-evident, because there does not exist a one-to-one relationship between advances in technology and increases in security. It is no doubt true that some of the time a technological lead contributes to Western security, but this need not always be so, for various reasons.

First, the Soviet Union may design around its technological shortcomings to achieve the same operational performance — the performance it needs to carry out a particular mission — on the basis of a lower level of technology. It has done this with its strategic missile force. In spite of serious lags in solid fuel and guidance technologies, for example, the Soviet Union has been able to develop ICBMs which could inflict immense destruction on the West in a retaliatory strike, and which possess some measure of counterforce capability as well.

Second, the striving after technological advances may prove detrimental to operational effectiveness, if it results in long development times and in 'baroque' rather than 'austere' weapons designs. There is a school of thought in the United States which argues that preoccupation with technological advances actually reduces American military power by fostering weapons designs that are too costly and too complex. Some critics of American policy point to Soviet design practices as a model to be emulated: simplicity, commonality and evolutionary (rather than revolutionary) development are said to yield good operational performance. The critics of American weapons development can support their case with some striking examples.[25] But it is a mistake to idealise the Soviet weapons design and development process and ignore the examples of Soviet systems that have been technologically overambitious (for example, the Mya-4 bomber, the *Galosh* ABM system, or — a civilian example — the Tu-144 supersonic airliner).

Third, when a technological lead does confer a military advantage, the security of the leading state may be reduced once the other side has caught up. A clear example is provided by MIRVs (Multiple Independently-targetable Re-entry Vehicles). The United States MIRVed its SLBMs and ICBMs in the late 1960s and early 1970s, before the Soviet Union did. But when the Soviet Union MIRVed its ICBMs in the late 1970s (more quickly than the United States had anticipated), the United States found itself worse off than if neither side had developed multiple warheads.

In spite of these considerations, however, one must suppose that technological advantage can make a substantial contribution to weapons performance, and hence to military power. Even though it is often the parameters chosen, rather than technological advantages, that are critical to the relative performance of weapons systems, technological superiority widens the range of options available to the weapons designer. The fact that this advantage is often poorly exploited does not detract from its potential significance.

Both the United States and the Soviet Union pursue technological advances relentlessly, in the belief that a technological lead enhances security, while a technological lag endangers it. Ever since the First Five Year Plan the Soviet Union has tried to overcome its backwardness in military technology. Starting from a weak base, it achieved considerable success in the 1930s. Large numbers of weapons were produced, some of which — the T-34 tank, for example — were of high quality. But the designers had to take account of the technological level of Soviet industry. The aircraft designer Tupolev said that 'the country needs aircraft like black bread. You can offer pralines, cakes and so on, but there's no point — there aren't the ingredients to make them out of'.[26]

The war with Germany showed that military technology was changing rapidly, and immediately after the war Stalin set up major programmes to develop nuclear weapons, rockets, radar and jet propulsion. From these programmes emerged weapons that were to lead to a transformation of Soviet military doctrine and organisation.[27]

The Soviet Union does not reveal what resources it devotes to military R&D, and considerable uncertainty attaches to Western estimates of the size of the Soviet effort. The CIA estimates that between 1967 and 1977 Soviet military R&D accounted for 20-25 per cent of defence spending, and was equal to 40-50 per cent of outlays on military equipment.[28] In the United States these proportions are about half: 10-12 per cent of the total military budget, and 20-25 per cent of the funds available for weapons acquisition. Even allowing for the Soviet stress on science and technology, the CIA's estimate shows the Soviet Union devoting a very high proportion of its outlays to R&D. Of course, the estimate may be wrong: the CIA acknowledges that its figures for military R&D outlays are the least reliable part of its estimates of Soviet defence spending. Perhaps the most that can be said is that the Soviet military R&D effort is large and that it has expanded greatly since the war, as part of the overall R&D effort.

Soviet military R&D policy is offensive in the sense that (until recently, at any rate) its avowed aim has been to attain military-technical superiority over potential enemies. The *Soviet Military Encyclopedia* contains an entry on 'military-technical superiority' which states that 'Soviet military doctrine ... gives a programme of actions for ensuring military-technical superiority over the armed forces of probable enemies'.[29] But this goal has not always been easy to attain, in spite of the very large R&D effort, and in practice Soviet policy has often been defensive, in the sense of countering or assimilating innovations made abroad.

Foreign Technology and the Soviet Military-Technological Effort

In the inter-war years the Soviet Union received a great deal of foreign help in developing its defence industry. Equipment was purchased abroad, foreign designs were copied, and technical assistance agreements were signed with foreign companies to help develop aircraft production. Antony Sutton collected a great deal of material on this technology transfer for his three-volume work on *Western Technology and Soviet Economic Development*, but he did not analyse this material carefully or systematically.[30] Consequently it is difficult to make a well-founded judgement about the contribution of Western technology to Soviet military power in the 1930s, beyond saying that it was considerable.

Between 1941 and 1945 the Soviet Union once again received a major infusion of foreign technology, first from its allies through Lend-Lease, and then from Germany in the form of captured equipment, plant and skilled manpower. It is difficult to say precisely what contribution German technology made to Soviet weapons programmes after the war, but captured equipment, production plants, engineers and technicians did play a substantial part in Soviet missile, radar and jet propulsion development.[31]

It was of course rational for the Soviet Union to acquire technology from abroad rather than try to develop it itself, but this policy carried two dangers: dependence on the West; and the possibility that the Soviet Union might end up doing no more than copying Western weapons designs. The Soviet Union has sought to avoid both of these dangers.

Since the late 1940s the opportunities for obtaining foreign military technology have been curtailed by the strategic embargo imposed by the West. It has generally been assumed that in the post-war period the Soviet Union has had to rely more on its indigenous R&D effort than before. This assumption has been challenged by the Reagan administration, which has argued that since the late 1960s the Soviet Union has used both legal and illegal means to acquire 'militarily significant technologies and critically important industrial ... technologies'.[32]

Evidence has been produced to show, first, that there is an extensive Soviet and Eastern European effort under way to obtain Western technology by both legal and illegal means; second, that Soviet weapons systems performance has been improved by the acquisition of Western technology; and third, that the technological level of 'militarily critical' industrial sectors in the Soviet Union — notably microelectronics — has been greatly enhanced by Western technology. This evidence needs to be considered briefly. In doing so it is useful to think of technology transfer as consisting of several different stages: the attempt to obtain technology; the transfer to the recipient country; assimilation by the recipient; and the resulting improvement in the recipient's military strength.

First, there is indeed extensive evidence of the Soviet attempt to acquire Western technology. Some of this effort is open and legal, some is covert and illegal. According to Admiral Inman, only a small percentage of the 'militarily useful, militarily related technology' that the Soviet Union has acquired from the West has come from direct technical exchanges between scientists and students. About 20-30 per cent has come through legal purchases and open source publications. About 70 per cent, according to Inman, was acquired by the Soviet and East European intelligence agencies, using 'clandestine, technical and overt collection techniques'.[33] It is not clear, however, whether all this activity by the intelligence agencies has been illegal.

Soviet legal and illegal methods should probably be understood as part of the same policy. In the late 1960s the Soviet Union increased its imports of foreign technology. In doing this it came up against export controls which prevented it from acquiring legally some of the technology it wanted. It has employed various illegal techniques, ranging from classical espionage to the use of intermediaries who are willing to evade export controls, to obtain this technology. A shady area exists where the undercover side of the Soviet economy meets the 'unacceptable face' of capitalism.

Sometimes controlled technology is diverted from legitimate trade channels to the Soviet Union. This is done through American or West European firms that are willing to evade the controls; through agents in such firms; through Soviet and East European firms in the West; or through foreign purchasing agents.[34] A recent example is provided by an advanced computer manufactured by the Digital Equipment Corporation, which was seized in Sweden in November 1983 before it was due to be shipped to the Soviet Union. The computer had been sold legally to a South African company which then seems to have tried to divert it to the Soviet Union (to which it could not have been sold legally) via West Germany and Sweden.[35]

Second, there is extensive evidence that technology of military value has been transferred to the Soviet Union. This is particularly true of microelectronics technology (see Table 8.1). The CIA claims that these acquisitions have enabled the Soviet Union to build a modern microelectronics industry: 'the acquired equipment and know-how, if combined, could meet 100 per cent of the Soviets' high-quality microelectronic needs for military purposes, or 50 per cent of all their microelectronic needs'.[36]

It should not be surprising if the Soviet Union has concentrated on acquiring microelectronic technology, for it has great military significance and can effect the performance of weapons of all kinds. The foreign acquisition of electronics technology has gone

Table 8.1: Microelectronic Equipment and Technology Legally and
Illegally Acquired by the Soviet Bloc

Equipment or Technology	Comments
Process Technology for Microelectronic Wafer Preparation	Many acquisitions in this area include computer-aided software, pattern generators and compilers, digital plotters, photorepeaters, contact printers, mask comparators, electron-beam generators, and ion milling equipment.
Equipment for Device Fabrication	Many hundreds of acquisitions in this area have provided the Soviets with mask aligners, diffusion furnaces, ion implanters, coaters, etchers, and photochemical process lines.
Assembly and Test Equipment	Hundreds of items of Western equipment, including scribers, bonders, probe testers, and final test equipment, have been acquired by the Soviets.

Source: Central Intelligence Agency, 'Soviet Acquisition of Western Technology'
(April 1982) in G.K. Bertsch and J.R. McIntyre (eds), *National Security and Technology
Transfer: The Strategic Dimensions of East-West Trade* (Westview, Boulder, CO, 1983),
p. 102.

hand in hand with expansion of the domestic R&D base in that
sector. In the 1970s the Soviet Union made a determined effort to
strengthen its own electronics R&D: the number of scientists in the
Soviet radio-electronics industry doubled between 1968 and 1977.
In 1978 the Deputy Minister of the Radio Industry, V.M.
Shabanov, was made Deputy Minister of Defence for Armament.[37]

The third stage in the process of technology transfer is the
assimilation of the acquired technology by the recipient. Here the
evidence is much poorer. All one can say is that assimilation is not
a straightforward process, and that at least some of the obstacles to
indigenous innovation will apply to the assimilation of foreign
technology too. Besides, the assimilation of illegally acquired technology may present problems of its own: the equipment or know-
how may not be complete; it may not come when it is needed; the
supplier will not provide help with starting it up. Illegal acquisition
of technology must be regarded as less desirable than legal acquisition, and it may cost more if intermediaries have to be paid for
the risks they take.

Fourth, the CIA report discusses some specific examples of
Soviet weapons development which may have benefited from the
acquisition of foreign technology. Two examples are quoted from

strategic weapons development. The first concerns the SS-13 ICBM silo: 'The striking similarities between the US *Minuteman* silo and the Soviet SS-13 silo very likely resulted from acquisition of US documents and expedited deployment of this, the first Soviet solid-propellant ICBM[38]. This was hardly a major technological gain for the Soviet Union, for only 60 SS-13s were deployed in the late 1960s and early 1970s, compared with about 1,000 liquid-propellant SS-11 ICBMs. The SS-13 is thought to have been deployed in small numbers because of technical problems with the solid fuel motors.[39]

The other example concerns a much quoted incident. In 1972 the United States approved the sale of 168 precision-grinding machines, manufactured by the Bryant Grinder Corporation, to the Soviet Union. Some US officials have insisted that these machines made it possible for the Soviet Union to produce the micro-ballbearings needed for the gyroscopes and accelerometers in missile guidance systems, and that without them the Soviet Union would not have been able to MIRV its system or improve so markedly its missile accuracy. On this issue the wording of the CIA report is ambiguous:

> Through the 1950s and into the 1960s the Soviet precision bearing industry lagged significantly behind that of the West. However, through legal trade purchases in the 1970s, the Soviet Union acquired US precision grinding machines for the production of small, high-precision bearings. Similar grinding machines, having lower production rate capabilities, were available from several foreign countries. Only a few of these machines, either US or foreign, would have been sufficient to supply Soviet missile designers with all the quality bearings they needed. These purchases provided the Soviets with the capability to manufacture precision bearings in large volume sooner than would have been likely through indigenous development. The Soviets probably could have used indigenous grinding machines and produced the required quality of bearings over a long period by having an abnormally high rejection rate.[40]

What this passage implies is that there is no firm evidence that these machines contributed to Soviet missile accuracy or MIRVs, although they may have speeded up the production of small, high-precision bearings needed for such systems.

These two examples illustrate the fragmentary and uncertain nature of the evidence about the military benefits the Soviet Union has acquired from foreign technology. To some extent the uncertain character of the evidence is inescapable, given the secrecy that prevails in this area. The third stage in the transfer process — assimilation by the recipient — is the weakest link in the chain of evidence.

Even in historical cases it can be difficult to trace the process whereby technology is transferred and incorporated into Soviet military equipment. The CIA report states that 'Soviet dependence on Western technology was visible and clear-cut in the years immediately after World War II, when the Soviets stole Western nuclear secrets leading to their development of a nuclear weapon capability ...'[41] But the issue of technology transfer was in fact much more complicated than this in the early Soviet nuclear programme. When nuclear fission was discovered, Soviet physicists were as excited as their colleagues abroad, and as quick to see that an atomic bomb with enormous destructive power might be built. In 1939, 1940 and 1941 Soviet physicists pursued research that paralleled what was being done in the West.[42]

When Nazi Germany invaded the Soviet Union on 22 June 1941 work on nuclear fission stopped. It was restarted in early 1943 when Stalin initiated a small project to see whether atomic energy could be used for military purposes. This project was set up because information was reaching the Soviet Union about British, American and German work on the atomic bomb. Klaus Fuchs' earliest reports seem to have played a role in this decision. So too did the awareness that research on nuclear fission was now shrouded in secrecy in the United States. This secrecy led to the conclusion that the United States was trying to build an atomic bomb.

The Soviet project remained very small by comparison with the Manhattan Project until August 1945. Then the Soviet project was expanded into a crash programme, after it had been demonstrated that an atomic bomb could be built, that it was immensely destructive, and that the United States was willing to use it. The Smyth Report on the Military Uses of Atomic Energy, which the United States government published at the end of the war, appears to have proved helpful to the Soviet effort: in any event 30,000 copies of the Russian translation were printed by the spring of 1946.

This brief outline of the role of Western technology in the

Soviet atomic bomb project suggests that espionage was important: most estimates indicate that Fuchs saved the Soviet Union between one and two years. But it was not the only way in which information was transmitted to the Soviet Union. Scientific journals played a key role; the fact of secrecy itself conveyed a crucial message to the Soviet Union; the Smyth Report contained significant information; most important of all was the demonstration that the atomic bomb was feasible.

This episode also shows that it is difficult to establish precisely what contribution foreign technology makes in specific cases. It suggests as well that foreign technology can be assimilated best when the standard of Soviet science and technology is high. Finally, it forces one to ask more carefully what can be controlled, if information can be conveyed through a variety of different channels.

Conclusion

Foreign technology has made a substantial contribution to Soviet military power. This was most evident in the 1930s and 1940s, but in recent years too the Soviet Union has made a serious effort, by both legal and illegal means, to acquire technology from the West in order to strengthen its own military-technological base, particularly in electronics. There is, however, a serious danger that the role of foreign technology may be overestimated, for the Soviet Union has a very strong R&D base, especially in the defence sector.

The Soviet effort to acquire 'military-related' technology abroad has presented Western governments with the difficult problem of devising an appropriate response. The problem has been made more complex by the way in which a number of different issues have been confused in the debate about technology transfer. For example, Soviet legal and illegal acquisitions of Western technology have been lumped together, even though the problem for Western policy-makers is quite different in each case. The 'military-related' technology that the Soviet Union acquires illegally cannot be stopped by toughening up export controls: the problem is one of enforcing existing controls. This is distinct from the problem of deciding what legal acquisitions to stop, except that the more controls there are, the harder enforcement may become.

A second difficulty with the discussion is that it tends to view the transfer process as unproblematic, and not to realise that assimilation of foreign technology presents many of the same problems as indigenous innovation. Philip Hanson has written in his study of 'The Soviet System as a Recipient of Foreign Technology' that 'certain features of the system, such as its tendency to inhibit domestic technical change generally, have been shown to have retarding effects on the absorption and diffusion of imported technology'.[43] It may be that assimilation of foreign technology is more effective in the defence sector, precisely because indigenous innovation is more effective there too. But the illegal acquisition of foreign technology is likely, in many cases, to impose new barriers to assimilation, most notably perhaps in making it difficult to have close personal contacts with foreign managers and specialists — something that most studies show to be crucial to the assimilation process.

Third, in the discussion of technology transfer it is important to distinguish clearly between technology that can be controlled and that which cannot. It is an illusion, and it may be a dangerous one, to suppose that the Soviet Union can be closed off completely from access to foreign technology. Many of the channels through which technology is transferred — scientific publications and exports to third countries, for example — could not be blocked without doing considerable harm to science and technology in the United States, or to United States economic interests.

Fourth, much of the rhetoric surrounding this issue has been grossly inflated. Admiral Inman has stated that

the Soviets are bent upon achieving world pre-eminence, dominance, if you will, in science and technology and are building a huge R&D infrastructure with that goal in mind. The technology they are acquiring from the West is an important input to that process because it allows them to compare and build upon the best of both worlds and they do.[44]

This is not an appropriate comment: it would have been relevant 50 years ago. The Soviet Union now has a huge R&D infrastructure and seems to be using foreign technology to further the development of individual sectors of industry: the chemical industry openly, the electronics industry in a more clandestine way.

Another US official has said that

the United States R&D establishment is viewed by the Soviets as a Mother Lode of important and frequently openly available [scientific and technological] information. In fact, they tap into it so frequently that one must wonder if they regard United States R&D as their own national asset.[45]

This too is a serious exaggeration: the Soviet authorities show considerable anxiety about their technological relationship with the West and their own poor technological performance. They would clearly rather rely on their own technology than be forced to acquire foreign technology.[46]

The rhetoric may seem unimportant, but it appears to reflect an overemphasis on the political significance of technology in the East-West relationship. It exaggerates the importance of Western technology to the Soviet military effort, and therefore exaggerates the pressure that can be put on the Soviet Union by stopping the flow of technology. It makes the same mistake as those who thought, in the early 1970s, that the Soviet leaders could be induced, through the expansion of trade, to make changes in their domestic and foreign policies.

Notes

1. Philip Hanson, 'The Soviet System as a Recipient of Foreign Technology' in R. Amann and J. Cooper (eds), *Industrial Innovation in the Soviet Union* (Yale University Press, New Haven and London, 1982), p. 450.

2. For a useful survey see Richard F. Kaufman, 'Changing US Attitudes Toward East-West Economic Relations', paper prepared for the NATO Colloquium on the External Economic Relations of CMEA Countries: Their Significance and Impact in a Global Perspective, April 1983.

3. Central Intelligence Agency, 'Soviet Acquisition of Western Technology' (April 1982), in G.K. Bertsch and J.R. McIntyre, *National Security and Technology Transfer: The Strategic Dimensions of East-West Trade* (Westview, Boulder, CO, 1983), p. 92.

4. Ibid., p. 94.

5. United States Senate, Committee on Governmental Affairs, Permanent Subcommittee on Investigations, *Transfer of United States High Technology to the Soviet Union and Soviet Bloc Nations* (US Government Printing Office, Washington, DC, 1982), p. 3.

6. 'Haemorrhage' — quoted by Eugene B. Skolnikoff in 'Technology Transfer and Security', *Europe/America Letter*, vol. 2, no. 1 (October 1982), p. 18; for other comments see US Senate, Permanent Subcommittee on Investigations, *Transfer of United States High Technology*, pp. 5, 7.

186   *Western Technology and Soviet Military Power*

7. CIA, 'Soviet Acquisition', pp. 94-5.

8. Kaufman, 'Changing US Attitudes', p. 24.

9. Philip Hanson, *Trade and Technology in Soviet-Western Relations* (Macmillan, London, 1981), pp. 223-6.

10. See comments quoted in Ehud Yonay, 'Washington Tries to Clamp Down With High-Tech Export Controls', *Defense Electronics*, September 1982, p. 87; see also James A. Dukowitz, 'A Business Perspective on Export Controls', *Signal*, August 1983, pp. 98-101; Lenny Siegel, 'Silicon Valley's Growing Disillusionment with Pentagon', *San Francisco Sunday Examiner and Chronicle*, 8 January, 1984, p. B2.

11. Kaufman, 'Changing US Attitudes', p. 19.

12. Richard Halloran, 'Pentagon Draws Up First Strategy for Fighting a Long Nuclear War', *New York Times*, 30 May 1982, p. 12.

13. R.W. Davies in R. Amann, J. Cooper, R.W. Davies (eds), *The Technological Level of Soviet Industry* (Yale University Press, New Haven and London, 1977), p. 66.

14. *The FY 1981 Department of Defense Program for Research, Development and Acquisition*, statement by the Honorable William T. Perry, Under Secretary of Defense, Research and Engineering to the 96th Congress, in United States House of Representatives, Research and Engineering, Title II, Hearings before the Committee on Armed Forces (US Government Printing Office, Washington, DC, 1980), p. 82.

15. *The FY 1983 Department of Defense Program for Research, Development and Acquisition*, statement by the Honorable Richard D. DeLauer, Under Secretary of Defense, Research and Engineering to the 97th Congress, Second Session (US Government Printing Office, Washington, DC, 1982), part 2, p. 21.

16. Robert A. Lewis, 'Some Aspects of the Research and Development Effort in the Soviet Union, 1924-1935', *Science Studies*, no. 2 (1972), p. 164.

17. Louvan E. Nolting and Murray Feshbach, 'R&D Employment in the USSR — Definitions, Statistics and Comparisons', in United States Congress, Joint Economic Committee, *Soviet Economy in a Time of Change*, vol. 1 (US Government Printing Office, Washington, DC, 1979), p. 746; see also Julian Cooper, *Scientists and Soviet Industry: A Statistical Analysis*, CREES Discussion Papers, Series RC/B17, University of Birmingham, England, p. 48.

18. For a discussion of these issues see R. Amann, 'Industrial Innovation in the Soviet Union: Methodological Perspectives and Conclusions' in Amann and Cooper (eds), *Industrial Innovation*, pp. 1-38.

19. See my 'Innovation in the Defence Sector' in Amann and Cooper (eds), *Industrial Innovation*, pp. 276-367.

20. D. Holloway, 'Military Technology' in Amann, Cooper and Davies (eds), *Technological Level*, pp. 407-89.

21. United States Congress, Joint Economic Committee, *Allocation of Resources in the Soviet Union and China — 1981*, Hearings before the Subcommittee on International Trade, Finance, and Security Economics, part 7 (US Government Printing Office, Washington, DC, 1982), p. 125.

22. United States Congress, Joint Economic Committee, *Allocation of Resources in the Soviet Union and China — 1976*, Hearings before the Subcommittee on International Trade, Finance, and Security Economics, part 2 (US Government Printing Office, Washington, DC, 1977), p. 67.

23. United States Congress, Joint Economic Committee, *Allocation of Resources in the Soviet Union and China — 1977*, Hearings before the Subcommittee on International Trade, Finance, and Security Economics, part 3 (US Government Printing Office, Washington, DC, 1978), p. 40.

24. See notes 14 and 15.

25. See James Fallows, *National Defense* (Vintage Books, New York, 1982), pp. 173-5; and Mary Kaldor, *The Baroque Arsenal* (Andre Deutsch, London, 1982).

26. Quoted in G.A. Ozerov, *Tupolevskaya Sharaga*, 2nd edn (Possev, Frankfurt-am-Main, 1973), p. 57.

27. See David Holloway, *The Soviet Union and the Arms Race* (Yale University Press, New Haven and London, 1983), pp. 15-28.

28. National Foreign Assessment Center, Central Intelligence Agency, *Estimated Soviet Defense Spending: Trends and Prospects*, SR 78-10121, June 1978, p. 3.

29. *Sovyetskaya Voyennaya Entsiklopediya*, vol. 2 (Voyenizdat, Moscow, 1976), p. 253.

30. Antony C. Sutton, *Western Technology and Soviet Economic Development, 1917-65* (3 vols., Hoover Institution Press, Stanford, CA 1968, 1971, 1973).

31. See Sutton, *Western Technology*, vol. 3 (1945-1965), Chapters 20 and 23.

32. CIA, 'Soviet Acquisition', p. 94.

33. Quoted in National Academy of Sciences, *Scientific Communication and National Security* (National Academy Press, Washington, DC, 1982), p. 140.

34. CIA, 'Soviet Acquisition', p. 95.

35. Warren Brown, 'US Computer Seized on Way to the USSR', *Washington Post*, 16 November 1983, p. D1.

36. CIA, 'Soviet Acquisition', p. 104.

37. The number of scientists in radio-electronics grew from 88,997 in 1968 to 173,055 in 1977; see Cooper, *Scientists*, p. 45. On Shabanov see *Voyennyi Entsiklopedicheskii Slovar'* (Voyenizdat, Moscow, 1983), p. 812.

38. CIA, 'Soviet Acquisition', p. 99.

39. Robert P. Berman and John C. Baker, *Soviet Strategic Forces: Requirements and Responses* (Brookings Institution, Washington, DC, 1982), p. 121.

40. CIA, 'Soviet Acquisition', p. 101.

41. Ibid., p. 98.

42. This outline of the early Soviet nuclear project draws on Holloway, *Soviet Union*, pp. 15-28, and David Holloway, 'Entering the Nuclear Arms Race: The Soviet Decision to Build the Atomic Bomb, 1939-45', *Social Studies of Science*, vol. 11 (1981), pp. 159-97.

43. Hanson, 'Soviet System', p. 449.

44. US Senate, Permanent Subcommittee on Investigations, *Transfer of United States High Technology*, p. 7.

45. Ibid., p. 5. The official is Dr Jack Vorona of the Defense Intelligence Agency.

46. This is made clear in Bruce Parrott's excellent book *Politics and Technology in the Soviet Union* (MIT Press, Cambridge, MA, 1983).

9 WESTERN POLICIES ON EAST-WEST TRADE AND TECHNOLOGY*

Stephen Woolcock

Introduction

This chapter discusses the East-West trade policies of the Western alliance. It considers briefly the general issues involved in Western policy-making which are seen as falling into roughly three categories; those concerning the strategic, political and commercial objectives of East-West trade policy. Although these general issues have changed little over the past 30 years, there have been important changes in the approaches of the major Western countries. These shifts and the problems they have caused for common Western policies are discussed in detail as are the current trends. The chapter also considers the question of who takes the lead in the West in trying to formulate Western policy and how this is likely to influence future developments. The general conclusion of the chapter is that whilst some of the tension has been removed from the transatlantic debate following the lifting of the US pipeline embargo in November 1982, important differences in approach still exist. A long-term and above all consistent effort will be needed if fundamental differences in the US and European perceptions of the strategic importance of East-West economic relations are to be contained and major rifts avoided. Greater consistency, above all in US policy objectives, is needed if progress is to be made towards reconciling differences of interest on more detailed policy issues.

The Issues Involved

The general issues in Western policies on trade with the European CMEA countries have changed little over the past 30 years, and have been extensively discussed.[1] Nevertheless, they need to be briefly restated because they continue to have an impact on how policy-makers influence the current general approach to trade with

188

the East as well as the detailed policy issues. Perhaps the most important issue is whether East-West economic relations should serve Western *strategic objectives,* and if so, how? Should the West adopt a general policy of, for example, denying the Soviet Union, or any other country, the benefits of trade? Such an approach is often based on the perception that Western denial of trade would weaken the Soviet economy and thus force it to make difficult choices between military and civil investment. It is also sometimes argued that this would force the Soviet Union either to reform its inefficient economic system, which would have important socio-political implications, or to reduce growth in military spending. This economic containment approach would in effect represent a return to policies pursued by the United States during the 1950s.

Opponents of this view argue that important military expenditure will take place no matter what happens in the Soviet economy, that the Soviet Union is well placed to survive economic autarky and is therefore unlikely to be significantly affected by such a Western policy even if it were possible to implement such a policy effectively. An alternative strategic approach, which is by no means shared by all those who oppose economic containment policies, is to use economic relations to enhance political stability or even encourage political *rapprochement.* Variants of this argument include the moderating effect of prosperity on Soviet policy. A common distinguishing factor about such strategic approaches is that they are of a long-term and general nature.

The second type of issue concerns shorter-term *political objectives,* such as the use of economic relations as a lever in order to induce a particular policy response from the Soviet Union on a specific issue. A common example of such a political objective is the attempt to use sanctions as an instrument in the pursuit of a particular foreign policy objective, such as the withdrawal of Soviet troops from Afghanistan. In many such cases sanctions tend to take the form of retribution. This use of economic relations is criticised by those who favour maintaining economic links as well as by those who believe that sanctions are most effective as a threat. The political objective pursued can also be to encourage the Soviet Union to do something, such as increase emigration, and can take the form of either positive inducements or sanctions. Even when sanctions are unlikely to reverse Soviet policy they are still considered necessary, on occasions, as a means of expressing condemnation of a particular Soviet act, or as a means of sending a signal that similar acts will be penalised in the future. Sanctions are also introduced for domestic political reasons, or quite simply to be seen to be doing something in response to a particular Soviet act.

The third set of policy objectives involves *commercial policy.* Here one is primarily concerned with the efforts of Western governments to devise rules for the conduct of trade and economic relations between economies of different political systems. The centralised nature of the CMEA countries' trade policy, and in particular the monopsonist powers of trade ministries, means that rules or norms have to be devised in the West to ensure that trade is mutually beneficial, and that the East does not play off one Western supplier against another in order to gain an unfair advantage. One area of particular importance in recent years has been that of credit, where the Western allies have been at pains to find a common interpretation of what constitutes sound commercial sense and what is a subsidy in the provision of credit to the East.

In addition to these general policy issues there are also a number of important subsidiary questions, such as the degree to which interdependence or dependence exists in East-West trade. There are also the difficult but important questions concerning the effectiveness of any given Western policy in terms of its impact on the Soviet economy and Soviet decision-making process. The ability of one country, no matter how large, to pursue unilateral policies on East-West trade is also an important issue when considering Western policy. Finally there is the whole question of whether a common Western front can be achieved on any given policy, and whether the costs of any policy for the West, in terms of its impact on West-West trade as much as East-West trade, outweigh the costs imposed on the East.

Fundamental Differences in Approach

The most enduring source of tension in the discussions on Western policies is the difference between the United States and the West European perceptions of the strategic role of East-West economic relations. The United States, with generally far less trade at stake but with responsibility for Western security, has always emphasised the strategic importance of East-West economic relations. European governments, with more trade and less responsibility for

general Western security, have tended to place far greater importance on commercial objectives. Whilst it is not always explicit,
West European governments believe that economic relations can
contribute to stability in East-West relations, even if, after the
demise of superpower detente, they seldom see trade as a means of
promoting better relations.

One area in which US and European approaches converge is in
the use of security export controls to deny the Soviet Union goods
and technologies of military importance. There has been a consensus on the need for such controls for some time, as has been
exhibited in the work of CoCom. It is important here to recognise
the distinction between the objectives of narrowly defined national
security export controls co-ordinated in CoCom, and economic
containment. There are of course considerable difficulties in
defining what is of military importance and therefore of importance
to Western security, and what is not.

Problems with the second group of issues concerning political
objective arise from the fact that the United States has generally
made far wider use of economic relations with the East as a means
of exercising leverage in the pursuit of particular political objectives. This compares with general European scepticism of the
effectiveness of such leverage. If one leaves aside the question of
effectiveness, the United States, in its role as a superpower, has
and will continue to find a need to use sanctions as a means of
responding to particular Soviet acts when there are few or no other
options. With more at stake in East-West trade the West European
governments have been far more restrained in the use of such
sanctions. While they recognise the need to respond to, for
example, the Soviet invasion of Afghanistan, they will generally
not introduce sanctions which cost the West more than the East.
When weighing up the use of sanctions, they also take more
account of the long-term costs of disrupting East-West economic
relations with on-off light-switch diplomacy than the United
States, which is generally more preoccupied with the short-term
political costs of doing nothing.

The differences on commercial policy objectives are, as with
CoCom, of a more technical rather than fundamental nature. The
structure of East-West trade and finance is, of course, of considerable importance here, especially when one considers that
East-West trade is very much a European affair. Western Europe
accounts for about 90 per cent of all OECD imports from the

European CMEA countries, and about 80 per cent of all OECD exports. West European banks also hold the bulk of Eastern debt.[2] Whilst the Europeans are more engaged in East-West trade it would be wrong to conclude that they are excessively dependent on the East. Apart from a slight increase in the mid-1970s, East-West trade as a proportion of total trade has remained at about 3 per cent for most of the West European economies since trade relations with the East were re-established in the 1960s. The one exception is the Federal Republic of Germany, for which trade with the East, including intra-German trade with the GDR, accounts for about 7 per cent of total trade. This reflects the FRG's pre-eminence in East-West trade in which it accounts for no less than a quarter of total OECD-CMEA trade.[3]

It is not only the level of trade which affects Western policies but also the structure of trade. Japan and the West European economies all export mainly machinery and industrial equipment to the East and import energy and raw materials. This is particularly the case with the Soviet Union, whilst trade with the other East European CMEA countries is less compensatory and more complementary. Industrial goods account for about 80 per cent of European and Japanese exports, and energy and raw materials account for most imports. In contrast, 80 per cent of US exports to the East consist of agricultural goods and raw materials, with imports being too small to have much effect on policy. These trade patterns are clearly reflected in Europe's reluctance to disrupt trade in industrial products, and, with the exception of 1979-80, US reluctance to disrupt trade in grain.

A further complicating factor in the formulation of Western policies is the question of leadership. As a superpower the US claims a leadership role in matters concerning Western security. When it comes to economic, and in particular trade issues however, Western Europe has become a power unto itself. The reason East-West economic relations are so problematic for the alliance is that more than any other field of policy they constitute a compound of strategic/security issues, in which US leadership prevails, and economic issues, in which Western Europe is equally powerful. In the absence of any clear leader the question of who determines the course of East-West trade policy is therefore a source of dispute within the alliance.

US Leadership

In the late 1940s the United States steered Western policy towards economic containment of the Soviet Union. A common approach to East-West trade was facilitated more by US economic and political dominance than by a genuine consensus with the Europeans.[4] Even at this time the French and British in particular had reservations about pursuing such a policy, but reconstruction of the West was seen as more important than trade with the East. As the United States linked the provision of economic and military aid to support for its policy of economic containment, the West Europeans were obliged to follow the US lead.[5]

As the West European economies gained in strength and sought to re-establish economic relations with the East, US leadership began a long process of erosion. Throughout the 1950s, and especially during the 1960s, the Europeans, again led by Britain and France, pressed for a liberalisation of CoCom controls. The pursuit of economic containment had never been supported with any conviction in Europe, and as the 1960s progressed competition for Eastern export markets increased. In so far as strategic considerations played any role there was a difference between US containment and a European desire to ease tensions in Europe and to build bridges with the East. There was, however, widespread support for the use of CoCom as a means of denying the Soviet Union goods and technologies which contributed directly to its military effort. The European governments sought to narrow controls to such items and liberalise other controls. Throughout the 1960s a *modus vivendi* developed within the context of CoCom. The US national controls remained more extensive than the national control lists in Europe, but differences over what should be controlled were generally reconciled through painstaking negotiations on the regular CoCom list reviews. There were very few issues concerning commercial policy objectives during this period. Western countries were still in the process of re-establishing trading links from a low base so there was less trade and thus less need to devise norms or rules. It was also not until the late 1960s that the CMEA countries started drawing on Western credit in order to finance trade with the West, thus creating a need for a Western policy on credit.

The 1962-3 Pipe Embargo

The striking parallels between the 1962-3 pipe embargo and the 1982 pipeline embargo help to illustrate how little the fundamental issues have changed. In 1962 the United States wished to prevent West European companies supplying pipe to help in the construction of the 'friendship' pipeline which was to carry oil from the Soviet oil fields to Eastern Europe. As in the later 1982 pipeline case, the US saw the construction of the pipeline as an issue of strategic importance, whereas the Europeans saw it mainly as a commercial proposition to sell large diameter pipe. American policy at the time, as expressed in the 1962 version of the Export Control Act, continued to be one of economic containment. The 1962 Act referred to the need to control exports of strategic and economic importance. US policy was summed up by W.W. Rostow as follows: 'From the standpoint of the United States the system [of CoCom controls] has been intricately interwoven into our overall strategic thinking about the cold war and in our cold war posture. Trade denial is looked upon as an effective weapon of cold war regardless of how large or how small the quantities involved may be, on the simple assumption that since the US is richer than the USSR any trade between the two must necessarily help the USSR more than the US.'[6]

In 1962 the United States first tried to embargo the pipe in CoCom but was opposed by the British. There was then a great deal of pressure exerted on the Federal Republic of Germany, which was the main supplier, and Adenauer finally agreed to support the US embargo. The US wished, however, not only to prevent the pipeline being constructed but also to 'coordinate and alter the East-West trade policies of its European allies',[7] who were at that time moving towards a more liberal approach to East-West trade. The West Germans, who were less able to pursue an independent policy than other European countries, supported the US embargo, but the British and Italians supplied the pipe. This lesson in the effectiveness of embargoes when they are not supported by all major exporters, is one the Germans did not forget when, 20 years later, they were again the main target of US pressure to prevent the 1982 Urengoy gas pipeline deal. The 1962 embargoes, it also illustrates that even at that time the ability of embargoes, it also illustrated that even at that time the ability of the US to exercise leadership on East-West trade issues was already on the decline.

During the 1960s a form of consensus emerged. Strategic issues were left largely in abeyance, and CoCom controls were more narrowly defined and economic controls relaxed.[8] During a brief period between 1969 and 1975 US and European perceptions converged during the period of US-Soviet detente. At this time the Kissinger-Nixon policy of linkage sought to use economic relations both as a carrot, to induce the Soviet Union into easing political tensions, and as a stick, to punish any actions the US disliked. Kissinger also envisaged a web of mutual interdependencies between East and West which would enhance stability and act as a mutual constraint on the two superpowers. The US linkage policies introduced a strong political element, in that progress in political detente was closely associated with continued trade and economic relations. Whilst Kissinger's approach to linkage or leverage was more subtle than could be implemented given the US political climate and involvement of Congress,[9] it still raised expectations about political progress, which, when not fulfilled, had a negative impact on US trade relations with the CMEA countries. In brief, US disillusionment with detente resulted in a reversion to restrictive approaches to trade in the mid-1970s. Throughout the 1970s an attempt was made to pursue forms of linkage policies or economic diplomacy,[10] but there was little evident success in the political objectives sought. There was also a progressive shift towards more general and more restrictive export controls. In Europe, economic relations remained largely insulated from the political setbacks because of a greater commitment to detente, and the fact that the European approach to detente also differed from that of the United States in the sense that Europeans saw it as a long-term process in which short-term setbacks did not totally invalidate the concept of wishing to seek a closer understanding with the East.[11]

Carter and Afghanistan

The Carter administration's policy on East-West trade pursued a number of objectives. On technology control the Carter administration was influenced by the so-called Bucy Report which was published in 1976.[12] This advocated a shift from controls on hardware to controls on technological know-how and led to the recommendation, made in 1979, that CoCom should monitor if not control large-scale compensation trade projects such as chemical or metallurgical plant projects, because these facilitated the transfer of 'critical technologies'.[13] The Bucy Report, and the Carter administration's policy which sought to put some of its recommendations into practice, was ambiguous on whether critical technologies were to be embargoed regardless of their use, or only if they had a military application. This ambiguity meant that the Europeans were not clear whether the proposed changes in CoCom represented a shift back towards an economic denial approach or merely an improvement on the existing controls.

Under President Carter the United States made increased use of foreign policy export controls in pursuit of political objectives. For example, in 1978 exports of computers were banned in response to Soviet treatment of dissidents. The 1978 foreign policy sanctions also involved making oil and gas equipment subject to US foreign policy controls, a move which opened the way for the Urengoy pipeline embargo. The Carter administration's policy was to deny exports of technology or machines to make equipment, but not the equipment itself. The West Europeans did not support this policy and even allowed their exporters to replace orders lost by US exporters due to unilateral US sanctions.

On the commercial policy front the US did raise the issue of the provision of subsidised Western credit. In the mid-1970s a number of West European countries had extended credit lines to the Soviet Union at preferential rates. As the United States provided no credit to the Soviet Union following the Stevenson Amendment in 1975, there was clearly concern about unfair competition from the Europeans. In the mid-1970s there was also a growing concern that Europe was becoming increasingly dependent on economic relations with the East. Seen from a US strategic point of view such interdependence was considered dangerous because it might eventually result in Western Europe becoming hostage to its economic ties with the East which would inhibit it in any crisis.

The reluctance of the Europeans to respond with economic sanctions following the Soviet invasion of Afghanistan in December 1979 also tended to confirm this view that the Europeans were becoming too dependent on trade with the East.[14] The United States, however, felt compelled to respond in some way to the Soviet invasion, and the only way of doing so was to introduce economic sanctions. These took the form of the grain embargo and a freeze on exports of technology followed by efforts to tighten up on CoCom controls on certain items such as computers. There was also increased effort to get the Europeans to stop providing subsidised credit.

The Europeans did not support the foreign policy sanctions, but only agreed not to undermine the US measures. With regard to at least two contracts for industrial plant, European suppliers did in fact take up orders similar to US orders stopped by the sanctions. In CoCom there appears to have been some support for improving controls but there were doubts in Europe about the United States objectives.[15] Some European countries stopped credit lines, but in the case of the United Kingdom, for example, it was already government policy to do so before the invasion took place. Rather than a convergence, Afghanistan resulted in a divergence between the US and European positions with the United States pursuing what was in effect an independent policy of sanctions. Europe recognised that the United States needed to respond with sanctions, but was not prepared to use sanctions as a means of signalling Western condemnation of the Soviet actions if it was going to be more costly for the West.

The Reagan Administration

The incoming Reagan administration also saw the reluctance of the Europeans to support US policy over Afghanistan as confirmation of the view that they were becoming too dependent on trade with the East, and that therefore only the United States could lead the West towards policies which took proper account of the real strategic issues involved in East-West economic relations. The inability to forge a common policy over Afghanistan was put down to the weakness of the Carter administration and its inability to provide strong leadership. In short, President Reagan was determined to re-establish US leadership in the field of East-West trade policy. Influenced by its tough anti-Soviet position, the Reagan administration sought to lead the West towards a far more restrictive approach to East-West trade.

The Reagan administration, or parts of it, had, however, learnt the problems of applying economic embargoes as a flexible instrument of economic diplomacy. Indeed the policy adopted by the Reagan administration was more consistent than previous administrations in the sense that the objective was strategic and therefore less changeable than the flexible economic diplomacy of the Carter administration. The Soviet economy was seen as being fundamentally flawed, and consequently the provision of Western technology or credits was merely delaying the inevitable demise of the Soviet economy and thus helping it in its military effort. As in the 1950s, the Reagan administration made the link between trade and the US defence budget, arguing that allowing the Soviet Union the benefits of trade meant the US had to spend more to match the resultant increased Soviet military spending.[16] The Urengoy pipeline was seen as 'an economic lifeline from the West which offers perhaps the final opportunity for the Soviet leadership to bail out a bankrupt and failing system'.[17]

Whilst this may have only been rhetoric, it gave the impression that the Reagan administration was pursuing a policy of economic containment. Consequently the Europeans were very suspicious of US initiatives in CoCom and on credit. The US initiatives stemmed from an internal policy review in 1981 and were launched at the Western economic summit in Ottawa because the Reagan administration was aware of the need to have a co-ordinated Western approach if its policy of neo-economic containment was to succeed.[18] The Ottawa communiqué included reference to an agreement to 'consult to improve the present system of controls on trade and strategic goods and related technology with the USSR', but little progress was made on this and other issues such as credit before the declaration of martial law in Poland, and the introduction, once again, of unilateral US sanctions in December 1981. The declaration of martial law in Poland was used by those seeking more restrictive policies as a justification for precipitative action. The original US opposition to the pipeline, repeatedly expressed during 1981, was justified in terms of the negative effects of increasing West European dependence on Soviet energy supplies.[19] In the event the main objective was in fact to deny the Soviet Union the hard currency earnings from exporting gas through the pipeline.

The nature of the initial December 1981 US embargo measures meant that its effects on the West European companies concerned took some time to work through. Most European contractors had delivery dates in the summer of 1982, so that the US ban on re-export of US parts allowed some time to negotiate a compromise. At a special NATO meeting in January 1982 the allies agreed to consider the 'longer-term East-West economic relations, particularly energy, agricultural commodities and the export of technology, in the light of the changed situation and of the need to protect [NATO's] competitive position in the field of military *and* technological capabilities' (emphasis added).[20] During the spring of 1982 negotiations were held with a view to reaching a compromise between the European and US positions. The Europeans hoped for an end to the US embargo on pipeline equipment because they wished to continue with the project and opposed US interference at such a late date in a project they believed did not clash with their strategic interests. In return there were suggestions that the Europeans might tighten up on CoCom controls and credit and thus satisfy at least the minimum objectives of the US policy launched in 1981. The United States also had proposals for improving the institutional framework of CoCom, including the creation of a special military advisory committee and a strengthening of the secretariat.

Some progress towards a consensus was made in the run-up to the Versailles summit. The West Europeans had agreed on limited economic sanctions in the form of import controls on certain marginal Soviet exports. This was as much a signal to Washington as it was to Moscow, and was done in the knowledge that it would not have the slightest impact on what happened in Poland. These sanctions were finally allowed to expire at the end of 1983. In CoCom there was an agreement to talk about ways of improving existing controls by reviewing the respective national control procedures and improving exchanges of information. The Europeans were also prepared to talk about US proposals on the use of critical technology as a criterion within the regular triannual CoCom list review which was due to commence in 1982. But this entailed detailed work which meant that results could not be expected to emerge for some months if not years. European governments also rejected the proposals for a creation of a military committee to CoCom, which would shift the bias in CoCom away from commercial to strategic concerns.

On the credit issue progress was also made. With some French reservations, the EEC agreed to reclassify the Soviet Union, and the GDR, so that they attracted the maximum rate of interest within the OECD arrangement on export credit guarantees. There was also support for higher interest rates to reduce the subsidy element in the provision of credit still further, but there was no increase in rates or agreement on the reclassification of the Soviet Union until after the Versailles summit. The delay was partly due to the complexities of the issue, and to the fact that other OECD countries resisted singling out the Soviet Union for special treatment, but, together with the inevitably slow pace of work in CoCom it resulted in frustration among the hard-liners in Washington.

At the Versailles summit itself, an attempt was made to move forward faster, but the summit communiqué referred only vaguely to the need for 'commercial prudence in limiting export credits'.[21] This was interpreted as introducing new limits on export credit by the US. When, however, the Europeans interpreted it as a definition of their present policies, it was clear that the US objective of bringing about a major reappraisal of East-West trade and financial policies was still no closer to realisation. In Washington there was temporarily no effective Secretary of State as Mr Haig was in the process of leaving the administration. Consequently the hard-line anti-traders had a tactical advantage in the interdepartmental turf battle over control of policy. With one or two policy advisors President Reagan decided to extend the pipeline embargo by seeking to apply US controls extraterritorially on licensees of US technology, US subsidiaries and other foreign companies with links in the US. This decision was taken despite knowledge of the fact that such measures would result in a direct conflict with the European allies.

Contrary to the earlier belief that strong US leadership would bring about a change in European policy, the major countries concerned openly defied the US legal measures and the embargo policy.[22] They did so for a number of reasons, the first being a continued belief in detente as defined in Western Europe. The Europeans believed that at times of heightened political tensions it was necessary both to respond to Soviet military build-ups but also to maintain channels of communication and seek to ease tensions, and trade was seen as one channel of communication. The Europeans were also concerned that breaking contacts for political reasons could set a dangerous precedent. Second, European policy-makers did not share the view that a Soviet economic collapse was imminent, or could be accelerated by a policy of economic containment or denial, nor did they believe that attempting to punish the Soviet Union would have any effect on political freedoms in Poland. In addition there were also economic and legal issues at stake. The contracts for equipment were clearly of economic importance to a number of companies. Furthermore,

European support for a restrictive US approach to East-West trade could have a general depressive effect on trade at a time when it was already stagnating if not declining. Probably most important, however, was the reaction to what was seen as a crude American attempt to force the European governments to follow the US leadership down a path the Europeans had no desire to follow. The interests of the various European countries varied, of course. Britain was probably more disposed to give the US case a sympathetic hearing but totally rejected the extraterritorial application of US controls because they infringed British sovereignty. France also rejected the attempt to impose US policy on Europe, whereas in the FRG and Italy economic interests were of equal importance.[23]

After the Pipeline

The ending of the pipeline embargo in late 1982 resolved neither the question of fundamental differences in approach, nor the more specific issues such as CoCom, credit or energy dependence. The only positive effect of the embargo and the major rift in US-European relations which resulted, was, at best, that the Europeans were forced to reappraise seriously their policy on East-West economic relations. The result of the reappraisal, however, was not the significant change of policy the US sought, but a strengthening of the European desire to continue, with a few minor changes, with the *status quo.*

In many ways, therefore, November 1982 saw the status of debate on Western policies back to where it was before the Versailles summit or possibly earlier. At the time the embargo was lifted Secretary of State Schultz was able to reach agreement to continue talks on these issues,[24] and six studies were initiated. These were to continue the work of CoCom on the 1982 list review process, discussions on 'other high technology', OECD studies on East-West credit flows and energy questions, and general studies by the OECD and the NATO secretariat on the general economic trends and strategic issues involved. There was initially some suggestion that the results of these studies would be needed before the Williamsburg summit in 1983, but in the event slower progress was accepted as a means of avoiding another transatlantic clash. Until shortly before the summit there was still some doubt about the US strategy. Some in the Administration argued for maintaining pressure on the European allies in order to get them to change their general approach to the issue; others, however, argued for a return to a less aggressive strategy. After President Reagan was prevailed upon by his closest West European political allies in the form of Mrs Thatcher and Herr Kohl, not to press the aggressive approach, the US relented. The fact that East-West trade was scarcely discussed at the Williamsburg and London summits in 1983 and 1984, was, however, more a recognition of differences rather a reflection of agreement.

The six studies produced little in the way of concrete results. They did, however, provide an opportunity for the United States to retract its embargo policy without an obvious loss of face. Three years after the lifting of the embargo, it now seems clear that it has been the United States rather than West European governments which has been forced to reassess its policy, or at least strategy, in the light of the 1982 transatlantic conflict.

Tension has been eased in a number of areas, but the potential for a renewed conflict over East-West trade policy remains. It would only take a major event in East-West political relations to once again bring out differences over the use of sanctions or foreign policy controls. Whether the ongoing debate on strategic exports (or national security controls) in CoCom will result in continued conflict will depend, to a very large extent, on the outcome of the current reassessment of US policy.

Tensions over credit and energy issues in East-West economic relations have eased because of economic needs. Western banks have changed their credit policy *vis-à-vis* the East so that if anything there is possibly a shortage of Eastern credit rather than competition within the West to supply cheap credit. There are still issues concerning credit, but the bitterness and urgency has left the debate. Similarly, on the question of energy, a decline in demand in the West has resulted in Western gas companies seeking to reduce the volumes of gas they are buying from the East. In the long or even medium term new gas contracts can, however, be expected, so that the potential for renewed tensions also exists in this field. There has also been some easing of tensions in the field of technology controls in CoCom, where agreement was finally reached in July 1984 on the revised lists for computers and telecommunications equipment.[25] This agreement effectively completed the list review process started in 1982 that had been delayed, largely by disputes within the US administration. In particular the Department of Defense clashed with the State Department in the autumn of 1983 over whether the US should cooperate with the Europeans and reach agreement on the new lists on a give and take basis, or whether it should continue to maintain pressure on the allies in order to get them to accept more restrictive policies.[26] Ultimately the US adopted a more conciliatory tactic, in order to get agreement. There should, however, be no confusion between strategy and fundamental policy. The United States has always been and remains in favour of generally more restrictive controls.

Differences continue to exist over security controls as they have for the past 40 years;[27] whether they will again flare up into a major transatlantic dispute depends very largely on the United States, because having followed the U-turns and inconsistencies in US policy under the Reagan administration, West European governments will be even less inclined to follow the US policy lead in the future than they have in the past. The debate within the United States has focused on the renewal of the export control legislation. After two years of work which produced two main bills, S 979 and HR 3213, the US Congress failed to agree on legislation before the end of the 98th Congress, despite a last attempt to reach a compromise. This failure to agree on new legislation was due to the resurgence of business and exporting lobbies, who returned to the policy debate, after their absence in the first two years of the Reagan administration, because of the threat to US export markets in the West caused by efforts to make East-West controls more effective.

Following the lifting of the pipeline embargo the interests of the still strong security lobbies in the United States shifted from foreign policy controls to national security controls. In order to make the existing controls more effective and prevent diversion of US technology to the USSR, the Department of Defense sought to tighten US licensing procedures. This involved a number of proposed changes in the way licences were granted, but most importantly it involved a greater role for the Department of Defense in reviewing licences for exports to other Western countries, as well as various steps to increase the amount of information available on the whereabouts of any piece of US equipment at any one time.

These proposals caused a number of problems for, in the first instance, US exporters. First, greater DoD review threatened to cause further delay in obtaining licences. US exporters, backed by other government departments such as the US Trade Representative and the Department of Commerce, were seeking to liberalise trade in high technology in order to capitalise on the US competitive advantage in such industries by increasing exports. Increased delays in obtaining licences therefore threatened to increase domestic controls on exports at a time when the rest of the government was trying to remove foreign constraints on US exports. There were also proposals to change procedures for granting general licences, which facilitate trade between US parent companies and their foreign affiliates without licensing delays.[28] These proposals would have tightened the general licensing procedures and also resulted in US companies becoming instruments of the extraterritorial reach of US export control legislation. This would have happened by US exporters having to obtain information about foreign customers before being granted a US licence. The proposals were modified in September 1984 due to the degree of domestic opposition. At present, however, the administration has discretion over rule-making in the field of licensing, with the result that some tightening has taken place even while Congress debates the issue.

The new requirements concerning information about the resale or movement of US technology once it has been sold to other Western customers caused considerable controversy in 1984. In the light of the requirements on information, IBM wrote to its customers reminding them of their obligations, under US export control legislation, to provide information. This provoked a strong reaction from European governments, who are totally opposed to the extraterritorial application of US export controls. As governments would refuse to provide such information themselves, access by US companies to public procurement markets, which are vital in sectors such as computers and telecommunications, was therefore threatened by the efforts to make existing controls effective. This led IBM, for example, to become openly engaged in lobbying for an easing of licensing requirements for trade with other Western countries. The presence of such powerful lobbies in the US debate therefore redresses the bias towards security interests that had existed in US policy for the first years of the Reagan administration; and this came about because of the threat to Western, not Eastern, markets. But although the balance has been redressed there is no consensus in the United States. Indeed the differences between the security and economic interests over the form of US export control policy are probably as deep-seated today as they ever have been.

This continued lack of consensus in the United States, which is likely to get worse rather than better when the debate reverts to the merits and disadvantages of trading with the East, contrasts with the stable consensus that exists in each West European country.[29] The current disagreement in the US is exacerbated by a ferocious turf battle within the Reagan administration between the traditional players of the Department of Defense in favour of tighter controls, the Commerce Department wanting to promote US exports, and the State Department wishing a co-operative rather than confrontational approach in talks with the allies. The future course of US policy will turn on this turf battle, as well as the related battle in Congress between the two different approaches represented by the House and Senate bills in the 98th Congress. The House bill was favoured by business interests, whereas the Senate bill was favoured by the security lobbies.[30] At the end of the 98th Congress in October 1984 an effort to find a compromise between these two approaches failed because of differences over the role the Department of Defense should have in the administration of US export licensing on a day-to-day basis, and in particular its role in reviewing licences for exports to Western countries.

The Department of Defense has been consistent in its efforts to make US export controls both more effective and more restrictive, even at the expense of US exports. It also believes that the West Europeans will not be persuaded to accept the more restrictive US approach to controls, unless some leverage is used. Consequently an effective veto over exports to the West in the hands of the Department of Defense could have far-reaching implications for US-European relations. It would in effect mean that exports to a Western country would be denied if the DoD felt the export control procedures of that country were inadequate. This would increase the potential for conflicts not unlike the 1982 clash over the pipeline embargo. The potential for such conflict would, however, be decreased if there were more checks and balances built into the US export control administration, such as those which have been proposed in the House bill (HR 3213). In the proposed legislation Congress would set new controls on executive discre-

tion, including its discretion to give the DoD more powers. As no
legislation has been passed, the administration is continuing to
operate on the International Economic Emergency Powers Act.
Under this law the executive has even more discretionary powers
than it had under the Export Administration Act of 1979. If this
stop-gap solution becomes permanent, which is not impossible
although there are complex legal issues involved, US policy would
be totally unrestrained by any checks or balances and would
depend heavily on the outcome of the turf battles within the
administration. Given the lack of consensus in the United States
on trade and economic relations with the CMEA countries, this
would be a prescription for continued uncertainty.

Notes

'This chapter is based on work conducted by the author while Research Fellow at
the Royal Institute of International Affairs (Chatham House), London.
    1. See Philip Hanson, *Trade and Technology in Soviet-Western Relations*
(Macmillan, London, 1981), for a recent evaluation of these questions.
    2. Klaus Schroeder, 'Rescheduling the Debts of CMEA Countries',
Aussenpolitik, vol. 34, no. 21 (1983).
    3. See Gunnar Adler-Karlsson, *Western Economic Warfare 1947-1967: A
Case Study in Foreign Economic Policy* (Almqvist and Wiksell, Stockholm, 1968).
For a current treatment of the topic of economic warfare, see also Reinhard Rode
and Hanns-Dieter Jacobsen (eds), *Economic Warfare or Detente? Ein Bilanz zu
Beginn der achtziger Jahre* (Verlag Neue Gessellschaft, Bonn, 1984).
    4. Hanns-Dieter Jacobsen, *Die Ost-West-Wirtschaftsbeziehungen als
Deutsch-Amerikanisches Problem* (Stiftung Wissenschaft und Politik, Ebenhausen,
1983).
    5. Ibid.
    6. W.W. Rostow, quoted in Angela Stent, *From Embargo to Ostpolitik: The
Political Economy of West German — Soviet Relations 1955-1980* (Cambridge
University Press, Cambridge, 1981), p. 93.
    7. Stent, *Embargo*, p. 94.
    8. This period has been termed the 'laissez faire' phase in East-West trade.
See Samuel Huntington, 'Trade, Technology and Leverage', *Foreign Policy*, no. 32
(Fall 1978).
    9. See, for example, Henry Kissinger, *The White House Years* (Weidenfeld
and Nicolson, London, 1979), pp. 150-5.
    10. Huntington, 'Trade, Technology and Leverage'.
    11. See, for example, Hans-Dietrich Genscher, 'Towards an Overall Western
Strategy for Peace, Freedom and Progress', *Foreign Affairs*, vol. 61, no. 1 (Fall,
1982).
    12. Office of the Director of Defense Research and Engineering, *An Analysis
of Export Control of US Technology — A DoD Perspective*, A Report of the
Defense Science Board Task Force on Export of US Technology, Washington, DC,
4 February 1976.
    13. Stephen Woolcock, *Western Policies on East-West Trade*, Chatham House

Papers 15 (Royal Institute of International Affairs/Routledge and Kegan Paul, London, 1982).

14. See Congressional Research Service, *An Assessment of the Afghanistan Sanctions: Implications for Trade and Diplomacy in the 1980s*, Report for the Subcommittee on Europe and the Middle East, Committee on Foreign Affairs, United States House of Representatives, US 75-985, Washington, DC, 1981.

15. *Financial Times*, 19 March 1980.

16. See, for example, the statement by Under Secretary of Defense Fred C. Ikle before the Subcommittee on International Economic Policy, Committee on Foreign Relations, United States Senate, 16 September 1981.

17. Assistant Secretary of Commerce for Trade Administration Lawrence Brady, quoted in *International Herald Tribune*, 15 January 1982.

18. The term neo-economic containment is more appropriate because there was never any prospect of returning to full containment given the economic links which have developed over the past decades.

19. There is in fact little evidence of any increased energy dependence. On this and the pipeline story in general see Jonathan P. Stern, 'Specters and Pipe Dreams', *Foreign Policy*, no. 48 (Fall 1982), and Angela Stent, *Soviet Energy and Western Europe*, The Washington Papers, vol. 10, no. 90 (Sage Publications, Beverly Hills and London, 1982).

20. 'Declaration on Events in Poland', NATO Press Release M-1(82)1, Special Ministerial Session of the Council, 11 January 1982.

21. See London Press Service, Verbatim Service, no. 98/82, 7 June 1982. On CoCom the participants agreed to 'work together to improve the international system for controlling exports of strategic goods ... and the national arrangements for enforcement of security controls'.

22. For the European Community's attack on the legality of these measures, see 'Siberian Pipeline: Note of the Ten to the US Government', *Agence Europe*, Europe Documents No. 1216, 12 August 1982.

23. *Financial Times*, 8 and 15 March 1983.

24. *Financial Times*, 31 April 1983.

25. *Financial Times*, 17 July 1984.

26. See William Root, 'Trade Controls that Work', *Foreign Policy*, no. 56 (Fall 1984).

27. See Adler-Karlsson, *Western Economic Warfare*.

28. See Department of Commerce, Amendments to Distribution Licence Procedure, *Federal Register*, vol. 49, no. 13, 19 January 1984.

29. For a comparative treatment of the respective policies of Western countries see Rode and Jacobsen (eds), *Economic Warfare*.

30. For details of the bills and the debate see Stephen Woolcock, 'US Export Controls: The Continuing Dilemma', paper presented to the UACES Conference, *US-European Relations and Technology*, London, October 1984.

10 THE STRATEGIC GOALS OF A TECHNOLOGY EMBARGO*

Hugh Macdonald

The essential peril of a strategic embargo that sought to comprehensively control technology over an indefinite period of time would be to become like the adversary against whom the embargo is directed. This is so, as I shall maintain, because for such an embargo to work, whatever its purported goals, an administrative and counter-espionage network would be required which could negate the technology gathering efforts of the enemy, control the behaviour of firms and individuals in the market place, and firmly align the ideas of foreign policy behaviour among allies in East-West relations. Moreover it is unlikely that such an embargo could succeed in attaining specific goals, for reasons which will be argued in what follows.

But to begin by stating the principal concern. Even so modestly stated a goal as 'the long-term, patient but firm containment of Soviet power' has two corollaries which are corrosive of liberty: it reduces knowledge and understanding of the adversary, and it inhibits those tendencies in one's own society which would seek to employ exchange to break the mould of containment. The loss of these capacities is dangerous to liberty because suppression of exchange in the name of interests which are managed by the State becomes tautologous: the controls that are allowed to the State in the defence of liberties the adversary is deemed to threaten extend the meaning of 'security' into realms of activity which States upholding open societies have no good cause entering, except in circumstances of 'clear and present danger'.

For 40 years during peacetime Western States have assimilated techniques of control and suppression that have been justified by the struggle against Soviet State communism. The ugliest and most intrusive techniques have been employed in foreign places; to uphold conservative regimes (Italy, South Africa, Saudi Arabia); to remove the odd dictator here and there when his enthusiasm exceeded its point of minimum usefulness (Mossadeq, Allende); to suppress revolutionary movements, particularly when they have sought common cause with Soviet Marxism (Cuba); and to deal with successful revolutionary governments when they have inclined to return to the bourgeois capitalist order (Libya). At home, fear and dislike of Soviet-inspired political ideas have justified a more restrained employment of the same methods (barring communists or sympathisers from public service, infiltrating socialist societies), though there have been occasional public outbursts (McCarthyism). Inexorably, in consequence of all this, the spectrum of political debate has become narrower, as it is filtered to exclude fellow-travellers and reward solid nationalists.

An apparatus for the strategic control of critical economic commodities fitted naturally into this wider and deeper fabric of state-centric containment: CoCom has been the tip of an iceberg of counter-intelligence security co-operation among NATO countries. But now the passive filtering of dangerous affiliations is being transformed, in the guise of proposals for a comprehensive technology embargo, into a positive vetting of knowledge that might be of use to an enemy. And how narrow will the definition of 'use to the enemy' be? We are told that Soviet citizens on academic exchanges are briefed to gather knowledge of Western science useful to the Soviet state; that the KGB and GRU run an enormously powerful mail-order apparatus for spotting, specifying, and extracting technology of interest to the Soviet military effort; that Soviet military trucks built in plants sold by Western firms, or Soviet naval vessels finished in dry-docks sold by Japan or Sweden, demonstrate the need to limit technology transfer according to the criterion of 'military significance'. But since the 'military significance' of the products of exchange is largely a function of the (increasing) economic and technological sophistication of the Russians, 'non-transferable' technologies come to encompass almost all commercial industrial products of modern design, particularly where these incorporate the widely diffused techniques of electronic micro-miniaturisation.

Hence the logic: the State is uniquely possessed of the authority to determine how an adversary *might* use the products of economic exchange; the adversary, the enemy, the Soviets, have a sophisticated system of identifying things which Western economies produce more effectively and cheaply than the Soviet economy; and for slotting these capabilities into the structure of the Soviet economy so as to directly or indirectly increase Soviet military power. And as *everything* is 'substitutable' in this way, so the greatest source of danger to the security of the West must lie at home, in the absence of a systematic policy, and monitoring apparatus, for preventing the transmission of knowledge or products which are, or might be, useful to the enemy.

There is, thus, a potent new correlation between the foreign policy criteria of containing Soviet power, and the domestic criteria of what is permissable individual and commercial behaviour. If a dominant criterion of foreign commercial policy is 'military significance', and if the image of 'military significance' is bolstered by untestable 'secret knowledge' about the implacable subtlety of the Soviet system, then it becomes *potentially* impermissable for citizen or firm to discuss any economically exploitable idea with any representative of the Soviet State. The logical corollary of the idea of the economic substitutability of Western resources for Soviet resources in the building of Soviet power, is the political theory that the Soviet Union should be quarantined, and its military power surpassed, until the Soviet system breaks down. All requisite efforts of Western States should be bent to that task, even to the extent of co-ordinating foreign, economic, and domestic policies beyond the limits of natural diversity produced by the bourgeois capitalist order.

The Credentials of Embargology

Regrettably, few if any of the best-informed protagonists of a strategic embargo against the Soviet Union have the courage of their convictions. Some, but not many, will argue for an embargo on virtually all exchange with the Russians; a few will point out that even a selective embargo will require a far greater apparatus of control, and intrusive new types of legislation. None, so far as I am aware, will honestly claim that the purpose of such an embargo is to make Western societies more like the Soviet society against which they are competing: more bureaucratic; more interventionist in the 'free market'; even more secretive; acting more (and in certain alarming ways for the first time) at the behest of Defence Ministries; less responsible to Parliamentary oversight; less free in the balance of the law between government and individuals.

Fortunately, however, not all protagonists of a strategic embargo against the Soviet Union take the same view of what ought to be the subjects and the objectives of that strategy. There is amongst them a number of differences and uncertainties which it is important to highlight. I shall indicate the most important of these shortcomings by referring here to the famous Bucy Report, and to a published paper by its current exemplar, Richard Perle. I shall also discuss the rather different approach taken by Peter Wiles.

The Bucy Report of 1976[1] is, as its title explains, an account of the criteria which the US Department of Defense might wish to see applied to technology exports to the Soviet Union and other communist countries. It defines 'strategic technology' as 'technology having military significance'.[2] The term 'significance' is crucial; it means 'mechanisms that transfer design and manufacturing know-how ... the detail of how to do things'.[3]

> Very early in their studies, the subcommittee confirmed that design and manufacturing know-how impacts [*sic*] a country's strategic capability far more so than applied research and development.[4]

The Report continues:

> These categories of export should receive primary emphasis:
> 1. Arrays of design and manufacturing know-how.
> 2. Keystone manufacturing, inspection, and test equipment.
> 3. Products accompanied by sophisticated operation, application, or maintenance know-how; [and as t]he more active the relationship, the more effective the transfer mechanism, [therefore] the more active mechanisms must be tightly controlled.[5]

Thus far one would be tempted to say, well, but aside from being a *Te Deum* for the prematurely demised new West-East economic relationship of the late 1960s and very early 1970s, what is new in any of this? The answer appears when one turns to two other areas of the Committee's findings: the strategic goals of the US embargo; and the principal means of implementation. As the principal strategic goal is

> to preserve strategic [i.e. military] US lead time, export should be denied if a technology represents a revolutionary advance to the receiving nation, but could be approved if it represents only an evolutionary advance ... When the US position results from a

revolutionary gain, export controls should focus on protecting all key elements of this gain.[6]

Such 'full-scope' controls on revolutionary technological advances having military 'significance' (not necessarily *direct* military use; not necessarily use to *Russians*; not necessarily an advance spawned by defence spending; but use which is deemed to be significant to the US military *by the US military*) would have to deny their exchange to all communist countries; to all neutrals (which should be treated the same as communist countries in the view of the Report); and to any CoCom country whose previous record in receiving exchange of embargoed technology is found wanting.

It is emphasised that 'US export control activity should place primary emphasis on control of the active transfer mechanisms',[7] which would seem to be opaque Department of Defense language for saying that 'full-scope' controls must apply to commercial enterprises, and through legislation as required. Even more gnostically, 'A simplified criteria [*sic*] should be developed in order to expedite the majority of licence requests'.[8] In context this means ways should be invented to embargo whole areas of technical innovation more quickly and with greater effect, not only in America but, through CoCom, in allied countries as well.

The strategic goals of Bucy's embargo can now be stated: to maximise the lead-time of the US and its allies in the utilisation of militarily significant technology where revolutionary gains have recently been achieved, through the imposition of 'full-scope' controls on the active *or* passive transfer of essential 'know-how', particularly where some 'know-how' may find its embodiment in Western commercial (non-military) applications (for instance, personal computers or industrial computerised manufacturing control processes for the production of non-military goods). Bucy's strategic technology embargo is an instrument of denial intended to implant consistent military-political values and behaviour in Western enterprises which might be tempted by political *naïveté* or the allure of the market place to sell or exchange know-how which is 'militarily significant'.

Of course, *indirectly* Bucy's embargo would (theoretically) affect the rate of Soviet economic development by cutting out some of those gains which derive from West-East technology transfer. But such gains are, or have been hitherto, limited by several major factors: the ability of the Soviet industrial structure to absorb imported technology; the capacity of the Soviet Union to afford to purchase advanced equipment from abroad; the unwillingness of the Soviet government to enter into the kinds of commercial arrangements which Western firms would find attractive; and the existence of Western controls on products which have military 'end-use'. Bucy suggests indeed, that it is *unnecessary* to justify the strategic goals of a technology embargo by reference to Soviet economic growth. What is at issue is simply Western self-denial in certain critical but narrowly definable areas of technology leadership.

What matters is controlling the active transfer of design and practical know-how. This is 'most effectively transferred when there is intent to do so, and the donor organization takes active steps in that direction'; and 'rapidly changing technologies are the ones for which export controls are most effective in slowing the flow of technology'.[9] The Department of Defense should take the leading role in evaluating the significance of technological change, the tactics appropriate to controlling this in each particular case, and the appropriate criteria for an efficient and pragmatic alliance embargo operated through CoCom.

This famous Report in its unclassified version presents no factual evidence of the extent or significance of the technology transfer 'problem' with 'high-velocity' technologies; its graphs and flow diagrams have no magnitudes attached to them; its research focus was four industries, air frames, aircraft jet engines, instrumentation, and solid state devices, all of which have significant or predominant military sectors for which by definition there are secret technologies whose transfer is highly restricted; and it avoids leading questions about the form and content of new export controls by blandly stating that these did not form part of its remit.

All of this therefore becomes unassailably virtuous: it speaks authoritatively; it appeals intuitively to reason; it explicitly claims to be moderate and pragmatic. Each and every word of the 39 pages produced by the 15 distinguished members, and numerous sub-committee experts, is, apparently, unanimously agreed.

But in practice what would be involved in the implementation of such a comprehensive strategic technology embargo? A short paper by Under Secretary of Defense Richard Perle, reflecting the policy of the Reagan administration, provides a number of important clues. In it we meet the following statement (to which we shall return):

A consistent [technology control] programme is needed to help create conditions for maintaining the balance of power and inducing genuine arms control. For example, if the Soviet Union had not used Western technology to improve her guidance systems, it might have been easier to convince her to accept reductions of strategic and intermediate-range nuclear missiles.[10]

The logic which underpins these statements is the logic of the Bucy Report, namely preserving lead-time and controlling 'militarily significant'[11] technology. The statement already quoted is immediately followed by this paragraph:

On the whole, the best way to prevent the Soviet Union from acquiring Western technology is by concentrating on protecting manufacturing techniques rather than products. By focusing on basic techniques we hope to slow the pace at which they can field new weapons. *And it should be the 'state of the art' in the Eastern Bloc, not in the West, that should serve as a guideline for what may or may not be transferred.*[12]

In practice, therefore, the rather neat conceptual division made by the Bucy Report between controlling critical military technology areas where the West holds revolutionary advantages, and permitting the diffusion of non-revolutionary technologies, is overturned. If the state of the art in the East does not yet include the techniques of microelectronic circuit production (or the production of plugs for bathtubs) which in the West are open and effectively diffused commercial technologies, exchange with the Soviet Union should be forbidden. The West should not sell, for instance, personal computers which may be bought for a few hundreds of dollars in Hong Kong, lest the open secrets which they contain are copied into improvements in the fire control systems of Soviet tanks.

Yet by the criteria of the Bucy Report, it is not *the products* of advanced technologies that matter; it is the know-how involved in the design of those products. And the design and manufacture of microcircuits remains quite secretive and extremely difficult: the kind of know-how which Western firms do not diffuse to one another except for very large amounts of money (more than the Russians could afford to spend in foreign exchange in a stock market take-over bid, for instance).[13]

This suggests that the distinction between 'know-how' and 'products' is not at all clear. Perle is interested in controlling the market-place, not just the boardroom. Hence, despite his formal denial, he begins to appear to want to use a comprehensive embargo as an instrument of compulsion for the promotion of American foreign policy goals. Industrial exchange in a very wide range of products is to be prohibited because the Soviet Union could benefit from such exchange and devote marginally greater resources overall to building military power.

Richard Perle believes that it is wrong that the Soviet Union should be allowed to do this: he thinks that if the United States dominates the balance of power between the superpowers, then the Russians will become more amenable. So much is clear from the first quotation given above, which links the specific goal of a technology embargo, namely to preserve 'lead-time', to the general strategic goals of an American administration espousing the kinds of values which are dominant in Washington today.

It is very important, therefore, to spot how this transformation works. First and foremost, there is the permissive ambiguity of the Bucy Report itself, which beneath its apparent clarity of purpose and unassailable virtue is a jumble of conceptual truths begging to serve any political ideology which cares to make use of them. And here is such a political ideology.

To take arms control, for instance. There is a clear desire to use arms control as an instrument to constrain Soviet nuclear power. But there is no good evidence from Richard Perle's period of office in the Pentagon that he considers the United States should trade any of its nuclear weapons programmes for the types of constraints that the Soviet Union might be willing to accept; indeed the administration which he serves has claimed time without number that the Soviets are not willing to accept meaningful constraints. Hence, the axiom which defines arms control bargaining between roughly equivalent great powers, as a process the goal of which is to turn interim pressures of a quite asymmetrical kind into equitable outcomes which both can live with, has no place in the Republican ideology. The place of arms control, like that of a strategic technology embargo, is to subserve the attainment of a *unilaterally* defined military power relationship with the Soviet Union. In such an ideology, arms control negotiations with the Russians are likely to remain fruitless. But their lack of fruit helps justify an economic embargo, and an expanding defence budget.[14]

Of course the option of American arms control policy doing nothing in the face of active Soviet anxiety would remain. But in that case the United States might recently have lost control of its West European allies, which was almost the outcome of its embargological approach to Soviet military power. Such an unplanned outcome was prevented only by the election, in the wake of an economic recession, of conservative governments in Britain and West Germany. But much damage was done to West European confidence in American defence policy, and new strains were created in several important West European societies. Thus Richard Perle is not speaking plain truth, or even common sense when he talks about the goals of his embargo; he is speaking partisanship. The same partisanship is evident in his use of history in this paper.

It is noted that in the 1920s: 'The Soviet Union obtained prototypes of numerous aircraft engines from Western manufacturers and built composite "Soviet" models incorporating the best features of each. She also imported military aircraft from Britain, France, Holland, Italy and Sweden, thereby gaining a design base for her own aircraft industry.'[15] All of this is true: but ...

In the mid-1930s, just as Hitler was embarking upon his extreme nationalist path, Russia had perhaps the largest air force in Europe; however, a technological revolution was affecting aircraft design and performance. As the 'Dreadnought' had rendered obsolete every other existing battleship, so the low-winged monoplane fighter and medium bomber swept away the strategic value of everything built before. The Soviet Union found itself facing the crises of the late 1930s isolated, not only geographically and by its strange political creed, but because its accumulated dependence upon imported technology left it incapable of competing in the savage arms race for superior air power. And this fact, as much as geography or distaste for Stalinism, influenced the considerations of Britain and France in their muddled reactions to Munich, the invasion of Czechoslovakia, and the Polish crisis.[16]

Another *canard* of history raised by Richard Perle is the plundering of German industry for Soviet reparations after the Second World War.[17] It was the Western democracies at the end of the First World War which first applied to Germany the criteria of war guilt and economic reparations. Moreover the concept of Soviet reparations from the whole of Germany after the Second World War had been agreed in principle by the allies. The extent of war destruction inside the Soviet Union did not leave many options for Soviet economic reconstruction. The ending of American Lend-Lease, the decision to drop discussions of a major American loan to Russia, and the cut-off of reparations from the Western zones of Germany, all added to the pressures on Stalin. In any case the Western allies had gone into 'their' parts of Germany intending to fillet German industry and science for the technology 'secrets' of its military performance; which they did rather thoroughly. Thus the making of the Cold War was accompanied not only by predatory behaviour on the part of Stalin, but by a growing Western embargo intended to force the Russians back on their own resources. And it succeeded rather well, as the present capability of Soviet power shows.

Richard Perle has produced historical facts as evidence for a long-term Soviet strategy of building military power by importing technology. These historical facts are not at all impressive when they are placed within their own wider historical contexts. As points of departure for a foreign policy of strategic technology embargo, they are useless. They serve only an *a priori* wish to depict the Soviet Union as devilishly clever. This I believe is what the social psychologists who have accounted for cognitive dissonance term 'proselytising after disconfirmation'.

And the evidence of disconfirmation is extremely strong, not only from periods when the Soviet Union was suffering from Stalin's paranoic economic priorities. There are also those technologically disastrous symbols of the high days of Franco-Soviet detente: the tacitly acquired imitations of *Concorde* (a Western achievement which works very well, if noisily, but has proved difficult for all others to copy); and a not very noteworthy attempt by Dassault to produce a VTOL fighter, the current nearly useless Soviet copy of which is the much-feared Yak *Forger*. In passing, let me point out the palpable sense of relief which accompanied the dissection of the first complete MiG-25 to fall into Western hands; and the comment of one government scientist on the intercontinental range capability of the *Backfire-B*, that 'without refuelling it could hardly get from one side of town to the other'. All of these well-documented technical and military shortcomings in Soviet air power and systems design were tragically confirmed by their incompetent handling of the intruding Korean airliner in September 1983.

The problem which the cognitive dissonants in the Pentagon do not recognise is that a State which has so far failed to master the economic art of military-technical innovation cannot have a successful and consistent long-term military build-up; and all the *historical* evidence is that the Soviet Union *was* (and maybe still is) such a State. This means that the Reaganites ought to stop stretching the credulity of the people whose support they want for a strategic embargo which they claim to be reasonable and prudent; and they ought to start producing good, sustainable, evidence for their cause, if such evidence exists.

And supposing for a moment that it does: my guess would be that if the Soviet Union *is* mastering the art of innovation, then the cause lies not in the success of its policy of importing 'Western' technologies, but in its secular, long-term, economic growth; in reforms of its educational system and distribution of trained intellectual resources; and in the degree of immunity from external sources of instability that it has built up. Patently then, if such evidence exists, it is foolhardy for Richard Perle and his colleagues to try to justify a strategic embargo by suggesting that the Russians need to beg, borrow, buy and steal 'Western' technology in order to compensate for 'the anomalies of central planning . . .' etc.

Some would perhaps contend that evidence has been adduced in the recent series of US Defense Department publications entitled *Soviet Military Power.* But the evidence presented in these publications is not worth the extremely expensive paper and promotion afforded it: consider, for instance, the proposition that expanding floor space in Soviet military industries is an indicator of the growth of *sophistication* of Soviet military power;[18] and then consider the likely reaction of a Western defence industry executive who was asked to believe that!

All historical evidence shows the failure of the Soviet Union to catch up with American military power (and indeed that, for Russia and the Soviet Union, warfare has been a very bad investment). Thus, the Reaganite use of history to justify a comprehensive strategic technology embargo is wholly disreputable. Indeed the most important and disheartening aspect of Richard Perle's paper is the number of times (at least six in just over seven pages) that it refers to 'enforcement', referring not to what a technology embargo will do to the Russians, but to what it will justify in terms of domestic and foreign controls upon technology transfer within the Western, the *Free*, World.

A different kind of approach to a strategic embargo is adopted by Peter Wiles.[19] His sense of the term 'strategic' is beyond exception; thinking and planning to produce significant, intended, effects upon the choices which face an adversary. The notable implication of this sense of strategy is that no *a priori* distinction exists between trade in general and trade in technology. Moreover in effect the argument focuses upon trade as well as technology, on the logical grounds that through 'trade' the Soviet Union can grow, and through growth invest more resources in military production, or at least avoid switching them out.

This is, explicitly, an argument in favour of completely boycotting the Soviet Union. But Wiles recognises two limiting conditions: the impossibility of obtaining consistent support for a logically extreme position; and the highly provocative nature of embargoes which, thus, 'should never go as far as Roosevelt's embargo on Japan'.[20] In effect he argues for a long-term, consistent, refusal to trade in a limited number of commodities, with the strategic objective of hampering Soviet economic growth and constraining Soviet behaviour in the choice between growth in defence versus growth in consumption: embargo technical know-how (Wiles supports a much expanded CoCom); tax the export of capital and grain; and boycott Soviet natural gas. It is not clear what he intends for the buying and selling of oil.

Wilesian philosophy is pessimistic: States are naturally rather aggressive entities, but contemporary capitalist democracies have become softened by enlightenment and material progress. Capitalism probably would sell the Soviets the rope with which it would be hung. The Soviet Union remains ideologically unreformed (and unreformable through enrichment), materially, culturally and morally backward; and physically aggressive when opportunity presents itself. Thus the West is open to continuous subversion from the East, because it has learnt to stop fighting for the future of history and to reason about it instead; whereas Soviet communism has as its *raison d'être* the ceaseless struggle to dominate the world, which if relinquished would mean the end of Soviet communism.

This theory says that on the plane of international economics there can be no peaceful co-existence between capitalist and socialist great powers; or at least that the only sensible form of peaceful co-existence for capitalism is not to help in important ways to enrich Russian communists. The strongest part of the theory is its mirror-image of Leninism; acceptance of the belief that all forms of co-existence are way-stations on the route to fundamental structural change. Communists should be taken literally when they tell us this is what they are working for; and consequently, as a deeply prudent principle, the West ought consistently to work in equally opposite terms.

Despite the transparent logic and well-tempered reason of Wilesian theory, here seems to be concrete evidence that the essence of a strategic embargo against communism is to become like the adversary against whom the struggle is directed. For instance, how in practice is the West to distinguish between 'the positive use of the economic weapon' (his term) because the West's scepticism about positivism tells it to be very wary of communist great powers; and the positive use of the same weapon, because those who employ it believe — despite all evidence to the contrary — that the future lies with, say, American Christian fundamentalism?

Whatever discomfort Peter Wiles may personally feel in company with such literal mirror-imaging, it seems to me that the subtlety of his position is too great to be consistently distinguished against the background noise of contentious domestic politicking in the West, or indeed against the quite different background hush of the permanently cloistered officials who may cultivate their beliefs without exposure to criticism. I think that this makes a West-East economic embargo much less desirable in the perspective of its consequences within Western societies.

'It is self-evident that if ... "doves" definitely take power in the Kremlin we must abandon our embargo. Indeed we must make the same point clear in advance, since precisely this event is the long-term hope of humanity.'[21] Self-evident in Wilesian theory means, however, self-evident to Peter Wiles. This is a serious shortcoming, since he insists that it is desirable and possible to have a long-term, consistent, embargo for the whole Western alliance. He numbers only one Soviet, one Hungarian, and one Czech 'dove'. Many would agree with his enumeration, but that is strictly beside the point, which is that many would not. The problem would seem to be that dove-like behaviour cannot be acurately separated out from the beliefs of genuine 'doves'. Thus the Wilesian condition becomes impossible to fulfil. I infer from this that the natural diversity of views within the foreign policies of different Western societies is inconsistent with a long-term embargo based upon the criterion of awaiting 'modified communism'.[22] Such a criterion is so elusive (and long term) that it requires a *philosophical* unity and orthodoxy of outlook, which is not to be found by reasoned consensus and is therefore only conceivable in other (and disreputable) terms, as indicated at the beginning of this chapter.

Moreover the logic on which Wilesian philosophy is based is not unimpeachable. A leading proposition is:

> The prospect of enrichment may entice the enemy into a broader international division of labour, but the main effect of this is ... dependence ... For this reason, and not because he has become richer, he no longer wants to make war on us. That means that he is, in the last resort, not softened but simply threatened.[23]

It is true that in the last resort he may have to be threatened, but that cannot be the point (which may be that good ends can be sought out of base motives). But it is surely incorrect to suggest that an adversary is threatened into enriching himself by becoming dependent on exchange. People and States who are not actually helpless seek some structural outcome beside that of not being struck (or embargoed), for of course this entails no security against being threatened again, and perhaps struck or embargoed despite having shown compliance.

Already then the threat is not simply that of an imposed outcome, but of a choice between that and the finding of an outcome which is less disagreeable. And this is the case even where one side is disproportionately dependent upon trade with the other. Just as the banker needs the overdraft, the embargologist needs trade to begin his search for a science: embargoes, like overdrafts, are not *ex ante.*

Another Wilesian proposition is that 'war springs more naturally from one's prosperity than from one's poverty'.[24] It is a truism that war requires resources (and organisation). But despite unprecedented prosperity, the states of the rich Northern part of the globe seem both rather content not to fight with each other, and, in East-West relations, rather impressively deterred from doing so. And even before the contemporary international system emerged, statesmen had become rather strongly convinced that prosperity and warfare were not compatible.

The British were the first to be convinced, because they had the most to hold on to. Louis Napoleon kept being swayed by opposite pressures, but was revolted by Solferino, and soon gave up in his later war with Prussia. The victorious Bismarck bent all the efforts of his later days to avoiding war that might jeopardise his creation, Imperial Germany. Most statesmen perceived that colonial adventures were categorically different from maintaining public order in Europe. By the early twentieth century it was uncivilised proto-nationalisms in the Balkans and the economically inefficient Empires of Austria-Hungary and Russia which entered wars with the greatest equanimity; all the most prosperous powers were appalled by the prospect, and co-operated quite successfully (but not successfully enough) to avoid it. The same was true in the inter-war period, even including some of the more avaricious dictatorships. But Hitler brought out the worst in everyone.

One might perhaps agree that prosperity unaccompanied by reason or a good system of deterrence leaves war too much rationality. But reason accompanied by mutual dependence through trade, *and* the ultimate prospect of nuclear destruction?

Finally, Wilesian theory postulates a logical alternative between a West-East embargo, and a continuing East-West arms competition. The logic is that an embargo will slow Soviet economic growth, constrain Soviet defence investment, and sooner rather than later allow the West to economise on its own defence effort.

There is no good evidence to show that the size of the West's defence effort is directly related to that of the Soviet Union. But there is quite a lot of evidence to suggest that the size of the Soviet effort is related to that of the West (and China), at least in certain categories of weapons and geographical areas. If this is a correct reading of the evidence, then the Soviet response to an economic embargo not accompanied in the short run by a decrease in Western defence spending probably would not be to diminish its investment in those areas of defence capability which are most critical to the security of the West; though the Soviets might attempt to shift resources out of other defence activities. Hence even if an embargo worked as effectively as predicted, the West would not notice because it would continue to see the Soviet Union matching its own capabilities in just those areas where it most wants to reacquire superiority.

Other possibilities exist also. The Soviets might sacrifice growth in civilian output in order to continue to have it in military production. Perhaps more likely, they could contemplate a counter-embargo, beginning with the indebtedness of the Soviet bloc countries. This would throw a considerable additional burden on to the Western taxpayer. Moreover the Russians might inform their allies that with some of the debt service resources saved by default, they could increase their investment in defence capabilities. This would be done in just that area where the European allies of the United States would feel it most, in Central Europe. In any case this is the area of the arms race which matters most; and if the Russians wanted to, they could make it very labour intensive at little or no cost to themselves, and probably heavily damage Western unity in the process.

There are very serious matters to ponder in all of this, and the lack of certainty which underlies the position of Peter Wiles does not mean that he might not be right after all about the relationship between a West-East embargo and an East-West arms race. But I think that he is wrong. In any case his science looks very experimental. And the costs of his experiment look high, and the risks too.

We shall see that further discussion of this matter will bring us again to the core of the problem highlighted by the preceding discussion of Embargology, namely whether or not an embargo would exacerbate East-West arms competition, and if so who would win. But that discussion must be situated in a context of international political analysis.

Ambivalent Intentionality

In the case of an implacable enemy, if I have a club which is useful for hunting and fighting and he does not, it is clearly foolish to give access to that to my enemy, even if he claims that he wants to use it exclusively for hunting and not for fighting; even if he is able to offer me economic inducements to exchange a club like mine for something which I rather desire; and even if, in consequence of my refusal to exchange, he goes hungry and this reinforces his enmity towards me.

But what if I do not know, and have difficulty in discovering, how far the intentions which underlie my adversary's political and military behaviour towards me are malleable? This is clearly a situation calling for judgement, involving discretion, but requiring some logic. Let me therefore try to make a number of propositions.

Firstly, if I decide that there is some possibility that using economic exchange may affect my adversary's choices between the accumulation of military and non-military goods, then refusal to exercise such influence by a deliberate withholding of exchange would be foolish: I would lose the benefit of exchange and would have to continue to bear the greater cost of the military effort required to defend myself. This is not to say that defence resources are wasted absolutely; but if a different mix of defence and non-defence production could produce the same security and release resources to alternative productive uses, then I am needlessly failing to optimise my allocation of resources.

Secondly, if I decide that refusal to exchange is likely to intensify my adversary's military efforts — by increasing either his enmity or his fear — then not only do I forgo the benefits of exchange and the possibility of a better allocation of my own resources, but, unless I can be certain of winning the ensuing arms competition, I also lose security and therefore act contrary to my interests. This is not simply foolish; it is irrational.

Thirdly, if I decide that there is no possibility of affecting my adversary's choices between the accumulation of more or less military power and more or less non-military production, at least in the short or medium term, then I am justified in treating my adversary as an implacable enemy. This does not mean that I should comprehensively forbear from exchange, but only that I should be careful about what is exchanged in structuring the situation and the utilities of my adversary, rather than attempting to influence his intentions.

Fourthly, if my adversary begins to show an ability, through observing my behaviour for instance, to himself develop the design of an effective club for hunting and fighting then, notwithstanding any substantive change in the structure of enmity, it becomes necessary for me to begin to relate my security concerns with my economic considerations.

It might pay me to trade my enemy one of my clubs. Firstly, this might discourage him from the expensive and time-consuming process of developing a club of his own: the consideration here is whether he will be stronger by having a club of his own, or by buying a club of my design. Properly grounded economic knowledge will be important in resolving this consideration, because I will want to know as reliably as possible what would happen to the resources which he might commit to designing and building his own club if, instead, he buys one from me. It might be that these resources would go into the activity of hunting, thus applying his gains from the exchange to improving his consumption, and replacing the items which he sacrificed in the exchange which gained him one of my clubs. This would not be incompatible with enduring enmity; it means only that my adversary gets fatter.

In any case it is not impossible that I can structure our enduring conflict somewhat through exchange, and that thereby my adversary will become both less committed to fighting with me in the short term, and stronger and therefore in principle more capable of fighting with me in the future. But in this case I have successfully affected the structure of his interests, and indeed the structure of the adversarial relationship: if I have priced my club right, then I have made a successful net addition to my own resources; I have obtained the security of knowing that I am not going to be fighting with my enemy at least in the short run; and I can consider how best to apply the gains from exchange to strengthening myself in terms of the uncertain future.

Now, I infer from this that even if my enemy will substitute economic gains from trade with me for additional defence production, I can structure the politics and the technological parameters *within which his intentionality operates.* Providing he is rational, the 'good' end of liquidating me will be offset by the 'bad' consequences of having to make the great effort of doing so, by the loss of the benefits of exchange which had been available, and by the risks involved in attacking me or pushing me beyond the limits of tolerance in a crisis. Thus even if I *suspect* that my adversary's intentions are not ambivalent, but implacably hostile, I cannot derive from this any necessary logic of Embargology. In the absence of a clear, present, danger to my security it is safer and more economical to work on the assumption that my adversary's hostility towards me can be structured by *his own* evaluation of circumstances.

Admittedly history provides examples of the ideological pursuit of victory, in which intentionality dispenses with the kinds of utilities that seem to be present in today's international conflict. But for every Crusader who persistently sought God there must have been a thousand who found contentment in the vanities of this world (actually, this historical fact is the basis of all modern economic science). It may then be, as Peter Wiles and others have argued, that a fat communist despises the West as thoroughly as a thin one, but this only proves that a sybarite tends also to be self-righteous; not that he is more likely to move himself against the enemies of his State. And that, surely, is the vital matter.

Nor is the persistence of ideological orthodoxy, despite material changes in its own and surrounding circumstances, decisive evidence of unchanging strategic intent. To demonstrate unchanging ideological hostility as a cause of unvarying intentionality towards the use of force, it is necessary to show *either* that the adversary's 'rationality' of force is indifferent to practical consequences of the kind considered previously; *or* that there are circumstances in its social structure which would precipitate latent hostility into the use of force in some set of external circumstances. In the case of the Soviet Union there is no particularly good evidence for either of these propositions. Aside from a certain loss of control in the immediate post-Revolutionary period, military intervention in Poland in 1939 and Finland in 1940, and Khrushchev's Cuban adventure, everything points to an enduring Soviet sense of military inferiority and circumspection. This of course does not cover all possible future cases. Nor does it dispute that if the West became very weak, Soviet communism might be tempted to act. But this is a universal propensity which can be explained without any reference to communism. If it does not justify an embargo in one case, why should it in another?

Although the notion of Soviet 'defectiveness' lends no historical credence to Embargology, there is another dimension to the problem of ambivalent intentionality: the long term itself. The problem is this; might *refusing* to withhold exchange, against the background of his accumulating military power, contribute to the creation of expectations about my behaviour which would affect his *future* strategic intentions? Can a comprehensive or selective long-term embargo on exchange find justification in this?

The answer is not an easy one, but I have suggested above that the beginning point cannot be the logic of my adversary's present or historic behaviour. It must therefore be some universal rule of prudence, such as that in the face of emergent, new, circumstances of strategic parity 'an adversary will only negotiate under duress'; or that 'it is better to be safe than sorry'.

If the prudential rule is to have an embargo in order to substitute the instrument of economic bargaining, which may have increasing usefulness, for the instrument of military power, which is of declining usefulness, then it is necessary to show how a strategy of withholding exchange *now* in order to exert leverage in the *future* is to be preferred on prudential grounds to a strategy of fostering exchange now with the implication that it would not continue without interruption if in future circumstances the strategic behaviour of the adversary changed.

If the prudential rule in withholding exchange is to seek safety against the uncertainties of how exchange might contribute to the military power of the adversary, then it must be shown how a strategy of withholding exchange can avoid lessening my safety by causing greater military competition, particularly if the dynamics of the arms race suggest that there will be a long-term equalisation of military power at any level of economic effort. Here we begin to return to the central questions of Embargology; but we have shown that neither history, nor economic analysis, nor philosophical logic can get around the issue of having to make judgements about uncertain and undetermined future circumstances.

What particular goal, what particular items, and what particular method of operation should characterise this long-term prudentialism, the essence of which is to temporise, rather than to dissuade, persuade, punish or penalise? The general answer appears simple, even recognising that in practice there will be difficulties: identify the sources of strategic power; do not actively aid the adversary in seeking access to these, unless the price is right and there is a margin of safety in doing so; and keep all options open, both in terms of extending and restricting exchange, as the development of the power of the adversary reaches and passes through these critical sources of power.

In terms of East-West relations the sources of strategic power include the following: a capacity to deter by assuredly being able to make an overwhelmingly destructive response; a capacity for the exercising of conventional military power beneath the threshold of assured destruction; domestic political stability; economic growth; allies or reliable political understandings with other States; access to 'high velocity' military technologies. This ranking is not beyond dispute; nor is it immutable. But fairly clearly the Soviet Union became a superpower through its nuclear and conventional military capabilities, without the wealth of America or Europe; in the absence of reliable allies; and without access to 'high velocity' technologies. Predictably *if* superpower competition continues, the equalisation of capabilities will increase the priority of access to 'high velocity' technologies; but it is difficult to envisage how this will overtake the importance of domestic stability and economic growth, or the value of reliable international understandings. Moreover *quantity* of conventional military power will remain capable of offsetting *quality*: this sets a dilemma for the West which is discussed in a later section of this chapter.

Thus the inferences which *may* be drawn in favour of a prudentialist strategy of embargo amount to two: in the short run, my adversary should not be sold the wherewithal to equalise his military power with mine; and in the long run the *uncertain* intentionality of my adversary indicates careful consideration of the sources of strategic power, among which economic performance and access to high technology have their rather different but perhaps increasingly important places. *The consideration of attempting to embargo Soviet access to these sources of power must turn, however, upon their relationship to other strategic considerations.* These concern two questions above all: can an embargo change Soviet domestic motivations behind the search for improved military power? And can the West win an arms race with the Soviet Union? These questions are crucial to the contention that a comprehensive embargo is primarily a matter of Western self-discipline and self-interest; that it would not exacerbate and would even serve to diminish arms competition.

The Domestic Constituents of Security

What are the constituents of security which will affect the domestic decision to reallocate resources towards, or away from, an existing pattern of defence production? Nearly all States seek to preserve a defence industrial base, and to maximise technological capacity (even if this means compromising short-run productive capacity). States seek to acquire technology from whatever domestic or foreign sources they may, and, providing that an awareness of the military strategic potential of given applications of technology has arisen, will usually pay higher than the 'market price' of the aggregate inputs in order to get a 'workable' output: indeed States are licensed to do precisely this because, as Adam Smith pointed out, the provision of defence is their 'first duty'.

This is apparently paradoxical in terms of the domestic economy; for why should the State — the monopolist of the provision of security and the monopsonist of the market for military goods —

pay above market prices for items of defence? There are probably three main parts to the answer. The State is an extremly bad provider of physical goods, and needs to be shown how, a felt need for which premium payments are available. Secondly, as the licensed monopoly provider of security, the State is also licensed to levy finance, usually on an extremely flexible ability to pay basis (in the West) or need to extract basis (in the East). Finally, as the meta-phorical creator of the boundaries of the domestic market place, and the literal defender of its values, the State is in competition with other States that are doing the same job, thus setting up a progressively more complex relationship between technology as both the cause of insecurity (the threat to be defended against) and the solution to its provision (the instrument to be employed to a given end).

Technology cannot solve technological problems in the realm of defence and security, because what is postulated by each State as a given end (the defence problem which technology is to solve) is not a given end in relations among States. It follows that if the application of technological advances to defence problems is *not* to result in an unending competition for relative security, then security must be given some non-relative dimension. This can only be done if adversaries decide that the values which they defend are compatible within the structure of their conflict and co-operation.

I wish to be clear at this point that by 'compatible' I do not mean convergent; compatibility could be defined as a 'stable' agreement to disagree, which would not be incompatible with con-tinued competition over values. The separate industrialised societies of the West have arrived at something like this arrange-ment, in which the resort to unstable violence, and even violent short-term changes in non-military policy, are precluded by co-operative institutions, yet accompanied by strong political competition and quite fierce socio-economic conflicts. A similar arrangement has been suggested for East-West relations, and for a time a rather basic working model seemed to be emerging: it was called detente. But detente has thus far shown the defect of being easily reversible. There therefore remains profound uncertainty about superpower compatibility in attempting to rule out the use of force in their continuing conflicts of value and interest.

In East-West relations, and superpower relations in particular, foreign trade (including technology exchange) is *not* going to be central to the determination of what level of defence is needed to achieve what degree of security, *because there is no strong inter-dependence between the economic systems of East and West, and therefore no basis for institutions of joint economic management to substitute for the place of military power in effecting security.* In the absence of detente — i.e. minus a politically directed effort to render the security interests of the two adversaries sufficiently compatible to rule out the perceived (historic) threat of force — within the framework of continuing conflict, there will be an indefinite competition to build military capabilities. The level and extent of this competition can be somewhat regulated by arms control, but not by any more fundamental means. The explanation for this was given above: technology relativises security, which engenders a search for technological solutions in the absence of political solutions.

From this situation it is possible to draw a number of provisional conclusions. First, short-run measurement of long-run investments in (and outputs of) military capability is not a good basis for making either economic or political judgements about the preferences or the intentions of an adversary. Second, States pursue technological improvements of their military capabilities out of fundamentally 'domestic' considerations and because of the relativity of international security, as well as because they sometimes actively intend to use force. Thirdly, some 'filtering mechanism' is needed in order to discriminate between these mixed motivations.

Fortunately, such a mechanism is available. In terms of capabilities the danger signal is a significant, discontinuous, *increase* in allocations to 'defence'. In terms of longer-run intentionality, the mechanism is a political dialogue about whether or not the use of force can be ruled out of the context of continuing conflict. The role of any strategic embargo on exchange between adversaries is therefore *consequential* upon the results of the application of these filters.

The strictly consequential role of a strategic embargo in the case where the intentions of the adversary are ambivalent must be emphasised. The *pre-emptive* imposition of a long-term strategic embargo on technology and trade will almost certainly be taken as decisive evidence of the *incompatibility* of the security interests of the adversaries in terms of ruling out the use of force. Thus, the imposition of such an embargo will have the consequence of stimulating military competition. The vital question then becomes: who will win?

Arms and Embargoes

Other things being equal, a qualitatively superior weapons system
such as an advanced tactical fighter aircraft provides greater defensive coverage in terms of range, speed, detection capability, armament and other such characteristics; and this establishes a cause
and effect relationship between the cost of including marginal
additional defensive qualities, and the procurement of a smaller
total number of systems within a given budget.

Operations research can build in such predictors as accident
rates, maintenance requirements, the consumption of fuel, munitions, and replacement sub-systems over a given life-cycle. But the
evidence of recent wars such as Vietnam, the Arab-Israeli conflicts, and the Falklands expedition, is that qualitatively superior
weapons systems meeting each other in combat conditions cause
higher rates of attrition, and munitions consumption, than have
been recorded historically. In practical terms, technological
improvement is a very dynamic process; each 'across the board'
increase in defensive military capabilities causes an escalation *both*
in the real cost of building in the next set of qualitative improvements, and in the total number of weapons systems required in
order to sustain the intensity of warfare beyond the initial stages of
hostilities.

A dilemma thus arises: to purchase even fewer yet further
improved weapons; or to cease adding improvements in order to
procure greater numbers? In practice each major new weapons
system presents this problem to Western governments at some
stage in its development. But to those who preside over such
decisions the substitution of additional numbers of *less* sophisticated platforms is unattractive (in nearly all cases): realistically, the
defence problem is seen (correctly) as an 'across the board' problem of dynamic technological improvement. It therefore seems
strategically more important to preserve comparative advantages
in technological sophistication, rather than 'opt out' by building
less capable systems; for to opt out on a particular stage of technological advance may be to lose that comparative advantage altogether. This is the Realist's dilemma.

The evidence of this syndrome in Western defence planning is
ubiquitous. In almost every category of major weaponry,
American systems are qualitatively superior to Soviet systems, or
to systems designed and built in other Western countries. Overall,

the level of defence expenditure undertaken by the NATO allies is vastly greater than that of the Soviet Union. Given favourable conditions for deploying its first line forces in Central Europe, it is quite possible that NATO forces would be able to destroy a Warsaw Pact offensive without resort to nuclear weapons. But it is questionable whether sufficient numbers of weapons systems or stockpiles of war material are there to staunch a Soviet offensive which caught the West off guard; to counterattack after a successful defensive action; or to fight a protracted conventional war. As the Falklands War showed, alterations in operational conditions or miscalculations in the operational effectiveness of qualitatively superior weapons systems can bring a qualitatively inferior enemy who manages to gain local superiority perilously close to humiliating the superior military power which lacks strength in depth or reserves.

Unless the adversary experiences the same phenomenon of *having* to trade off numbers against qualitative improvements, then, practically, pursuit of the logic of technological superiority becomes *unrealistic.* According to the evidence provided by enthusiastic American proponents of strategic technology embargoes (and hence the technological arms race), the Soviet Union is improving the quality of its military systems without suffering (to the same extent) loss of equipment numbers. Clearly this is not happening by magic.

Soviet technological advances tend to be restricted in their application to certain categories of weapons systems; the overall impact of improvement is spread thin; and in overall terms defence spending has been kept up against a trend of declining overall economic growth. This implies that currently or very shortly the Soviet Union must choose whether to make economies within its defence spending which could affect development or production or both; or to sacrifice investment and consumption in its civilian economy. Yet despite these obvious Soviet problems, and notwithstanding the windfall effect of a military-technological revolution in Western research and development (to which the embargologists hope to deny the Russians access), it is not clear that the United States and its allies are capable of funding both the systems development which the new technologies require in order to bring them to operational usefulness, and the procurement of numbers of weapons systems needed to replace existing systems on a one-for-one basis.

Let me try to be more specific here: whereas qualitative improvements in nuclear weapons are important, and are occurring, it is in terms of conventional military power that the new technologies will have their most radical effects upon the strategic problems of NATO. It is in this realm that the West must outstrip the Soviet Union if it is to reap tangible benefits from a long-term strategic embargo accompanied by an arms race. Of course there has been a conventional arms race in Central Europe for the last 30 years or so — just as for much of that time there has been some variety of Western embargo on technology and trade with Russia. But during more than three decades the West has failed to raise enough resources to provide a durable conventional defence against Soviet conventional military power. Is it reasonable to believe that this time things will be different?

It has been estimated that the cost of bringing critical new conventional weapons technologies to maturity will be around $30 billion in current dollars. *In addition* to this very large R&D effort would come the costs of procurement. General Bernard Rogers, NATO Supreme Allied Commander, has suggested repeatedly that procurement of sufficient new conventional systems could be provided if all NATO countries were to increase defence spending by 4 per cent per annum in real terms for a period of eight to ten years. What is being called for, essentially, is an increase in defence expenditures of between one-third and one-half over present levels;[25] in the case of Britain, about an extra 2 per cent of GNP, *plus* a research and development down payment. It is altogether unclear whether a comprehensive long-term technology embargo would diminish these demands, or would merely serve to justify them. In the latter case, the effects of such added effort on Western societies have not been calculated. But the argument presented above is that in the face of an embargo the Soviet Union would be most unlikely to reduce its defence expenditures in areas which would allow the Western powers to economise on the burden of expenditures on new conventional weapons capabilities.

As much of the new technology is of American origin, West European governments would insist upon collaborative development and production regimes in return for such vast additional investment. Not only would this exercise by its very nature run counter to a widespread technology embargo against Russia — as the existing evidence of development 'leakages' indicates — it would also lead any sensible economist to infer that considerable inefficiencies would accompany the establishment of joint ventures in design and production. The programme costs — and performance shortcomings — of the multinational *Tornado* lead one to treat with profound scepticism the claims which are currently being made about NATO's prospects for rectifying its conventional deficiencies.

It is not clear what is happening to the technological level of Soviet military power. According to American official publications, the Russians are improving the quality of their weapons systems with increasing, or not diminishing, equipment numbers.[26] The traditional Soviet problem in developing the quality of military power has been the absence of critical resources such as machine tools, special metals, electronic components, and educated human skills; while other resources — land, labour, and basic raw materials — have been relatively abundant (albeit provided at the cost of other forms of production).

The Soviet answer to these impediments has been to produce large numbers of equipment that are rather basic in performance; to select between different types of system on the evidence of in-service performance; and to further refine selected models over lengthy time scales, meanwhile developing further 'generational' improvements in research and design bureaux. The most chronic problems in this centrally managed system appear to be how to acquire and sustain conceptual innovations at the stage of research and development; and how to acquire the skills to produce actual equipment items which conform to design standards of manufacture and operating efficiency. In these terms technology transfer — commercial, scientific, and illicit — has always been sought; and its influences on Soviet military power have been clear. But *dependence* on technology transfer has never been a goal of the system, which has persistently sought to induce independence and self-sufficiency in military design and production.

The Soviet system has now provided itself for the first time in its history with what will soon be an adequate innovative base of educated researchers and designers, and with something approaching an adequate base of workers' skills. What it continues to lack is access to certain raw materials; adequate practical knowledge of certain groups of applied technologies (for example turbines, turbo-fan engines and compressors); high productivity and consistency of production standards; and a broadly based (as opposed to unevenly specialised) interrelationship between conceptual innovation, investment, and industrial application.

This problem is now and for the future the most significant source of lag in general Soviet economic performance, including the military-industrial sectors. But is it a reflection of the *transient* or of the *permanent* absence in Soviet development of the social and economic conditions for self-sustaining qualitative improvement? In other words, can this problem be solved rationally and productively by economic decisions, albeit of a complex and unusual kind? Or is the problem that fundamental errors have been made in economic organisation, in personnel selection, in the educational system, in the dynamic process of production, or in the fostering of an unconscious dependence upon the importation of 'disembodied' technology? I have seen no clear, convincing, scientific answers to these questions. But in the absence of answers, a technology embargo accompanied by an arms race is a strategy without any coherent goal.

Moreover although the aims of such a Western embargo turn upon Soviet economic performance, a policy based on such slender empirical foundations must be compared with the amply documented problems of cost-effectiveness which affect the defence economies of the Western adversaries of the Soviet Union. The national defence programmes of the West, including the United States, have become institutionally inefficient: typically, not more than 25 per cent of a given year's budget will be devoted to the acquisition of new equipment. Moreover, the existing evidence of cost-inflation in defence construction suggests that realising the new technologies in terms of *minimal* equipment numbers might require vast investment and a large overall increase in NATO countries' defence expenditures. Thus there are grave doubts as to whether the West could win an arms race which its embargo might well exacerbate.

Furthermore, one must predict that the Soviet Union will respond to a strategic technology embargo accompanied by continued arms competition by pressing the West at its weakest strategic point — in terms of numbers of operational military manpower and equipment in Central Europe. The situation for the West would then become paradoxical: if NATO did not seek to capitalise on new weapons technologies, whatever the cost, then the Soviet Union would narrow the 'qualitative' gap, as it has been doing over the last few decades, and it would then possess a *numerical* military superiority within a qualitatively even balance

of power. But if NATO sought to draw ahead in military competition by heavy investment in new technologies which it comprehensively denied to the Soviet Union, without *somehow* greatly
increasing the output of its own defence production systems, and
without being sure that the Soviet Union could not compete in
quality, then the cost of this competition might escalate to a point
where, despite its advantages, numbers of equipment on the
NATO side would fall below the critical level of substitutability
between quality and quantity.

Conclusions

When advocacy of a long-term comprehensive strategic technology
embargo is subjected to an analysis of strategic behaviour between
roughly equal adversaries, its claims are found sorely wanting; in
ideas and goals; in logic; and in predictive strength.

There are only two unshakeable principles by which exchange
between adversaries may be regulated in the absence of a clear and
present danger. One is that in the short run the adversary should
not be sold the club with which to beat — or the rope to hang —
the West. The other is that with regard to the longer term, the
West should carefully hedge about Soviet access to the principal
sources of strategic power.

These principles must be translated into practical policy-making
in their proper context, which this chapter has argued as follows.
On existing public evidence the West is not inferior to the Soviet
Union in military technology or innovation, and is not becoming
inferior. Even if it is suspected that Soviet intentions are
implacably hostile, a logic for a comprehensive embargo cannot be
derived, because it can be shown that (providing exchange prices
are right) it is more economical to work on the assumption that
Soviet hostility can be structured by the Soviet Union's own evaluation of circumstances. For the long term, a careful eye must be
kept on whether economic performance is coming 'up' and
military performance going 'down' as sources of strategic power;
but even if so, a comprehensive embargo would have to show that it
would be efficacious in impeding Societ economic development, and
in winning the accompanying arms competition.

The important work of Peter Wiles has attempted to show that
these very demanding conditions can be met. The central tenets of

Wilesian theory are that the intentionality of Soviet behaviour can be disregarded because it is implacably hostile, and anyway objective constraints can be placed by the West on Soviet domestic economic choices; and that, other things being equal, a successful, consistent, comprehensive Western embargo would induce a reduction of arms competition after a period of time (and would not seriously increase it meanwhile).

Such a contention usefully reveals the core of what a 'scientific' economic policy would need to account for: the manner of the disposition of resources to 'defence'; the consequential effects of exchange upon domestic economic *decisions*; and the rate and direction of increase (if any) of Soviet innovative capacity in military technologies.

But the theory of Embargology concentrates almost entirely upon incomplete evidence about Soviet political and economic behaviour, while largely ignoring the implications, for Western society and foreign policy, of conducting a long-term embargo. The most plausible hypothesis which it generates is that an embargo *may* influence Soviet domestic economic choices in a direction favoured by the West. It covers itself against the fragility of such a claim by discounting the possibilities that an embargo might make things worse.

This chapter has tried to amplify the implications of proceeding to embargo the Soviet Union without knowing with precision what consequences would flow from this. On inductive grounds it has been suggested that domestic decision-making for the pursuit of advanced military technologies may be rather insensitive to other economic priorities; that if we look at our own policies we find that what stimulates action in short-run circumstances is not the amount or rate of change of defence expenditure (or vice versa); and that anyway the Soviet Union can probably easily avoid losing any arms race which accompanied an embargo, as the 'qualitative' gap is closing not because of Soviet innovation or West-East technology transfer, but because the political parameters of *military* competition are static. Yet the Soviet leadership could easily stimulate arms competition, and stress the Western alliance, by emphasising quantitative (and for them rather cheap) factors.

More fundamentally, I have argued that the consideration of intentionality should not be disregarded; and is indeed critical to any co-existence which is going to be both stable and at the same time preserve the values upon which the West distinguishes itself.

Indeed the dynamics of conflict as they are broadly understood by Western reasoning *prescribe* certain aspects of properly managing a *modus vivendi* with a major adversary. These aspects have been spelled out in the foregoing, but can be summarised: if you think the conflict in which you are engaged is impervious to change, you are kidding yourself; therefore, prepare for change.

Such a position does not deny that Soviet ideology and socio-economic structure require careful thought and special treatment. It does suggest that if we ignore the overwhelming probabilities of change, the flexibility offered by consideration of intentions, and the pragmatic criterion of 'clear and present danger', then the West will set itself upon a course to becoming like its adversary, and will anyway lose out in a competition involving prohibitions on exchange, cohesion in alliance foreign policy norms, and psychological strength derived from building military power.

Finally, the worst outcome of all would be for Western policy towards the Soviet Union to become dominated by those whose claims to scientific rigour are in fact rooted in deformed theology. The proselytising approach to a West-East embargo is disreputable: it pretends to have answers to questions about what is happening to Soviet economic performance and strategic goals which it is not prepared to air fully in public policy debate; it abuses historical evidence in building an effigy of Soviet military-political performance; and it relies for corroboration upon a rather strongly entrenched semi-enclosed order in our societies, the civilian and military professionals whose ethical values and socialisation are deliberately anti-communist, but whose knowledge of Communism, or for that matter of Democracy, falls into doubt by the measures which they espouse.

Notes

'I would like to thank the Editor, Mark Schaffer, for many interesting conversations about this subject.

1. Office of the Director of Defense Research and Engineering, *An Analysis of Export Control of US Technology — A DoD Perspective*, A Report of the Defense Science Board Task Force on Export of US Technology, Washington, DC, 4 February 1976 (hereafter, 'Bucy Report').
   2. Ibid., p. v.
   3. Ibid.
   4. Ibid.
   5. Ibid., p. xiii.
   6. Ibid., p. xiv.

7. Ibid.

8. Ibid.

9. Ibid., p. 34.

10. Richard Perle, 'The Strategic Implications of West-East Technology Transfer' in *The Conduct of East-West Relations in the 1980s, Part II*, Adelphi Papers, no. 190 (International Institute for Strategic Studies, London, 1984), p. 24.

11. In Richard Perle's paper the term 'militarily significant' as used in the Bucy Report is dropped in favour of the term 'militarily critical'. I assume the change is due to the development by the US Defense Department of a Bucy Report-inspired 'militarily critical technologies list', and is not a matter of definition.

12. Perle, 'Strategic Implications', p. 24 (emphasis added).

13. And supposing they could raise the money, say, to buy ICL, and were allowed to do so, how could they afford to buy the grain to supplement their own harvests ...?

14. Ample support for this view exists, but a particularly good recent documentary can be found in Strobe Talbott, *Deadly Gambits* (Alfred A. Knopf, New York, 1984). See especially Chapter 16 on the famous 'walk in the woods' episode.

15. Perle, 'Strategic Implications', p. 20.

16. The economic nationalism of the inter-war period is, altogether, sad testimony to the philosophy of constraining adversaries by juxtaposing competitive economic values. One lesson is that there are no permanent enemies; so there should not be any permanent embargoes. But there is another.

When Germany was a disadvantaged loser after the First World War, it made use of Russia's ideological isolation to begin rebuilding its own military power; Stalin, finding himself in 1939 militarily weak (because of the purges as well as the redundancy of the Red air force), made a temporising pact with Hitler; Japan in 1941, isolated by American economic sanctions, decided to begin a pre-emptive war. Embargoes are laden with political significance. The political consequences of their economic effects are very difficult to predict. But the most severe strategic embargoes produce the greatest discontinuities of political risk-taking.

17. Perle, 'Strategic Implications', p. 21.

18. United States Department of Defense, *Soviet Military Power* (US Government Printing Office, Washington, DC, 1984), pp. 91-3.

19. Peter Wiles, 'Is an Anti-Soviet Embargo Desirable or Possible?' in *Conduct of East-West Relations*.

20. Ibid., p. 46.

21. Ibid., p. 45.

22. The *aim* of his embargo is of course Soviet economic weakness; but 'modified communism' is his *criterion* for ceasing to embargo.

23. Wiles, 'Anti-Soviet Embargo', p. 39.

24. Ibid., p. 43.

25. That is to say, an increase of either 36.9 per cent over eight years or 48.0 per cent over ten years, in real terms, over the current aggregate of NATO defence expenditures, which in 1983-4 amounted to perhaps $300 billion. Presumably having attained the projected new plateau, the equivalent of some $400-$450 billion annually, it would be necessary to hold expenditures at that level in real terms.

26. The highest priority in Soviet acquisition policy remains long-range missile guidance and propulsion. In terms of conventional military power, the Soviet Union needs to develop weight-efficient aircraft materials' designs; engine technologies for high bypass turbo fans; airborne inertial navigation systems; electro-optical ranging systems for tactical missiles; and remote sensors and seekers.

In more general terms, the Soviet military industrial sector has acquired the ability to apply large scale integration of microelectronic components to high volume production, but it still lacks in development of very high speed integrated circuits. The Soviet Union is well behind in the development of large scientific computers, and in the production of microcomputer systems with large memory capacities and fast disk-drives.

11 SOME GENERAL PATTERNS IN TECHNOLOGY TRANSFER IN EAST-WEST TRADE: AN EASTERN VIEWPOINT*

Péter Margittai

The fact that technology — or interpreted dynamically, innovation — has become a magic word, has important reasons related to the outlook on international trade. It is well known that following the price explosion of the 1970s, importers of raw materials could not balance the price increase in raw material sectors either with products of the declining industries, or with products of the progressive industrial branches which were already in the falling section of the product life cycle.

In innovation activity and technology-intensive products two points have been emphasised. On the one hand there is the aim of rationalisation of the manufacturing industry in order to save labour, raw materials and energy. But these achievements refer not only to the process of technology itself but also to increasing the value of the product.

It is in this economic context that we must note a new characteristic of the world economy: the specialisation which has linked together internationally — through economic integration and the transnationalisation of national firms — the R&D sector of the production process. The means which promote this linkage have been called 'technology transfer'.

But before analysing the role in East-West trade of Western technologies, I want to make clear what the term 'technology' means.

Generally speaking, technology is the material form of machines and equipment, the material conditions of production. More commonly, technology is identified as 'industrial property', that is, all human knowledge in a particular field. Of course, even that definition confines the meaning of 'technology'. Turning out any product requires knowledge of production and of organisation and management, both of which are technology. The former concerns bringing together the technical papers, labour, machines and components, the latter ensuring that the norms of planning, production

241

and control are observed by the participants of the production process. Recent views originating in the study of the transnational company (TNC) classify as technology even market knowledge, and consequently all notions connected in some way with development, production and market knowledge.[1]

It is therefore a complicated task to define precisely not only technology, but its components, and its share and contribution to economic growth. Estimates of the latter at most refer *indirectly* to the development of technology and its consequences, designating the growth effect of technology by analysing the residual that remains after all other production factors are accounted for.

It is quite natural that while the interest in the 1950s and 1960s was focused on technical progress, that is, on the relationship of technical knowledge to growth, in the last decade more attention has been paid to the forms and effects of technology transfer among countries. These studies used the same terminologies used for technical development and technology deals within a single country. Thus, as in technology deals within a country, these studies began to distinguish between horizontal and vertical deals; embodied and disembodied technologies (know-how, licences, etc.); negotiable and non-negotiable technologies (patent protected or embargoed); and system-specific (mainly sectoral), process-specific (factory level) and product-specific technologies, the latter being both the most difficult to obtain and the most profitable.

Previously, the view prevailed that there should be a correlation between the development of science and the level of industrial technology. It has become clear, however, that new scientific discoveries stem mostly from previous scientific achievements and new technologies from previous technological research results. Thus, a country with a significant scientific programme may lag in industrial technology.

Furthermore, technological development is not a static environmental condition of an industry, but a process in which the boundaries of development extend continuously. At present the CMEA countries are proceeding to a development stage which the developed capitalist world has already achieved.[2]

I now want to try to classify the forms of technology transfer in East-West trade, and appraise the expectations raised by them.

Embodied Technology Transfer

One way to measure the impact technology transfer among countries at different levels of development is by the flow of the material transfers, by the pure product balances. Here it is interesting to compare two research-intensive industries, machinery and chemicals.

The unfavourable position of CMEA countries is obvious when high technology trade in these industries is compared. The most developed countries in general have an export level which is roughly twice that of their imports. In East-West trade, however, there are manifold differences in favour of the Western countries. In 1981-2, the ratio of exports to the CMEA to imports from the CMEA in these categories was 22 for Japan and Switzerland, 13 for the FRG, 8 for Austria, 6 for Sweden, and 4 for France, Italy and the Netherlands. Even those smaller Western countries which have overall trade deficits in these industries have major surpluses in trade with the CMEA countries. (See Table 11.1. In this table, as elsewhere in this chapter, CMEA means the European CMEA members.)

The amount of technology embodied in a machine can be measured by the ratio of the value of the machine to the weight of the machine. Table 11.2 demonstrates clearly the low technology content of CMEA machinery exports to the EEC countries compared to the technology content of Western machinery sales to these countries.

Four points should be noted here. First, it is very difficult to measure the growth effect of Western technologies embodied in machinery. There is the problem of measuring not only the direct benefit from imported machines, but also the indirect effects, such as the gain from using in other sectors the products made with the imported machines.

Second, the productivity difference between domestic and foreign machines is strongly influenced by the share of imports in investment. The disparity between the productivity of domestic and foreign machines diminishes as the share of imports in investment increases.[3]

Third, when examining the consequences of technology transfer it is important to look at the import share in investment by industry. For example, it is not correct to draw from the low average import share of Soviet investment the conclusion that the

Table 11.1: Ratio of Exports to Imports (Per Cent) for the Trade of Machinery and Chemicals with a High Research Intensity by Developed Western Countries

| | Machinery | | | | Chemicals | | | |
| | Total Trade | | CMEA Trade | | Total Trade | | CMEA Trade | |
	1958/9	1981/2	1958/9	1981/2	1958/9	1981/2	1958/9	1981/2
United States	557	244	2,000	119b	537	226	122	148
Japan	.	269	.	2,225	.	96	.	444
FRG	654	153	3,575	1,366	386	153	1,444	169
United Kingdom	765	142	850	647	205	130	61	342
Italy	80	102	733	443	108	81	244	292
France	210	103	411	442	251	104	1,100	193
Finland	.	28	.	169	.	53	.	166
Austria	72	61	1,385	818	62	150	280	215
Sweden	60	85	637	581	39	63	22	26
Netherlands	120	109c	414	428c	193	225c	387	400c
Belgium	105	82	600	238	146	188	100	198
Switzerland	197	228	633	2,196	.	208	.	487
Norway	20	25	20	109	143	120	83	73

Notes: a. Each column contains the ratio for two years. For the years 1958/9 SITC classification numbers for goods are as in the ECE report cited below. For 1981/2, because of slight modifications in the nomenclature in the meantime, SITC categories 561, 581, 599.2, 729, and 734 are left out, and thus machinery relates to SITC numbers 714, 724, 726, 751, 774, 778, 792 and 87, and chemicals to 515, 524, 541, 562, 58 and 591.

b. The 1981/2 drop in US export coverage presumably stems from the embargoes introduced in the high technology sector, mainly against the Soviet Union.

c. 1981 only. (. not available).

Sources: *The European Economy from the 1950s to the 1970s*, UN Economic Commission for Europe, 1972, for the years 1958/9, and *OECD Foreign Trade Statistics Series C*, 1981, 1982.

Table 11.2: Technology Content as Measured by $US per kg in the Export of Machinery to European Community Countries[a]

	1965	1970	1975	1978	1979	1980
Non-EEC OECD total	2.17	2.53	4.92	6.71	7.48	8.44
United States	4.99	8.65	12.36	18.21	19.54	23.31
Japan	3.15	3.65	5.16	7.56	7.78	8.04
FRG	1.84	2.24	4.56	6.29	7.00	7.85
CMEA total	1.07	1.14	1.79	2.46	2.67	2.92
Soviet Union	1.00	1.09	1.45	1.92	2.16	2.43
Hungary	1.64	1.81	2.49	3.65	3.95	3.98

Note: a. The enlarged Community is reckoned from 1973 onwards. 1965-75: SITC 7 (−735) + 861 + 891.1; 1978-80: SITC 7 (−793) + 87 + 881 + 884.
Source: 'Problemü razvitija vnesnej torgovli v usloviah nautchno tehnitseskovo progresa', VUZO, Prague, 1983.

USSR is less involved in technology transfer. Soviet imports of capital have been concentrated in key sectors; for example, the modernisation of the Soviet chemical industry was based almost entirely on imports of Western machines.

Fourth, the growth and productivity effects of imported technologies and machines are not entirely of foreign origin, because all installations need internal outlays as well. This means that importing embodied technologies is successful only when it is supported by complementary domestic efforts.

Licence Contracts

The very low share of the socialist countries in world trade is reflected in East-West licensing, which is marked by marginality and asymmetry.

In several socialist countries, emphasis has shifted many times from self-sufficient research programmes on one extreme, to over-estimating the significance of buying licences on the other. Simplifying slightly, the considerable efforts of numerous CMEA countries is evidence of the former strategy,[4] and the frequent campaigning for licence-based development is evidence of the latter. However, the question is much more complicated than, for instance, the augmentation of high technology exports through an increase of licence expenditures within R&D expenses.

In the past two decades the world licence trade has developed a number of key characteristics. First, there is the still extremely strong licence-exporter position of the US *vis-à-vis* other regions of the world, including the OECD countries.[5] Second, the territory outside the developed countries participates only marginally in the world licence trade. According to statistics for 1977-9, the share of the OECD area in this trade was 97-99 per cent.[6] Finally, a relatively new development in this trade has been the rapid increase in internal licence transactions within transnational companies. The income derived from licence sales to affiliated firms with majority ownership amounts to up to 80 per cent of total American licence exports.[7] This means that nearly two-thirds of the world licence trade is constituted by sales between American sister companies.

This has a number of consequences for the role that technological products from Western countries might play in the socialist world. The first consequence is that the area outside the OECD is forced into the peripheries of the world intellectual product flow. Furthermore, the 'technical culture' of some developed countries — mainly that of the US — is increasingly on the way to covering the globe: world licence turnover and related trade are covered by the US norms and standards, and licence delivery is more and more frequently arranged in conjunction with capital investment. Although the world licence trade can be divided into that trade controlled by transnational companies and that beyond this circle, in both fields the big companies control the key technologies. However, in this respect it can also be mentioned that the 'choice' of whether to join the technological division of labour or to choose 'backwardness' — like the choice of whether to join the international division of labour as a whole — is ruled increasingly by political decisions. Under such conditions, actual licence policies appear to move on a limited course, defined both by the commercial and economic strategy of a country and by political considerations.

In a technological industry which is dominated by large enterprises and where the outflow of licences is governed by a central strategy, outsiders can less and less easily find a place for themselves in a technological division of labour which is organised within a framework of transnational companies. A licence buyer must face market, application and development restrictions, as well as the factors of the price and the technological level of a given licence. The characteristic feature of the licence connection is that it creates single ties between seller and buyer, and involves

the danger of making the buyers indolent or just freezing them at
the level of the imported technology (through development restrictions). All this leaves fewer possibilities to share in the technological results of the most developed countries.

Furthermore, one of the main purposes of politically motivated
interferences in the technology market (for example, embargoes) is
to make the technology available only within a specific circle, and
to maximise the return for a small group of source and applying
countries. Both the company strategy of product and technology
development, and purely political strategies have thus become
increasingly dependent on each other. This meant that joining in
the technological division of labour became for the outsider company or country a political task as well.

The import substitution and/or export creation choice also has
important consequences for the question of how to buy technologies. Not only is the importance of the import-substituting
technologies in the R&D activities of the socialist countries growing at the expense of the export-creating technologies, but in the
case of the export-creating technologies themselves the socialist
countries are hardly gaining on the leaders. If purchases of licences
do not enlarge the commodity structure in a way which increases
the export capability to Western markets, then this import substitution strategy becomes a dead-end. But if licences are not
purchased, relative productivity (as acknowledged by the world
market) is not increased and the handicap remains.

The connection between the level and expenses of the technology has another important aspect. Primary technologies are
much more expensive than secondary technologies, especially in
technology-intensive industries. Both the price of a technological
solution which rationalises production, and the price of basic technical information necessary for a brand-new product, are much
higher than the price of the secondary technologies. The fact that
this group of primary technologies is practically unreachable determines the licence purchases of the socialist countries, the level of
technologies specified in licence agreements, etc.

The licence buyer thus has two choices. First, use the secondary
technology in conjunction with an indigenous R&D effort to produce a first-rate product, and possibly eliminate the lengthy
adaptation process which occurs when importing primary technologies from abroad. The alternative is to use the secondary technology to produce second-rate products. In this case, however, the

licence purchase will not lead to an improvement in export market prospects.

Besides the above, indirect expenses also increase the burdens for socialist countries which buy licences. In many cases it is even unnecessary for a partner to request a tie-in sale, because such a demand often arises naturally on the side of the buyer. Without such purchases, a patent with alien technical norms becomes unadaptable. This is why licence purchases are frequently linked to the sale by the licence-owner of machinery, material and part-pieces, or machine lines. Though purchasing such machinery may facilitate the adaptation process, from the point of view of the buyer it may also result in long-lasting dependencies which lessen the role the licensed product can play in the trade balance. This is especially true because the licence seller usually excludes from the licence buyer the most valuable export markets for the licenced products.

Finally, it is worth remembering that a licence-based development strategy requires a comprehensive approach. Those expenses in the innovation process which are necessary for the commercial application of an invention[8] face the licence purchaser as well. Also, licence purchases have an impact on investment policy as well, and the two can be effective only in a consistent system.

East-West Co-operation Agreements

Due to the necessity to change their growth strategy and because of their exhausted internal growth reserves, the CMEA countries searched for new ways to join in trade with the most developed part of the world. Inter-firm co-operation agreements multiplied as a result, being aimed primarily at increasing both the trade in convertible goods and the proportion of goods manufactured in high technology sectors, and thus improving the commodity structure and the adaptability of the socialist partners.

Nowadays, the different forms of inter-firm co-operation have been more or less clearly identified: countertraded[9] licence purchases, turn-key factory purchases, joint ventures, third market ventures, etc. Co-operation preceding or following actual prodecution, i.e. that which arises in the development stage of the production process or in marketing and selling, may be added to this list. The question is whether these forms of inter-firm co-operation really enable the Eastern partners to join the mainstream of world trade.

First, it should be mentioned that the co-operation-type trading, having spread rapidly in the first half of the 1970s, has recently slowed down. This slack, at first judged transitory, now appears more permanent. Due to slow rates of growth and problems of unemployment, Western enterprises have not been interested in giving up technology in favour of the socialist countries. There have been some changes in the political background of inter-firm relations, too. Business interests have been sacrificed more frequently to political arguments, and this did not spare inter-firm partnerships.

The unprecedented acceleration of technology development in the 1970s required each participant in inter-firm co-operation to keep up with the technological level of the others. This explains why inter-firm co-operation is very often restricted to second-rate technologies rather than peak products or technologies. The majority of co-operation contracts are countertraded licence contracts and machinery deliveries. In the former case, however, the licence or market rights of the socialist partners are often restricted, blocking them on the level of the introduced technology. Third market ventures, subcontracting, and especially inter-firm specialisation, can hardly be realised between partners of different levels of technological development.

Of course, it is risky to judge the technology transfer effects of this co-operation for the CMEA countries. There is a big difference, for example, between small CMEA countries and the Soviet Union in the frequency, volume and structure of co-operation agreements. Though many co-operation agreements were concluded by the trade-sensitive smaller countries such as Poland, Romania and Hungary, agreements concluded by the USSR, though less frequent, refer as a rule to a much larger basic transaction as well as to a much greater continued bilateral or multilateral flow of goods. These latter agreements have involved investment programmes in key sectors of the economy, and usually involved the latest achievements of industrial technology.[10]

It is also difficult to appraise the co-operation which precedes or follows the stage where actual production occurs. In the development stage, for example, co-operation may be established between partners which are at a similar level of development and which have more or less the same innovation capacity. Similarly, it is very unlikely that marketing partnership in the post-production stage would help the socialist partners to get nearer to the technological level of the most developed nations. Sales co-operation at most eliminates or decreases the losses that otherwise would arise from a lack of market experience.

Beyond this, it is extremely speculative to rank industrial co-operation agreements by technology transfer methods, because of other purely methodological points. For example, the proliferation of co-operation agreements is demonstrated mainly by the growing number of the agreements, and not the trade volume, which would be much more relevant. Even this number is only partly reliable, because of the cancellation of agreements or their transformation into more complex forms of trading. It is essential to emphasise that the volume of trade realised through East-West industrial co-operation does not exceed at present even 0.2 per cent of world trade.[11] It is also impossible to avoid the uncertainty concerning how to determine and categorise inter-firm co-operation agreements. This is not a simple theoretical question, for in the absence of definite rules of classification, it will be more difficult to understand the phenomenon, to measure the economic benefits attached to it, and to formulate appropriate economic policies. Even more significant than the problems of classification are those of analysing the motivations of, and conflicts between, partners when planning market strategy and settling the bills.[12]

Joint Ventures

How have joint ventures, frequently considered the most organic ties in East-West partnership, actually performed?

First of all, in the areas of the most advanced technology, strictly controlled market planning and the specialisation policy of the mother company in producing parts and components allow only a modest role for joint ventures. A joint venture is possible in cases when co-operation does not involve a key technological process. The chance for a successful partnership will be the greatest with small and mid-sized enterprises, mainly in technologies which the transnational companies do not yet control. From the viewpoint of the foreign investor, joint ventures should not transfer much technology from the centre to the periphery. There is, however, no reason to view joint ventures as a recipe for integration into the world economy, as is often claimed.[13]

It is very rare to see joint partnerships in industries where the technological units are strongly vertically integrated (chemicals), in industries sensitive to innovations (electronics, computers), or in industries producing consumer goods and which are compelled to adjust frequently their production programmes in response to a sudden change in market demand. Joint ventures are found more often in industries using local resources, or in sectors meeting local demand, in protected or subsidised industries, or where just from a political point of view there is an emphasised sensitivity to foreign ownership.

The possible role for joint ventures is connected to the outward-looking perspective of a host country. It is quite common for investment regulations, even in 'classical' joint venture rules of developing countries, to require local majority ownership. Parallel with the rise of joint ventures in the East, as part of a strategy of import substitution, that is, ventures aimed at export markets, these ventures — especially in advanced technology sectors — gradually came under the control of a transnational market structure of Western origin. In other words, East-West joint ventures came to meet the requirements of market strategies centrally controlled by the transnational companies.

It must be stated here that contracts may contain elements which substitute for co-operation or even joint ventures. In developing countries a joint venture involvement was frequently changed into looser contractual forms — servicing agreements, assumption of risk, product or technology development agreements, marketing contracts, etc. — but which at certain scales of production created interactions of the same degree as a common venture.[14]

With the complexity of scientific and technological development noted above, it has become more difficult for partners to enter into co-production. The receiver of the technology could leave out of the investment package the unwanted parts and components of the investment goods and services. Regardless of the fact that the sellers' competition for orders of each component gave advantages to the buyer, the latter did not get into a better situation. It has been worthwhile to obtain via contracts the materials and the technical knowledge indispensable to a higher technological level only if components of the process were available, and if an investment package could be made from the components. Of course, even the techniques for such integration were available on the market; however, this method thus became more expensive and cancelled the supposed advantages.

In sum, the success of technology import policy — that is, the chance to join fully in trade with the most developed nations — became strictly dependent on how the receiver countries were related to the transnationalisation of the production process and to the transnationalisation of market strategies.

However, the transnational corporations are not only seldom inclined to establish joint ventures in advanced technology sectors — they are even the main actors in the international division of labour in the most developed areas of the world. This is clear from Table 11.3; although data for the period after 1970 are not at the disposal of the author, these figures have probably not changed significantly and are of interest even today. The table shows a rapid increase and high level of TNC-related trade, especially trade with majority-owned foreign affiliates (MOFA) and trade in high technology industries. In short, the transnationalisation of US companies and the flow of embodied technologies form the main channel for transferring American technologies.

Table 11.3: Aggregate and TNC-Related Performance in 25 US Industries in the Period 1966-70, by R&D Intensity Class (Per Cent)

	High	Medium technology industries	Low
Ratios based on levels of trade			
Total US exports to total US imports	168	232	62
TNC related exports to TNC related imports	396	191	142
Exports to MOFA to imports from MOFA	473	294	88
Exports to MOFA to total US exports	45	15	12
Imports from MOFA to total US imports	16	12	8
Ratios based on increases in trade			
Total US exports to total US imports	124	171	81
TNC related exports to TNC related imports	433	149	193
Exports to MOFA to imports from MOFA	425	167	120
Exports to MOFA to total US exports	46	11	11
Imports from MOFA to total US imports	13	11	7

Source: TC publication 537, Tariff Commission, Washington, DC, 1973.

Moreover, the transnationals' so-called company-internal sales among affiliated firms and shared companies in different countries represent about 25-30 per cent of total world trade. This not only exceeds the less than 1 per cent of international trade represented by co-operation-type trading between East and West, but even surpasses by two or three times the total weight of the socialist countries within world trade.[15]

To enter the world economy means for the smaller CMEA countries to be integrated with the world economy at the level of the firm. This implies increased involvement by transnationals, especially in the key technology sectors.

Of course we may only guess what it would mean for the smaller CMEA countries to turn to transnationals: what economic diplomacy would be needed, what controlling means would be required from the host country, or what management formations would bring about affiliated firms (majority-owned foreign enterprises, partial fusions with the partner, take-overs, etc.). It is worth mentioning here that host countries have proceeded in two directions in their policies towards transnationals. Those countries with a traditionally high share of foreign ownership are focusing on restrictive practices and on eliminating the disadvantages of the foreign control. Meanwhile, the countries with a much lower share of foreign ownership now urge speeding up the liberalisation process.

The socialist countries can be placed in the latter group. In Yugoslavia — the first socialist country to introduce joint venturing — the related legislation has been continuously transformed and eased — in 1971, 1973, 1975 and 1976 — in the favour of the foreign partner. Laws allowing majority-owned foreign assets have been enacted by other socialist countries, such as China, Bulgaria, and for certain special cases, Hungary and Poland.

The request of the foreign partner for majority ownership in the key technology sectors and frequently even in the follow-up transfer deals, and the desire of the host country to control a joint venture, do not necessarily conflict with each other. Mixed ownership rights in joint ventures are by themselves only one means of control; others are protection of key industries, foreign exchange controls, monitoring capital flows, management participation, and regulation of joint venture decisions. With foreign majority ownership, these other means of control grow stricter. However, due to its technological supremacy, foreign capital may maintain control even when restricted to minority shares.

Of course, the control conflict is only one of the reasons for the small progress in joint venturing. The inclination of foreign capital to participate also depends on market size, putting the smaller countries at a disadvantage except for cases when they are connected with neighbouring markets. The control question also varies markedly with respect to the size of the transnational partner, whether the common venture is directed to dynamic or to falling industries, what technological level is permitted the venture within the constraints of the transnational structure, etc.

Inter-governmental Technology Transfer Agreements

Different terminologies have been used to depict these inter-governmental agreements — scientific, technical, technological, development — depending on what the co-operation referred to. In any case, the 1970s gave a new impetus to the spreading of such contracts, because of the depletion of labour reserves, the pressure to shift to a strategy of intensive rather than extensive growth, and the increasing problems of selling on the world market.

It is necessary to stress two factors in this respect. The first is that the increasing cost of basic research and the revolutionary results of applying scientific achievements to the production process (genetics, compact physics) meant that these achievements were largely unavailable from open scientific literature. New basic achievements were protected and were released only as part of an exchange.

The other factor is of political origin. Discoveries which advanced military as well as civilian technologies and which figured in strategic planning, were often prevented from being offered in scientific exchanges. In other words, communication in the field of science and technology became in all its forms conditional upon, and motivated by, non-economic factors. This is why the Soviet Union first successfully concluded exchange agreements with countries with less 'political motivation': in 1966 with France and Italy, in 1968 with the United Kingdom, and only much later on in the years of 'detente' with the US and Japan in 1972, and with the FRG in 1973. It is not by chance that in the 1980s, with the deepening of mutual distrust, the realisation of these contracts has advanced slowly. On the other hand, smaller and larger countries are not equally concerned in building up these contract forms. It was precisely political detente that gave a decisive impetus to the spread of East-West agreements, inter-governmental and otherwise.

The basic feature of these agreements has been, however, a two-way channel of technology. In 1972-4, as stipulated in eleven Soviet-American agreements on science and technology, experts of both countries were to take part in 150 common projects in the fields of space technology, ecology, oceanographics, and non-military nuclear research, among others, i.e. precisely in those fields where each partner could gain from the advances of the other.[16] The reason these common research efforts were shortened or abandoned later on was not deficiencies in the agreements themselves. In many fields, however, bilateral agreements resulted in only minor advances and restricted the technical research to a bilateral basis. Differences in national juridical and technical stand-ards and differing consumer behaviour were some of the causes.

The Relationship Between Planning and Technology Transfer Policy

What conclusions might be stressed for technology transfer policy, when trying to summarise some points of this paper, with an eye to internal factors?

First, there is a strong relationship between technology and industrial structure. The price explosion of the 1970s made inexact the question of what level of technology is needed. Rather, the question was raised concerning what industries and structures required the most up-to-date technologies. Regarding the price of output, or the productivity of labour, a leading technology will have a totally different impact in, say, metallurgy or electronics.

The possibilities of access to leading technologies are certainly not the same in all industries. Since even the most up-to-date tech-nology may not help a failing industry, the quality of the intel-lectual product is of less importance than the fact that technology is usually product- and branch-specific and linked to particular industries.

The question of which industry requires technology imports is more important than, for instance, the question of whether to choose a leading or a mature technology. It is particularly important because the hierarchy of leading and backward industries, and their relative importance, is a measure of economic development.

What role might economic policy have in choosing the proper direction of technical progress? In countries with a diverse and strongly technology-intensive manufacturing industry (for example Hungary), where domestic companies face significant fixed costs and barriers to entry, and where competitors can rely on regaining their expenses through global market organisations, neither the development of a proper technology, nor the import of intellectual products, nor both together, is a sufficient starting point.

It is of no use to import technology for a definite manufacturing stage, if in the other stages the additional costs caused by poor organisation, supplier failures, etc., decrease the benefits from foreign technologies. But the discriminative rules imposed on the export of final goods have the same effect.

Branch-specific technology imports, especially when in material form, are closely connected with the investment structure of the importing country. In this respect, it is important to note that technical progress tends to become more expensive in all industries — and not only because of the increasing cost of R&D. Because the marginal productivity of capital tends to decrease, it becomes more and more difficult to maintain steady growth in productivity. Finally, R&D fixed costs rise in parallel with the increase of investment requirements in almost all industries, but particularly in key technology sectors.

The growing risks faced when developing a new product and the growth of fixed costs have let research policy slip into an ominous position. Research and innovation policy, and thus technology import policy, should include consistently those principles which show where and how economic policy has to deviate from the standard economic regulations in order to ease technical development. But just choosing the right directions for market demand and technical progress will not ensure their realisation. To achieve this, it must be known quite precisely whether both the direction of technical development, and the means chosen for a decisive leap forward, are selected correctly.

The solution to this must be looked for in the creation of an economic environment in which the price system, the exchange rate and the budgetary connections make real market judgements effective. A company should be able to measure exactly how much industrial property or the imports necessary for the technological improvement should cost it, and ensure that the gains from this venture remain in its possession. It should therefore be worthwhile for a company to undertake the costs and risks of turning to the toughest partners and to learn the methods of selling to their markets.

The problem of organising research and technology imports brings forward a more general question, that of the organisation of centralised programmes. Evidently, if high technology industries and companies are predominant in an economy, and require central support, then state intervention cannot be limited to giving priority to certain medium- and long-term research programmes, when the state budget is distributed. The preference system, that is, state interference, must accompany the full innovation cycle, up to the marketing of the research product. Naturally, this does not excuse state interference, investment and credit preferences, price and exchange rate juggling, counter-trade guarantees in bilateral trade agreements, etc., but it does explain them.

Here some other points must be underlined. The socialist countries are bound by many inter-state agreements, which add a stabilising effect to the planning of trade and are thus a positive factor in the environment of crisis in the world economy, but which also presumably limit the means at the disposal of enterprises and planners to meet the liabilities stemming from these agreements. Even if an enterprise saves company income, the problem remains that the intermediaries, machines and foreign exchanges indispensable for efficient transfer deals are often in shortage; in a period when planning becomes more and more difficult their distribution should be realised in a way which proves sufficient means for the state to meet plan targets.

The uncertainty of estimation explains why, in intergovernmental relations of the CMEA countries, major decisions on the purchase of basic technologies are derived from internal decisions on how to balance the structure of bilateral trade, that is, from the decision of what to give in exchange. Similarly, the problem of reconciling interest in purchases at all economic levels remains an unsolved problem.

At the same time, sudden changes in the world economy and the sharpening of competition, especially in prices, have accelerated the obsolescence of trade and technology agreements and, especially in smaller countries, have devalued their manufactured goods. This compelled them either to suffer losses in income, or to make the required technical improvement by undertaking new investments which further impair the terms of trade and long-term investment efficiency.

The next serious problem is that the lack of convertibility of national currencies of the CMEA countries complicates settling the bills for Western technology. The paradox is that exports to the West realised in the framework of co-operation agreements are very often uneconomic, either because partners are of a very different size, and the Eastern partner cannot penetrate the world market because it has no adequate marketing technologies, or because the co-operation venture refers to technologically obsolete products.

Even now it is not fully recognised in the socialist countries that in key industries the technology market, in the form of either embodied technologies or industrial knowledge, is almost entirely controlled by transnational companies. The oligopolistic nature of the technology markets inhibits meeting the technological requirements of regional markets, and this problem may increase further. Transnational partners are only interested in the transfer of technologies which raise as little as possible the general technological level of the CMEA region, that is, in selling second-rate technologies or imposing market and development restrictions on their use. The difference in transnational and CMEA market planning cannot be easily accommodated.

The above indicates that, especially in the smaller countries, importing technology, controlling the technology flow in and out of the country, and setting up conditions of equal partnership in all kinds of transfer channels, should be seen from a strategic viewpoint. This may imply a readjustment of not only the technology factor but also of any factor of the production process (labour, capital, etc.), in order to eliminate the conflicts between, among others, planning at the enterprise level, market planning by transnational companies, and the national planning and market policy of Eastern partners.

At the very beginning of this chapter I referred to the price explosion of the 1970s, and the difficulties the smaller countries have faced in compensating for the price increases of their raw materials imports. The aim of equalising the resulting trade deficits by increasing export volumes has become more and more costly and entails an ever growing national sacrifice. This is true of both the Western and the Eastern trade of the smaller countries, the latter because of the steadily increasing requirements of CMEA partners. This challenge may be met only by applying market planning to these two channels. Failing to dissolve this conflict would mean in practice a growing share of Western imports (especially in high technology goods) in the foreign trade of the socialist partners, and the danger of growing deficits in both East-West and East-East trade for the smaller CMEA countries. Meeting this challenge facing the smaller countries requires in the long run improving their integration within the world economy, and with the CMEA area.

It is none the less obvious, however, that progress in inter-firm relations and the economic environment, and progress in the political climate, are possible only if pursued jointly.[17]

Despite the temporary cooling in East-West political relations, the subject of technology is very topical, since political, economic and, within the latter, inter-firm relations are closely interrelated. Mutually advantageous economic ties can hardly be developed without the easing of actual tension in the political field, and preserving the results that derive from detente urges strengthening economic contracts, especially in the field of technology.

Last but not least, we must note that the pursuit of an efficient technology transfer policy depends on the economic, social and political structure of the receiving country as a whole. For technology importers the choice is to take or to miss the opportunity to form an efficient internal infrastructure in any respect.

Notes

*The author is Senior Economist at the Institute for Economic and Market Research (KOPINT), Ministry of Foreign Trade, Budapest, Hungary.

1. See *Technology Transfer through Transnational Corporations* (UN-CTC, NY, 1979).

2. See, for example, C. Gati, *The Politics of Modernization in Eastern Europe* (Praeger, New York, 1974), p. 22.

3. See, for example, Philip Hanson, 'International Technology Transfer from the West to the USSR' in United States Congress, Joint Economic Committee, *Soviet Economy in a New Perspective* (US Government Printing Office, Washington, DC, 1976).

4. The R&D expenses of Hungary increased from 1.5 per cent to 3.7 per cent of national income in the years 1960-80. In 1980 only 3 per cent of the research budget was spent on buying licences. *Statistical Yearbook* (KSH, Budapest, 1981).

5. According to one estimate, nearly two-thirds of world licence sales, valued at eleven billion dollars in 1980, were of US origin. See, for example, *The*

Experiences of Buying and Adapting Foreign Licences (OMFB, Budapest, 1984), Ch. 1 (in Hungarian).

6. See, for example, B. Madeuf, *L'ordre technologiques international* (Notes et études documentaires, Paris, 1981), p. 87. The percentage relates to the proportion of licence payments to OECD member countries which originate in the OECD area.

7. The polarisation in the licence flow coincides with the R&D efforts of the countries in the Western hemisphere. In 1978, the OECD accounted for 70 per cent of world R&D. Half of this was done by the US. (*Donnees de l'enquête sur les depenses mondiales de RD* (OECD, Paris 1978), or B. Madeuf, *L'ordre technologiques international*, p. 49.) Similar patterns are in evidence when companies are examined. For example, in the US 20 per cent of R&D performed by the private sector is done by four companies, and 53 per cent by 20 companies. (*Science Indicators* (NSF, Washington, DC, 1978), p. 82.)

8. For example, specification, tooling, setting up the pilot plant, marketing costs, and so forth. R&D expenses — which are roughly equivalent to the price of a foreign licence — cover only 5-10 per cent of the total expenses in the innovation process. (See, for example, J.E.S. Parker, *The Economics of Innovation* (Longman, London, 1974), p. 40.)

9. This terminology was first precisely defined in United States Department of Commerce, Office of East-West Trade, 'Counter Trade Practice in East-West Trade', Washington, DC, 1977.

10. This is detailed in Eugene Zaleski and Helgard Wienert, *Technology Transfer Between East and West* (OECD, Paris, 1980), and in Economic Commission for Europe, *Trends in East-West Industrial Co-operation* (ECE, Geneva, 1981).

11. This is a rough estimate based on the percentage that East-West trade (CMEA-OECD) has in the world total (in 1983 less than 3 per cent) and the estimated role of industrial co-operation in East-West trade flows (approximately 5 per cent).

12. This issue was first raised in C.H. McMillan, 'East-West Industrial Co-operation' in United States Congress, Joint Economic Committee, *East European Economies Post-Helsinki* (US Government Printing Office, Washington, DC, 1977).

13. See, for example, R. Vernon, 'Organizational and Institutional Responses to International Risk', Harvard University, 1982, p. 26. This is also supported by the fact that two-thirds, and in some West European countries four-fifths, of foreign (mostly American) investments have been realised in majority-owned foreign affiliates. (See, for example, 'Foreign Capital in Belgium', KOPINT, Budapest, 1975.)

14. This practice is detailed in, for example, *Transnational Corporations in World Development*, Third Survey (UN-CTC, NY, 1983).

15. See, for example, *Reciprocity in Transnational Ventures* (KOPINT, Budapest, 1980), p. 9. The estimates of the share of company internal sales in total world trade are in *Transnational Corporations in World Development*, First Survey (UN-CTC, NY, 1978).

16. L.H. Theriot, 'US Governmental and Private Industry Co-operation with the Soviet Union in the Fields of Science and Technology' in US Congress, Joint Economic Committee, *Soviet Economy*.

17. See *Technical Gap and the Means of Transferring Technology in East-West Trade* (KOPINT, Budapest, 1978), and the summary of 'Innovation Process, Transnational Companies, and International Forms of Joint Ventures', KOPINT, Budapest, 1978, both by the present author.

NOTES ON CONTRIBUTORS

Julian Cooper is Lecturer in the Centre for Russian and East European Studies at the University of Birmingham. His publications include *The Technological Level of Soviet Industry* (Yale University Press, 1977), edited with R. Amann and R.W. Davies; *Industrial Innovation in the Soviet Union* (Yale University Press, 1982), edited with R. Amann; and articles on various aspects of Soviet industry, science and technology.

Stanislaw Gomulka is Senior Lecturer in the Department of Economics at the London School of Economics. His main areas of research are the economics of technological change and the economies of Eastern Europe and the Soviet Union, and his writings include *Growth, Innovation and Reform in Eastern Europe* (Wheatsheaf Books, forthcoming).

Malcolm R. Hill is Senior Lecturer in the Department of Management Studies at Loughborough University of Technology, where he teaches production management and international business. His research interests include East-West trade and technology transfer, and is the author of *East-West Trade, Technology Transfer and Industrial Co-operation* (Gower, 1983).

David Holloway is Lecturer in Politics at the University of Edinburgh and Senior Research Associate at the Center for International Security and Arms Control at Stanford University. He has written on various aspects of Soviet military and technological policy, and his publications include *The Soviet Union and the Arms Race* (Yale University Press, 1982).

Neville March Hunnings is Editor of *Common Market Law Reports* and Editorial Director at the European Law Centre Ltd, London. He is a member of the Law and Technology Committee of the *Union Internationale des Avocats* where he heads a working party on international telecommunications law, and is the author of *Gazetteer of European Law* (European Law Centre, 1983).

Alastair McAuley is Senior Lecturer in Economics at the University of Essex. He is the author of *Economic Welfare in the Soviet Union* (University of Wisconsin Press, 1979) and other books and papers on Soviet economics.

Hugh Macdonald is Lecturer in the Department of International Relations at the London School of Economics. Among his writings are 'Military Power and Arms Control' in L.S. Hagen (ed.), *The Crisis in Western Security* (Croom Helm, 1982), and a forthcoming book, sponsored by the Ford Foundation, on the structure of European security.

Péter Margittai is a Senior Economist at the Institute for Economic and Market Research (KOPINT) of the Hungarian Ministry of Foreign Trade. His main research interests are innovation, technology transfer and transnational marketing, and his publications include *Technical Gap and the Means of Transferring Technology in East-West Trade* (KOPINT, 1978).

Mark E. Schaffer is a former Editor of *Millennium: Journal of International Studies,* and is currently a graduate student in the Department of Economics at the London School of Economics.

John A. Slater is an international civil servant based in Geneva.

Stephen Woolcock is currently Spaak Fellow at the Center for International Affairs at Harvard University. His publications include *Western Policies on East-West Trade* (Royal Institute of International Affairs/Routledge and Kegan Paul, 1982), and 'British Policy on East-West Economic Relations' in R. Rode and H. Jacobsen (eds), *Economic Warfare or Detente?* (Verlag Neue Gessellschaft, 1984).

AUTHOR INDEX

SUBJECT INDEX

Academy of Sciences, USSR 84
Adenauer, K. 194
AEG-Kanis 164
Afghanistan, Soviet invasion of 8-9,
    125, 134, 153, 161-2, 191, 196-7
agricultural equipment 64-5t, 66-7t,
    73, 74, 75, 76
    Soviet Union 64-5t, 66-7t, 94t,
        95t, 96, 97
agricultural goods, trade in 192, 199,
    219
aircraft 11n2
    Backfire-B 217
    Boeing 747 85
    C-141 85
    Concorde 217
    MiG-25 217
    Mya-4 176
    Harrier 151
    Il-76 85-6
    Il-86 85-6
    Tornado 234
    Tu-144 176, 217
    Yak *Forger* 217
    see also aviation industry
Albania 11n1
Aleksandrov, A.P. 109n22
Alsthom-Atlantique 134
Armco 134
arms control 215-16
Arms Export Control Act, US
    168n11
arms race 7-8, 222, 228, 230-5
Australia 155
Austria 155
    trade with East 93, 243, 244t
Austria-Hungary 222
aviation industry, Soviet 89, 96,
    141n32, 216
    see also aircraft

ballistic missiles
    Galosh ABM system 176
    Minuteman 181
    MIRVs (Multiple
        Independently-targetable
        Re-entry Vehicles) 176, 181

SS-11 181
SS-13 181
SS-18 145n75
    see also Soviet military
Battle Act, US 154
Belgium 148
    trade with East 243, 244t
Bismarck, O. 222
Brady, L. 129, 207n17
Bryant Grinder Corporation 126-7,
    143n47, 181
Bucy Report 108n5, 144n72, 195-6,
    211-13, 214, 215, 239n11
    and goals of strategic embargo
        211-12
    definition of 'military significance'
        196, 211
Bulgaria 3, 55, 79n5, 253
    imports of investment goods from
        CMEA 60-1t, 63
        allocation by end-use 66-7t
    imports of investment goods from
        West 58t, 60-1t, 74, 75
        allocation by end-use 64-5t
    and total investment 70, 71,
        71t, 72
    residual in trade statistics 59
Bull SA 134
buy-back agreements *see* countertrade

capital goods imports *see* individual
    country, region and industry
    listings
Carter administration, policies on
    West-East technology
    transfer and trade 195-7, 198
Caterpillar Tractor 134
Central Intelligence Agency (CIA)
    143n47, 155, 170-1, 174, 177,
    179, 180, 181, 182
central planning
    characteristics of 38-9
    incentives and penalties 15-17,
        24-5, 36-8, 40-3, 45, 48-6,
        173
    innovation under 14-18, 24-5,
        35-43, 173, 174, 218, 234-5

265